OFFICE-HOLDERS IN MODERN BRITAIN

IV

Admiralty Officials

1660–1870

OFFICE-HOLDERS
IN MODERN BRITAIN

IV

Admiralty Officials
1660–1870

compiled by

J. C. SAINTY

UNIVERSITY OF LONDON
INSTITUTE OF HISTORICAL RESEARCH
THE ATHLONE PRESS
1975

Published by
THE ATHLONE PRESS
UNIVERSITY OF LONDON
at 4 Gower Street, London WC1

Distributed by
Tiptree Book Services Ltd
Tiptree, Essex

U.S.A. & Canada
Humanities Press Inc
New Jersey

© *University of London* 1975

0 485 17144 9

Printed in Great Britain by
WESTERN PRINTING SERVICES LTD
BRISTOL

Contents

CONTENTS

CONTENTS

Abbreviations

Add. Additional
app. appointed, appointment
Bart. Baronet
BL British Library
     (formerly British Museum)
c. circa
cr. created
d. death, died
dis. dismissed
ed. edited, edition
f., ff. folio, folios
HC House of Commons Paper
Hon. Honourable

kt., ktd. knight, knighted
MS, MSS manuscript, manuscripts
occ. occurrence, occurs
pd. paid
pt. part
reapp. reappointed, reappointment
Rept. Report
res. resigned
ret. retired, retirement
succ. succeeded
TM Treasury minute
vac. vacated office, vacation of office

References

IN MANUSCRIPT

Bodleian Library, Oxford
Rawlinson MSS
British Library, London
Add. 31144   Strafford Papers
Naval Library, Ministry of Defence, London
Corbett MSS   Corbett, Naval Precedents.
SPB   Naval Salary and Pension Books.
National Maritime Museum, Greenwich
Sergison MS   Sergison MS, vol. i (Patents and Privy Seals).
Pepys Library, Magdalene College, Cambridge
Pepys Library MSS
Public Record Office, London
Adm. 1   Admiralty In Letters and Papers.
Adm. 2   Admiralty Out Letters, etc.
Adm. 3   Admiralty Minutes.
Adm. 6   Admiralty Registers, Returns and Certificates.
Adm. 7   Admiralty Miscellanea.
Adm. 12   Admiralty Indexes and Compilations for Official Reference (including Digests).
Adm. 17   Admiralty: Accountant General's Department: Accounts, various.
Adm. 20   Admiralty: Accountant General's Department: Treasurer's Ledgers.
Adm. 46   Admiralty: Accounting Departments: Admiralty Orders.
Adm. 47   Admiralty: Accounting Departments: Record Books.
Adm. 116   Admiralty Cases.
AO 1/1710/102–
   AO 1/1783/296   Declared Accounts: Treasurer of Navy 1660–1827.
C 66   Patent Rolls.
HCA 50   Admiralty Court: Muniment Books.
PC 2   Privy Council Registers.
PMG 24   Paymaster General: Salaried Officers: Civil Pensions.
Prob. 11   Prerogative Court of Canterbury: Registered copies of wills.
T 29   Treasury minutes.
T 52   Treasury: King's warrants.

WORKS IN PRINT

Barrow, *Autobiography*   J. Barrow, *Auto-biographical Memoir*. London 1847.
BIHR   *Bulletin of the Institute of Historical Research.*

REFERENCES

CSPD	*Calendar of State Papers Domestic*. 94 vols., 1547–1704. London 1856–1964.
CTB	*Calendar of Treasury Books*. 32 vols. 1660–1718. London 1904–69.
Ehrman, *Navy*	J. Ehrman, *The Navy in the War of William III 1689–1697*. Cambridge 1953.
Gent. Mag.	*Gentleman's Magazine*.
Hist. Reg. Chron.	*Historical Register . . . Chronological Diary*.
James and Shaw, Admiralty Administration	G. F. James and J. J. S. Shaw, 'Admiralty Administration and Personnel 1619–1714', *BIHR* xiv (1936–7), 10–24, 172–80.
Murray, Admiralty	O. A. R. Murray, 'The Admiralty', *Mariner's Mirror*, xxiii (1937), 13–35, 129–47, 316–31; ibid. xxiv (1938), 101–4, 204–5, 329–52, 458–78; ibid. xxv (1939), 89–111, 216–28, 328–38.
Royal Kal.	*The Royal Kalendar*.
17th Rept. on Finance	*Seventeenth Report of Select Committee on Finance 1797*. Reports of Committees of House of Commons 1797–1803, xii, 328–43.
3rd Rept. on Fees	*Third Report from Commissioners for Enquiring into Fees in Public Offices* (HC 1806, vii).
27th Rept. on Finance	*Twenty-seventh Report of Select Committee on Finance 1798*. Reports of Committees of House of Commons 1797–1803, xiii, 199–343.
Vesey Hamilton, *Naval Administration*	R. Vesey Hamilton, *Naval Administration* (London 1896).

Note on Editorial Method

This volume is designed to make available lists of the officials who served in the Admiralty between the Restoration in 1660 and the year 1870 which witnessed the introduction of the system of open competition for entrants into the Civil Service. The term Admiralty has been understood to cover the Secretaries, Clerks and other officials in the immediate service of the Lord High Admiral or Commissioners of the Admiralty. Also included are the staffs of the Marine, Marine Pay and Naval Works Departments of the Admiralty and the officials of the Admiralty court. The lists do not cover the officials of the various other agencies concerned with naval administration, the Navy Board, the Victualling Board, the Transport Boards or the Commissioners of Sick and Wounded nor do they include the staffs of the Principal Officers of the Navy at Somerset House who took over the functions of the Navy and Victualling Boards after their suppression in 1832.

The material is presented in four parts: an introduction, lists of appointments, periodic lists of officials and an alphabetical list of officials. The purpose of the introduction is to provide a short account of the development of the Admiralty during the period in order that the various offices and grades may be related to their general context. The lists of appointments give the dates of appointments to these offices and grades. They are preceded by introductory notes which bring together information concerning such matters as the method of appointment, remuneration and the relevant statutes and minutes. The periodic lists enable the complete establishment to be seen at selected dates.

The alphabetical list is not intended to be a biographical index. Its purpose is confined simply to providing summarised accounts of the offices held by each individual within the Admiralty during the period. No information has been included unless it is directly relevant to this purpose. Thus dates of death are only included if the individual in question was in office at his death. Appointments to offices outside the Admiralty have been ignored unless they occasioned, or can reasonably be held to have occasioned the departure of the official from the Admiralty. In general the accounts of the careers of the 'political' officials, the Lord High Admiral and the Members of his Council, the Commissioners and, during the nineteenth century, the First Secretary, have been confined to a simple statement of their periods of service in these offices; information concerning resignations and retirements is provided only in the case of those holding 'permanent' offices. Where an individual held an additional office within the Admiralty such as a private secretaryship, which was not directly related to the ordinary course of promotion, the details of his period of service in this additional office have been placed in a separate paragraph. The accounts of the careers of those who were in office at the end of 1870 have not been continued beyond this point.

All references have been concentrated in the alphabetical list except in the cases of the Commissioners and Members of the Lord High Admiral's Councils where they are included in the relevant lists of appointments. Where printed calendars of manuscript material exist they have been used as authorities provided that the calendaring is sufficiently full. Peers and holders of courtesy titles have been indexed under their titles. In the case of changes of name or status appropriate cross-references have been inserted. Unless otherwise noted, information concerning peers and baronets has been taken from the *Complete Peerage* (ed. G.E.C. 2nd ed. 13 vols. London 1910–59), the *Complete Baronetage* (ed. G.E.C. 5 vols. Exeter 1900–6) and Burke's *Peerage*.

Certain conventions have been adopted for dating appointments. The year is taken to have begun on 1 January throughout the period. In the case of those offices which were conferred by an instrument, whether this took the form of letters patent under the great seal or under the seal of the Admiralty court, Admiralty commission or Admiralty warrant, the date is that of the instrument. Where appointment was by Admiralty order or minute, it is that of the order or minute. The task of determining the periods of service of 'political' officials presents considerable difficulty particularly in the nineteenth century when their appointments were frequently canvassed in newspapers and elsewhere several days before their formal entry into office. For the sake of consistency the latter date has been adopted throughout the period. All officials are taken to have remained in office until the appointment of their successors unless there is clear evidence to support the selection of an earlier date. Where there is no indication of the date of appointment of an individual, his period of service is dated by reference to the time during which he received a salary or other remuneration or, failing this information, by reference to the earliest and latest date at which he is found occupying a particular office. Before 1714 there was often a considerable discrepancy between the date of the order requiring the payment of the salary of an official and the date from which that official was to be paid and until this year both dates are included in the alphabetical list; thereafter the discrepancy is usually small or non-existent and, where available, the date of the order or minute alone has been selected.

Introduction

At the Restoration in 1660 the office of Lord High Admiral was re-established. The powers and functions of the Admiralty were vested in this office until the end of the period covered by these lists, except for the years 1684–9 when they were exercised directly by the crown acting through a Secretary for the Affairs of the Admiralty. The office was occupied by individuals only during the years 1660–73, 1702–8 and 1827–8; at other times it was placed in commission. Both Prince George (1702–8) and the Duke of Clarence (1827–8) were provided with a Council to assist them in executing the office of Lord High Admiral.[1]

The judicial functions of the Admiralty were of considerable antiquity. The offices of the court of Admiralty, those of Judge, Registrar and Marshal, had long been established.[2] The officials appointed by the Lord High Admiral or the Admiralty Board to represent their interests in the court, the Advocate and the Proctor, were in existence at the Restoration. During the reign of Charles II the offices of Judge Advocate and Deputy Judge Advocate of the Fleet, which were concerned with the conduct of naval courts martial, were placed on a permanent basis. A Counsel, attached originally to the Navy Board but later to the Admiralty as well, was first appointed in 1673; the office of Solicitor had its origin in 1692. Although these officials were in varying degrees subject to the authority of the Admiralty, they were distinct from the Admiralty office itself which is the principal concern of these lists.

The Admiralty office in its limited sense comprised those officials who served in a secretarial, clerical or subordinate capacity under the immediate direction of the Lord High Admiral or the Admiralty Board. This organisation had remained relatively undeveloped. The Secretary had been an important figure in Admiralty administration since the early seventeenth century. During the Commonwealth salaries from public funds had been made available for him and two Clerks. At the Restoration, however, the Secretary reverted formally to the station of a personal servant of the Lord High Admiral, deriving his remuneration exclusively from fees.[3] In 1664 he was accorded, in consideration of the abolition of the fees arising on commissions and warrants, a salary of £500 payable by the Treasurer of the Navy.[4] A salary was also provided for a Messenger from 1666 and, at various periods after 1676, for a Porter.[5]

Very little information has survived concerning the clerical organisation of the Admiralty before 1694 when salaries were provided for the Clerks from public funds. Statements about it during this period must, therefore, be of the most tentative kind.

---

[1] For the Admiralty generally, see Murray, *Admiralty*; James and Shaw, *Admiralty Administration*; G. F. James, 'Some Further Aspects of Admiralty Administration, 1689–1714', *BIHR*, xvii (1939–40), 13–27; Ehrman, *Navy*, 186–98, 651–6; D. A. Baugh, *British Naval Administration in the Age of Walpole* (Princeton 1965), 61–81; Vesey Hamilton, *Naval Administration*.

[2] For the court of Admiralty, see *27th Rept. on Finance*, 334–7; W. Holdsworth, *A History of English Law*, 7th ed. (London 1956–72), i, 544–68.

[3] James and Shaw, *Admiralty Administration*, 167–8.

[4] MS Rawlinson A 185 f. 451.

[5] AO 1/1711/106; AO 1/1715/120; AO 1/1717/127; AO 1/1719/132.

It seems that the Secretary was in origin entirely responsible for recruiting such Clerks as he needed for the conduct of business and that he either paid them salaries out of his own receipts from fees or allowed them to retain certain fees on their own account. The Clerks held their positions at the pleasure of the Secretary who could dismiss them at will as is illustrated by the case of Burchett in 1687.[6] The experience of Atkins who failed to retain his place in the Admiralty on Pepys' removal from office in 1679 indicates that Clerks appointed by one Secretary had at this date no claim to be continued in service by his successor.[7] Nevertheless there are some signs that there was a degree of continuity in the composition of the clerical staff. Thus Southerne, who had originally been appointed by Coventry in 1660, is found in the service of Pepys in 1673.[8] John Walbanke, who had served Pepys during his first period as Secretary, also acted as Clerk to Brisbane between 1680 and 1684 and again served Pepys from the latter year until his death in 1686. Burchett, although dismissed by Pepys in 1687, returned to serve his successors, Bowles and Southerne, at various periods between 1689 and 1694.

The earliest surviving list of the Admiralty establishment is dated 1 January 1687 and indicates that, in addition to the Secretary, Messenger and Doorkeeper, there were four Clerks in the office at that date, Atkins, Richard Walbanke, Burchett and Skinner.[9] There are indications that one of the Clerks was customarily given greater responsibilities than his colleagues and acted as Chief Clerk. The most obvious function of this Clerk was to sign the Secretary's letters in his absence. Southerne may have occupied this position continuously from 1660. By about 1674 he was replaced by Hewer who is the only Clerk to be specifically referred to as Chief Clerk before 1694. John Walbanke appears to have been Chief Clerk from 1680 to 1686 when he was succeeded by Atkins who appears first on the list of 1687. Samuel Pett seems to have served as Chief Clerk to Bowles in 1689 and Burchett acted as Southerne's principal subordinate in 1693. It must be emphasised that this reconstruction of the succession to the position of Chief Clerk rests on no greater authority than a series of scattered references but it derives some support from the fact that, of those mentioned, Southerne, Hewer, John Walbanke, Atkins, Samuel Pett and Burchett all held the office of Deputy Judge Advocate of the Fleet which may at this period have been regarded as a perquisite to which the Chief Clerk had a special claim. That the Chief Clerk was an official of some consequence is indicated by the fact that Atkins' association with the Admiralty began in 1674 when he became personal Clerk to Hewer as Chief Clerk in which capacity he served for three years before being appointed a Clerk by Pepys as Secretary.[10]

The transfer of the office of Lord High Admiral from the Duke of York to a Board of Commissioners in 1673 probably accelerated the growth of routines of business which in turn required some degree of specialisation on the part of the Clerks. Developments of this kind were undoubtedly encouraged by business-like Secretaries such as Pepys and Bridgeman. The demands made upon the office as a result of the

[6] *Letters and Diary of Samuel Pepys*, ed. R. G. Howarth (London 1932), 181.

[7] MS Rawlinson A 181 f. 250.

[8] References to the evidence for the careers of Clerks will be found in the Alphabetical List of Officials.

[9] Pepys Library no. 2867 p. 13.

[10] Pepys, however, was anxious to dispel the idea that John Walbanke undertook any more than merely routine duties. See the letter printed in A. Bryant, *Samuel Pepys: the Saviour of the Navy*, 2nd ed. (London 1949), 207–8.

continuous period of war between 1689 and 1698 necessitated the introduction of new regulations for the conduct of business and a further definition of the duties of the Clerks.[11]

In 1694 the decision was made to abolish the office fees and to provide all the staff with fixed salaries, borne on the ordinary estimate of the Navy and paid by the Treasurer of the Navy.[12] At the same time the Board adopted a proposal, which had originally been made in 1690,[13] and appointed two joint Secretaries, each with salaries of £800. Next in seniority were two Chief Clerks, with salaries of £200. The appointment of a second Chief Clerk may have been an innovation at this date and was possibly designed to correspond with the new secretarial arrangements. It may be significant in this connection that Burt, one of the Chief Clerks, was transferred directly to the Admiralty from the Navy Office. Under the Chief Clerks were six other Clerks, each with salaries of £80, a Messenger (or Head Messenger), two Servants (or Messengers), a Porter, a Watchman and a Necessary Woman.[14] Shortly afterwards the salaries of a Housekeeper and a Gardener were transferred to the establishment from the contingent fund.[15]

From 1694 it is possible to obtain a much clearer picture of the identity and periods of service of Admiralty officials than is the case earlier. The authorities for the payment of salaries are recorded in the Naval Salary and Pension Books[16] and the payments themselves can be traced in the Treasurer of the Navy's Ledgers[17] and Declared Accounts.[18] New appointments and increases in salary were quite frequently authorised directly by letters from the Admiralty Board.[19] Although the office continued to be known officially as the 'Secretary's Office' down to the end of the nineteenth century it seems clear that, whatever may have been the case before, the Secretary's discretion in establishment matters was increasingly circumscribed after 1694 as a result both of the intervention of the Board and of the growth of conventions within the establishment itself. The mere fact of receiving salaries from public funds tended to give the Clerks a more 'public' character and the accumulation of records associated with their remuneration provided them with a body of precedent to which appeal could be made should any arbitrary interference with customary conventions be contemplated. These conventions finally received full recognition by the Board as a result of the practice, increasingly observed after about 1720, of recording in the Minute Books decisions relating to appointments and other establishment matters.[20]

Two external factors particularly affected the development of the Admiralty establishment. First, as a service department its business was inevitably subject to substantial fluctuations according to whether conditions of war or peace prevailed.

[11] Ehrman, *Navy*, 557, 564–5.   [12] ibid., 562–3; Adm. 2/16 p. 332; Adm. 2/174 pp. 452–3.
[13] Ehrman, *Navy*, 657–61.   [14] Adm. 2/16 p. 414; Adm. 2/385, 27 Oct. 1694.
[15] SPB, i ff. 10, 20.

[16] This series of books (SPB), which originally formed part of the records of the Treasurer of the Navy, extends from 1694 to 1832 when the responsibility for paying Admiralty salaries was taken over by the Accountant General of the Navy, whose principal series of records are the Admiralty Order Books (Adm. 46).   [17] Adm. 20.
[18] AO 1/1710/102–AO 1/1783/296.   [19] Adm. 2/169–376.

[20] Adm. 3. The series of Minute Books was discontinued in 1802. After 1763 minutes relating to establishment matters and appointments were rather unsystematically entered in the series of Admiralty Digests (Adm. 12) under head 5 (Admiralty) in the section entitled 'Appointments of Clerks, &c.'. All references to the Digests are to this section unless otherwise specified. After the discontinuance of the Salary and Pension Books in 1832 the Digests constitute the principal source of information concerning the establishment.

Secondly, because the amounts necessary for the payment of its officials had to be voted annually by the House of Commons, its establishment was subject to the possibility of parliamentary scrutiny to an extent which did not apply to the civil departments until the nineteenth century. At the conclusion of hostilities in 1698 retrenchment was demanded; one of the Secretaries was dispensed with and the number of Clerks was reduced.[21] Following the accession of Anne in 1702 war broke out once again. A second Secretary was again appointed and in the following year the clerical establishment was fixed at one Chief Clerk at £400, the other Chief Clerk having been dispensed with in 1696, and nine other Clerks with salaries ranging from £60 to £150.[22] In the years immediately following it was customary to employ a varying number of other Clerks, sometimes known as Extra Clerks, at £50 a year.[23] In 1705 one of the Secretaries was replaced by a new official of inferior standing, designated the Deputy Secretary.[24] In 1712 the establishment was again modified and provision was made for a Chief Clerk at £300, eight other Clerks with salaries ranging from £60 to £120 and four Clerks at £50.[25] On the termination of the war in 1713 the Chief Clerk's salary was fixed at £200, the number of Clerks on the establishment reduced to six with salaries from £60 to £100 and the Clerks at £50 discharged.[26]

Following the accession of George I the establishment of the Admiralty was revised. The basic structure of the office as settled in January 1715 endured in its essentials until the end of the eighteenth century. A short survey of the principles which governed its organisation may therefore be appropriate at this point. The office was presided over by the Secretary. In the years immediately following the Restoration the Secretary enjoyed a relatively insecure tenure. During Burchett's long period of office which extended from 1694 to 1742 it came to be accepted that the Secretary was a permanent official who remained in office until his death or voluntary retirement.[27] In the latter event a pension was customarily provided.[28] The security enjoyed by the Secretary was not in practice affected by the fact that he was usually a member of the House of Commons.[29] The salary attached to the office remained £800. In 1717 Burchett made a successful application to the Privy Council to have restored the Secretary's fees which had been abolished in 1694.[30] In the following year it was laid down by the Board that the Secretary should receive half of the product of these fees while the remainder should be divided up amongst the Clerks, the size of whose shares was calculated by reference to the amount of their salaries.[31]

[21] Adm. 2/179 pp. 4–5, 24–7.   [22] SPB, i f. 1; Adm. 2/183 pp. 189–90, 218.
[23] Adm. 2/184 p. 52; AO 1/1725/147–AO 1/1729/155.
[24] Adm. 2/185 f. 205.
[25] Adm. 2/191 p. 98; AO 1/1729/155.   [26] Adm. 2/191 pp. 417–18; AO 1/1731/158.
[27] For Burchett's career, see G. F. James, 'Josiah Burchett, Secretary to the Lords Commissioners of the Admiralty, 1695–1742', *Mariner's Mirror*, xxiii (1937), 477–97.
[28] As in the case of Burchett (1742). Retiring allowances were also granted to the Deputy Secretaries, Milnes (1759), Fearne (1766) and Jackson (1782) and to the Second Secretary, Ibbetson (1795).
[29] Before 1800 the following individuals sat in the Commons while holding the office of Secretary: Coventry, Wren, Werden, Pepys, Burchett, Corbett, Stephens and Nepean.
[30] Order in council 31 July 1717 (PC 2/86 pp. 13, 26, 482).
[31] Adm. 3/31, 8 July 1718; *3rd Rept. on Fees*, 96. This arrangement was made at a time when the official next in seniority to the Secretary was the Chief Clerk with a salary of £400. Thereafter the share of the fees of the person enjoying this position in the office was calculated on the basis of this salary, even when he occupied the office of Deputy, joint or Second Secretary. Between 1741 and 1742 Corbett also received half the Secretary's share of the fees as a result of a private arrangement made with his colleague, Burchett (Adm. 3/45, 2 Dec. 1741 and 23 Feb. 1742).

Before 1783 the arrangements for providing the Secretary with assistance in his duties were relatively fluid. The Secretary acted alone from 1715 to 1728. Thereafter he usually had an associate who was either Deputy Secretary (1728–41, 1744–6, 1756–9 and 1764–83), joint Secretary (1741–2) or Second Secretary (1746–51 and 1759–63). The appointment of Corbett as joint Secretary in 1741 was occasioned by the need to provide the ageing Burchett with support;[32] the appointments of Clevland and Stephens in 1746 and 1759 respectively by the increased burden of work which fell upon the Secretary as a result of conditions of war.[33] The standing of all three was more or less comparable to that of the Secretary himself[34] and each of them ultimately succeeded to the senior position. All Secretaries who held office between 1715 and 1795 had had some experience of naval administration before their appointment to the Admiralty. However, the post was not one to which the Admiralty Clerks could ordinarily expect to be promoted. Corbett became Secretary in 1742 after having served successively as Clerk, Chief Clerk, Deputy Secretary and joint Secretary since 1715. Stephens, who was appointed Second Secretary in 1759, had entered the Admiralty as second established Clerk in 1751 after a career in the Navy Office.[35] On the other hand, Clevland, appointed Second Secretary in 1746, had served for the whole of his earlier career in the dockyards and the Navy Office.[36]

The standing of the Deputy Secretary approximated more closely to that of the Chief Clerk than to that of the Secretary. The salary attached to the office was £500 with an additional £100 in time of war. In ordinary circumstances it was the highest post to which the Clerks on the establishment could aspire. With the single exception of Jackson (1766–82) whose previous career had been in the Navy Office,[37] all Deputy Secretaries had served for long periods as Clerks and it was the usual practice for them to be promoted to the post after having occupied the position of Chief Clerk. Before 1783 the office of Chief Clerk to which a salary of £400 was attached was only filled when the Secretary was acting without the assistance of a joint, Deputy or Second Secretary. When there was a Deputy Secretary he appears to have undertaken the duties of the Chief Clerk which included immediate responsibility for the clerical staff and for the contingent fund. In these circumstances no special position was accorded to the senior established Clerk. However, during the periods when there was a Second Secretary (1746–51 and 1759–63), the senior established Clerk was a more important figure. Although Fearne's salary was not raised from £200 to £400 until 1763 it seems clear that he undertook at least some of the duties of Chief Clerk from 1759.[38]

Under the immediate direction of the Deputy Secretary or Chief Clerk were the

[32] Order in council 23 April 1741 (PC 2/96 pp. 442, 447–8).

[33] Adm. 3/55, 1 Aug. 1746; Adm. 3/67, 16 Oct. 1759.

[34] Corbett, as joint Secretary, was granted a salary of £800 on his appointment. The subordinate position of Clevland and Stephens as Second Secretaries was marked by the fact that they were accorded salaries of £600 on appointment. In each case, however, this sum was later increased to £800.

[35] Stephens had occupied the offices of Clerk to the Comptroller of Storekeeper's Accounts 1739–40 and Clerk in the Ticket Office 1740–51.

[36] Clevland had occupied the offices of Clerk to the Comptroller of Storekeeper's Accounts 1722–31, Clerk of the Cheque at Plymouth Dockyard 1731–43 and Clerk of the Acts 1743–6.

[37] Jackson had served in the office of Clerk of the Acts as Clerk 1743–55, Chief Clerk 1755–8 and Assistant Clerk of the Acts 1758–66.

[38] Adm. 3/67, 16 Oct. 1759; Adm. 3/71, 4 July 1763; G. F. James, 'The Admiralty Establishment 1759', *BIHR*, xvi (1938–9), 24–7.

established Clerks. In 1715 their number was fixed at seven with salaries of £200, £150, £120, £100, £80, £70 and £60.[39] After 1718 the Clerks received, in addition, shares in half the product of the office fees in the manner already described. By 1786 it had become the practice for them to demand personal fees as well.[40] Before 1715 there was a certain amount of flexibility in the clerical organisation of the office. Clerks like Lynn were brought in and immediately granted relatively high salaries; others like Parmiter, Oldner, Cole and Oakes were appointed to responsible posts in other branches of naval administration. Of the six Clerks in the office in January 1715 two, Crosfield and Allen, were appointed to posts elsewhere; two, Barnett and Newson, were discharged; while only two, Pembroke and Crickett, remained. Five new Clerks, Corbett, Hawes, Edwards, Hinsom and Westcomb, were brought in of whom only Hinsom had previously served in the Admiralty. Corbett and Hawes were appointed directly to the first and second places on the establishment.

However, the events of 1715 were unusual. In the years that followed the appointment of Clerks to posts outside the Admiralty became much rarer and it was accepted as the rule that Clerks should be appointed in the first instance to the junior position on the establishment after which their advancement should be governed by the principle of seniority.[41] Exceptions were, however, made from time to time. In 1717 Young, Secretary to Berkeley, the First Lord of the Admiralty, was appointed to the third place while in 1751 the Board, seeing the need to bring in an experienced naval administrator to undertake a particular branch of Admiralty business, appointed Stephens directly to the second place. This caused considerable resentment amongst the Clerks who had been overtaken. They embodied their grievances in a petition to the Board stating that this departure from the rule of promotion by seniority both injured them materially and damaged their reputation in the eyes of the world. In answering the petition the Board, significantly enough, did not attempt to deny that promotion by seniority was the rule of the office but justified their action not by insisting on the superior merits of Stephens but by maintaining that the vacancy which he had been appointed to fill was of such a special character that it could not be regarded as an occasion for the application of that rule.[42] Other departures from the ordinary course of promotion occurred in 1759 when Fearne was promoted from fourth to first place on the establishment and in 1763 when Borrodale was passed over for the first place on the grounds of age and infirmity. Borrodale was, however, compensated by being given an allowance out of the contingent fund that was equivalent to the increase of salary that he would have received had he been promoted.[43]

The Clerks, like the Secretaries, enjoyed a secure tenure. There were only two cases of dismissal during the period under discussion and they were occasioned by serious misconduct.[44] Allowances were provided for Clerks who retired after long

[39] Adm. 2/193 pp. 127–8.　　[40] 3rd Rept. on Fees, 98.
[41] See, for example, the minutes of 19 Dec. 1728 (Adm. 3/37), 14 Oct. 1742 (Adm. 3/46), 18 June 1743 (Adm. 3/47) and 2 May 1751 (Adm. 3/62). In two cases, those of J. Corbett, jun. and Alcock, the Board gave promises of clerkships before vacancies on the establishment had occurred (Adm. 3/55, 1 Aug. 1746; Adm. 3/63, 5 May 1753). See also F. B. Wickwire, 'Admiralty Secretaries and the British Civil Service', Huntington Library Quarterly, xxviii (1964–5), 235–54.
[42] Adm. 3/62, 6 April 1751.
[43] Adm. 3/67, 16 Oct. 1759; Adm. 3/70, 4 July 1763.
[44] Hinsom was dismissed in 1716 for forgery (Adm. 2/194 p. 8); Barkham was dismissed in 1790 for persistently incurring debts (Adm. 3/107, 13 March 1790).

service. These usually took the form of annuities to which the Clerks who benefited from the retirement contributed from their salaries.[45]

In addition to the established Clerks there was after 1715 a fluctuating number of Extra Clerks. At first they appear to have been employed as writers and copyists without salary. From 1738 they received £50 a year from the contingent fund.[46] Before 1740 their number and identity cannot be precisely determined. In that year when there were five, their salaries were transferred from the contingent fund to the ordinary estimate and made payable by the Treasurer of the Navy like those of the established Clerks.[47] Thereafter the identity of the Extra Clerks can be determined without difficulty. Unlike the Clerks on the establishment, the Extra Clerks did not have a secure tenure. Their number varied according to the pressure of work. Some of those who had been engaged during periods of war were liable to be discharged after the cessation of hostilities. On the other hand those Extra Clerks who had remained in the service of the Admiralty for a considerable time could look forward to promotion within the office. An Extra Clerk was appointed to the establishment in 1721 and from 1738 to 1800 vacancies on the establishment were with only one exception filled by Extra Clerks.

The first detailed evidence of the manner in which the work of the Admiralty was undertaken is to be found in a document of October 1759.[48] This records the changes in the distribution of functions which were made necessary by the promotion of Stephens from a clerkship to the office of Second Secretary and shows that it was the practice for branches of business to be assigned to particular established Clerks who were assisted by Extra Clerks. It is evident from a number of scattered earlier references that the practice of dividing up the work in this way was of considerable antiquity.[49]

A number of changes were made in the Admiralty office in the course of the eighteenth century. In 1731 an Inspector of Repairs was attached to the department.[50] In 1738 a Clerk of the Journals was appointed with the function of inspecting and making abstracts from Captains' journals so that the Board could inform itself as to the manner in which its instructions were being carried out. However, this post was discontinued as a separate office in 1741.[51] From 1755 it was usual for one of the Extra Clerks to be employed as Translator of French and Spanish Languages.[52] In the same year the establishment of the Marines was placed under the immediate authority of the Board.[53] This gave rise to the creation of two new sub-departments, the Marine Department and the Marine Pay Department. The Marine Department was placed under the Secretary who was granted an additional salary on this account and salaries were made available for two Clerks and two Extra Clerks. These salaries were paid out of the marine contingencies fund. A third Clerk was appointed in 1778. The two Extra Clerks were dispensed with in 1782 and in 1784 the number of Clerks was reduced to two.[54] The Marine Pay Department had its origin in the Clerks employed

[45] Adm. 3/62, 6 April and 17 July 1751 (Ram); Adm. 3/69, 31 July 1761 (G. A. Burchett); Adm. 3/76, 5 Oct. 1768 (Borrodale); Adm. 3/80, 25 Aug. 1773 (Alcock).
[46] Adm. 3/43, 30 May and 7 Nov. 1738, 25 Sept. 1739.
[47] Adm. 3/44, 13 Nov. 1740; SPB, vi f. 7.   [48] James, *BIHR*, xvi, 24–7.
[49] Adm. 3/43, 25 Sept. 1739; Adm. 3/55, 17 Oct. 1746; Adm. 3/62, 14 March and 6 April 1751.
[50] Adm. 3/39, 1 April 1731.
[51] Orders in council 30 Nov. 1738 (PC 2/95 pp. 21–3, 33) and 7 March 1741 (PC 2/96 pp. 447–8, 455).   [52] SPB, vii f. 7.
[53] Order in council 3 April 1755 (PC 2/104 pp. 364–7).   [54] *3rd Rept. on Fees*, 116–17.

by the Paymaster of Marines. In 1756 three Agents of Marines were appointed. In 1763 they were reduced to one.[55]

In 1783 changes were introduced into the more senior offices of the department. The office of Deputy Secretary was abolished and replaced by that of Second Secretary which was now established on a permanent basis and also given the title of Second Secretary of the Marine Department. Thereafter the Admiralty office was presided over by a First and a Second Secretary until the end of the period covered by these lists. At the same time the position of Chief Clerk was also established on a permanent basis and conferred upon the senior established Clerk.[56]

In 1786 the Admiralty office was investigated by the Commissioners on Fees. The Commissioners examined twenty-seven officials of the department whose testimony was included in their third report which was made in the following year.[57] The Commissioners found the office presided over by two Secretaries who were, under the Board, charged with the oversight of all the business of the department. The immediate conduct of the work was entrusted to a Chief Clerk who was responsible for the direction of the other Clerks and who also acted as Paymaster of Contingencies. The business of the Admiralty was divided into six branches which were placed in the charge of the Chief Clerk himself and the next five established Clerks. The junior established Clerk was attached to the Chief Clerk as his assistant. Nine of the eleven Extra Clerks were attached to the Clerks in charge of the various branches; the remaining two were placed at the disposal of the Secretaries, one acting also as Translator of French and Spanish Languages.

The subordinate staff consisted of a Head Messenger, two Assistant Messengers, a Porter, a Housekeeper, a Necessary Woman, three Watchmen, a Gardener and an Inspector of Repairs, most of whom were accustomed to receive perquisites in addition to their salaries.

The Marine Department was under the direction of the two Secretaries of the Admiralty. Two Clerks were employed in the Department who were distinct from the ordinary establishment. There was also a Paymaster of Marines who was assisted by two Clerks, and an Agent of Marines. The Commissioners also extended their enquiry to the offices of Receiver and Comptroller of Admiralty Droits.[58]

Reviewing the organisation of the office the Commissioners began by commending the fact that the Secretaries 'contrary to the custom observed in other departments into which we have enquired, appear to be stationary Officers'. In their view the Clerks and other officials appeared to be efficient and to perform their duties in person although they felt that the amount of work that arose in peace-time was hardly sufficient to provide them all with full employment. However, the Commissioners were of the opinion that this consideration was outweighed by the advantage of having a body of experienced Clerks in readiness in the event of an outbreak of war when they were likely to be fully extended. The Commissioners deprecated the manner in which the Secretaries and established Clerks received their remuneration and were of the opinion that the Extra Clerks were inadequately paid given the nature and amount of work that they were called upon to perform.

The first recommendation made by the Commissioners was that the Secretaries, Clerks and other officials should all receive fixed salaries which should replace all existing forms of remuneration. They proposed that the First and Second Secretaries

[55] *3rd Rept. on Fees*, 117–18.   [56] Adm. 3/96, 13 Jan. 1783.   [57] *3rd Rept. on Fees*, 93–129.
[58] ibid., 95–102.

should receive £2000 and £1200 respectively and the Chief Clerk £800. The remaining six established Clerks should form a class of Senior Clerks with salaries ranging from £300 to £500. Eight of the Extra Clerks should be added to the establishment as Junior Clerks with salaries ranging from £150 to £250. The three junior Extra Clerks should retain their existing title with salaries of £90 and be placed on the establishment when vacancies occurred according to 'seniority and merit'. Special allowances were proposed for the Receiver of Fees and Paymaster of Contingencies and for the French and Spanish Translator.

The Commissioners deprecated the fact that the first Clerk in the Marine Department was also Chief Clerk to the Paymaster of Marines since this involved him in some degree in the responsibility of checking the accounts of his own principal, the Paymaster. They also commented unfavourably on the fact that the same official was a Purser of a ship, a post which he executed by deputy, and that he acted as agent for a number of marine officers.

Amongst the subordinate staff the Commissioners recommended the abolition of the office of Housekeeper as a sinecure and that of Inspector of Repairs as 'unnecessary'. Otherwise they approved this part of the establishment on the understanding that remuneration should be confined to fixed salaries and that all other emoluments should be discontinued.[59]

The Commissioners proposed that the office fees should continue to be received by one of the Senior Clerks, subject to certain accounting safeguards, and that they should constitute a fund to be applied towards defraying the expenses of stationery and contingencies.[60]

The Commissioners recommended that those officials who were obliged to retire on account of age or infirmity should receive pensions not exceeding half the amount of their salaries. Officials should take an oath of secrecy and fidelity before a Baron of the Exchequer and also enter into a bond to the amount of three times their salaries for the proper performance of their duties. To prevent abuse the bond should make clear that the official in question would not directly or indirectly take any fee or other perquisite for business done in the office, other than his established salary nor act as agent in connection with the purchase of naval supplies, on pain of dismissal.[61] Finally the Commissioners recommended that the office of Paymaster of Marines should be amalgamated with that of Agent and provided with an establishment of two Clerks, two Extra Clerks and a Messenger with salaries payable out of the marine contingent fund.[62]

The report of the Commissioners was referred to the Admiralty Board for comment in 1792. However, in 1797 the Commons Select Committee on Finance found that no system of regulation had been introduced into the office by the Board in consequence of its recommendations on the ground that the establishment proposed by the Commissioners was 'inadequate to the execution of the duties of that important and extensive department; and that the Salaries proposed to be allowed to the Secretaries and Clerks were by no means sufficient to compensate them for their constant and laborious services'.[63] The Committee observed that there had been a substantial increase in the cost of the department since the Commissioners reported. This was

[59] ibid., 102-3.   [60] ibid., 103-4.   [61] ibid., 104-6.   [62] ibid.
[63] *17th Rept. on Finance*, 328. See also P. K. Crimmin, 'Admiralty relations with the Treasury, 1783-1806; the preparation of naval estimates and the beginnings of Treasury control', *Mariner's Mirror*, liii (1967), 63-72.

due partly to war but was principally occasioned by the creation of three new offices. Of these that of Hydrographer, first appointed in 1795, survived to become a permanent feature of the department.[64] The Inspector of Telegraphs, appointed in the same year, was intended only to be a temporary official for the duration of the war and his post was discontinued in 1816.[65] Finally, there was the sub-department concerned with naval works, which was established in 1796. This was under the direction of an Inspector General, assisted by an Architect, a Mechanist and a Chemist and served by a Secretary, a Draftsman, two Clerks and a Messenger at a total cost of £2700 a year. This sub-department remained under the immediate direction of the Admiralty until 1807 when it was transferred to the Navy Board.[66]

The Finance Committee were not unfavourably disposed towards these new offices but strongly urged that, as soon as conditions of peace returned, the Admiralty Board should make a determined effort to reduce the size and cost of the establishment generally and also to implement the recommendations of the Commissioners of 1786 with regard to the fees.[67]

The Board finally submitted its observations on the recommendations of the Commissioners in 1799.[68] It acquiesced with a marked lack of enthusiasm in the proposal that fixed salaries should be substituted for the existing system of remuneration. It reiterated its view that the salaries proposed for the Secretaries and Clerks were inadequate. Instead of £2000 for the First Secretary it recommended a salary of £3000 with an additional allowance of £1000 in time of war and instead of £1200 for the Second Secretary it proposed £1500 with an addition of £500 in time of war. The Board agreed that the salary of the Chief Clerk should be £800 and suggested that this official should undertake the duties of Receiver of Fees and Paymaster of Contingencies, receiving in time of war the allowance of £150 attached to this post.

With regard to the succession of Extra Clerks to vacancies on the establishment and the question of promotion generally the Board observed that 'it does not appear to us that any fixed rule should be laid down, as due attention will always be paid to the services of persons who have been in that capacity, if their conduct should merit approbation. The Junior Clerks on the Establishment, if competent to higher situations, will rise in succession as a matter of course'. The Board was of the opinion that the clerical establishment proposed by the Commissioners was inadequate both in terms of numbers and remuneration. It recommended that there should be six Senior Clerks with salaries ranging from £300 to £500, ten Junior Clerks with salaries from £150 to £250 and six Extra Clerks who were to receive either £90 or £100. The salary scale of one of the Clerks in the Marine Department should be assimilated to the class of Seniors; the salary scale of the other to that of Juniors. The Translator should receive £100 and the office of Secretary (or Private Secretary) to the First Lord should be inserted in the establishment at a salary of £300. The Board recommended that the Clerks should receive the addition of a fifth to their salaries in time of war.

[64] Order in council 12 Aug. 1795 (PC 2/144 pp. 51–3).

[65] SPB, ix f. 11; Adm. 12/178, 9 March 1816; SPB, xii ff. 55–6.

[66] Order in council 23 March 1796 (*17th Rept. on Finance*, 342–3); *4th Rept. of Commissioners on Civil Affairs of the Navy* (HC 120 pp. 12–14 (1809) vi, 12–14); order in council 27 Oct. 1807 (PC 2/174 pp. 274–6). [67] *17th Rept. on Finance*, 329.

[68] These observations are contained in the order in council 15 Jan. 1800 (HC 138 pp. 1–14 (1816) xiii, 169–82). See also P. K. Crimmin, 'The financial and clerical establishment of the Admiralty Office, 1783–1806', *Mariner's Mirror*, lv (1969), 299–309.

Turning to the subordinate staff the Board agreed to the abolition of the posts of Housekeeper and Inspector of Repairs but urged the necessity of increasing the salaries of the established Messengers and of retaining the services of certain other additional officials until the end of the war. The Board agreed to the tightening up of the procedures for accounting for the fees and also to the proposal that the fees themselves should form a fund to be applied towards the payment of the contingencies. It rejected the suggestion that retiring officials should receive pensions amounting to half their salaries in all cases and proposed instead that the amount of the pensions should be related to length of service. The Board accepted that Clerks should take an oath of secrecy on entering office but felt that the proposal that every Clerk should give security to the amount of three times his salary was impracticable; this safeguard should apply only to the Chief Clerk who as Receiver of Fees and Paymaster of Contingencies was the sole official entrusted with public money. So far as the other Clerks were concerned, the sanction of dismissal in the case of misconduct remained.

The recommendations of the Commissioners of 1786 as thus modified by the Admiralty Board were embodied in an order in council of 15 January 1800 which provided the basic framework of the establishment until the end of the period.[69] The first significant change in the office to occur after this reorganisation related to the position of the Secretaries. As has been seen, it was an established principle during the eighteenth century that the Secretaries should be 'stationary' or permanent. However, the convention of permanence was broken in the case of the second secretaryship in 1804 when Tucker was turned out in favour of Barrow, in 1806 when Barrow was turned out in favour of Tucker and once again in 1807 when Barrow was reappointed. After this episode, however, the post reverted to its permanent character which was consolidated during Barrow's long second term of office which lasted until 1845. The permanent character of the first secretaryship was maintained until 1807 when Marsden, who had occupied the post without a seat in parliament since 1804, resigned. It was then agreed that the holder of the office should invariably be a member of the Commons. Thereafter it was accepted that the first secretaryship should be governed by the conventions which applied to the 'political' members of the administration and be vacated on a change of government.[70]

In 1807 it was agreed that the remuneration of the Clerks should be increased in view of the rise in the cost of living and also that the size of their salaries should be governed by the length of their service rather than by the particular position that they happened to occupy in the office. A system of progressive salaries was introduced with maxima of £600, £400 and £140 for the Senior, Junior and Extra Clerks respectively. The practice of paying additional allowances in time of war was continued. The new system was extended to the Clerks in the Marine and the Marine Pay Departments.[71]

In August 1809 the Board turned its attention to the condition of the Admiralty records. It was found that many rooms were filled with official documents which were

[69] HC 138 pp. 1–14 (1816) xiii, 169–82.

[70] Barrow, *Autobiography*, 254–5, 291–2, 298–9. This would appear to be a fair summary of the case although Croker, First Secretary 1809–30, tried to suggest that he enjoyed a 'permanent' tenure. In doing so he was guilty of disingenuousness. The truth was that, during his long period of office, there had not been a change in the complexion of the government sufficiently radical to require his removal. In the event he recognised this fact by 'resigning' in 1830 in order to forestall his almost inevitable dismissal by the Whigs. See H. Parris, *Constitutional Bureaucracy* (London 1969), 44.

[71] Orders in council 28 Oct. and 11 Nov. 1807 (PC 2/174 pp. 284–6, 483–5). At the same time the salaries of the officials of the Marine Pay Department were made payable by the Treasurer of the Navy.

almost inaccessible as a result of a lack of proper indexes. To deal with the problem authority was obtained for the appointment of a Keeper of Records and Papers with a salary of £500. The post was given to John Finlaison who was responsible for introducing into the Admiralty the distinctive system of digests and indexes.[72]

In September 1809 the separate existence of the Marine Department was brought to a close and its two clerkships integrated into the ordinary establishment.[73] In 1811 the Board, having found it necessary to increase the branches into which the business of the department was divided from seven to nine, was authorised to raise the number of Senior Clerks to nine and that of the Junior Clerks to twelve.[74] Between 1811 and 1816 Supernumerary Clerks were temporarily employed and paid on a weekly basis.[75] In 1812 allowances were made available for two Clerks for acting as Private Clerks or Private Secretaries to the First and Second Secretaries.[76] In 1815 it was provided that the distinction between war and peace salaries should be abolished and that the salaries both of the Secretaries and the Clerks should be fixed permanently at the war level.[77]

In 1816 the clerical structure of the office was subjected to a major reorganisation.[78] The avowed purposes of the reorganisation were to bring about uniformity in the conduct of business, to ensure that salaries were relevant to the responsibility assumed and to the amount of work performed and to maintain the distinction between the Clerks of the Admiralty and those of the subordinate naval departments, a distinction which the Board felt to be well founded 'in the superior political importance and responsibility of the duties of this department'. The existing grades of Senior, Junior and Extra Clerk and also the office of Keeper of the Records were abolished and replaced by three new classes. The First Class Clerks were eight in number. Seven of these were to preside over the various branches into which the business was divided: military, civil, legal, commission, record, miscellaneous and marine, while the eighth was to act as Reading Clerk or Reader to the Board. The First Class Clerks were accorded a progressive salary scale ranging from £600 to £850. Provision was made for eleven Second Class Clerks with salaries ranging from £400 to £600 and for fourteen Third Class Clerks with salaries ranging from £150 to £400. At the same time the order in council authorising this new establishment laid down that 'the removal from a lower class to a higher shall be the reward of qualification for the duties of the higher class without any reference whatsoever to the seniority the person may hold in the lower class'. The principles of the reorganisation of 1816 were extended to the Marine Pay Department in 1819 and continued to operate there until the abolition of that department in 1831.[79]

In the years following the end of the war parliamentary pressure forced the Admiralty, like other departments, to give serious attention to the question of cutting down the cost of its staff. In 1818 criticism in the House of Commons led to a reduction

[72] Order in council 16 Aug. 1809 (PC 2/182 pp. 474–6); SPB, xii ff. 55–6; R. B. Pugh, 'The Early History of the Admiralty Record Office', *Studies presented to Sir Hilary Jenkinson*, ed. J. Conway Davies (London 1957), 326–36. [73] SPB, xii ff. 57–8.

[74] Order in council 14 March 1811 (PC 2/192 pp. 98–100).

[75] SPB, xii ff. 45–6.

[76] Adm. 12/154, 5 Feb. 1812. After 1832 Clerks were also allocated to the junior Lords of the Admiralty as Private Secretaries.

[77] Order in council 21 June 1815 (HC 125 pp. 1–2 (1816) xiii, 167–8).

[78] Order in council 30 Jan. 1816 (HC 139 pp. 1–12 (1816) xiii, 183–94).

[79] Orders in council 3 Dec. 1819 (PC 2/201 pp. 595–6) and 31 Jan. 1831 (PC 2/212 pp. 34–5).

in the salaries of the Secretaries to the former peace-time level.[80] In 1822 a new scheme was introduced which 'reduced the establishment to the very lowest scale consistent with the due execution of public business'. The number of Clerks was reduced to six in the first class, to six in the second class and to twelve in the third class. The salaries of the First Class Clerks remained unchanged; those of the Second Class Clerks were reduced to a scale ranging from £350 to £550 and those of the Third Class Clerks were reduced to a scale ranging from £100 to £350.[81] In 1823 it was provided that Clerks should serve for a year on probation after appointment before being fully established.[82] In 1827 the right of appointment to clerkships was transferred from the First Secretary to the Duke of Clarence as Lord High Admiral, vesting subsequently in the First Lord of the Admiralty.[83]

In 1824 the Board reviewed the position of the Private Secretary to the First Lord. The duties attached to this post were, in the view of the Admiralty, 'very different in many respects from those of a similar description in the other principal departments'.[84] The Private Secretary was never selected from amongst the Clerks in the office as was often the case elsewhere but was usually an individual of considerable experience and standing. As the nineteenth century proceeded it became common for First Lords to appoint senior naval officers as their Private Secretaries. The Private Secretary had the duty of presiding over the First Lord's private office which came to include several of the Clerks on the establishment and a Messenger.[85] The post, which had carried a salary of £300 since 1800, had often been held in conjunction with another office to which few or no duties were attached. With the general reduction of establishments it was becoming increasingly difficult to find offices suitable for this purpose. It was, therefore, provided in 1824 that, when the Private Secretary had no other form of remuneration from the government, the salary scale should begin at £500 and rise to £600.[86]

During the Whig government of 1830–4 far-reaching changes were introduced into naval administration. In the first place the work of the Admiralty Board was re-organised.[87] Originally there had been no fixed principle governing the proportion of junior Lords who were naval officers. From 1804, however, it was the rule for there to be an equal number of 'civil' and 'naval' Lords. Until 1822 there were thus three civil and three naval Lords. When, in that year, the size of the Board was reduced, one civil and one naval lordship were abolished. In 1830 all the junior lordships were filled by naval officers. Two years later a Civil Lord was added and from then until 1869 it was the usual practice for the Board to be composed of four Naval Lords and one Civil Lord in addition to the First Lord. Originally all the Admiralty Lords had been eligible for election to the Commons; in 1832 the number so eligible was reduced to five.[88] It was apparently while Barham was First Lord (1805–6) that the first steps

[80] *Parliamentary Debates*, 1st ser., xxxiii, cols. 476–514; Adm. 12/178, 11 June 1816; *6th Rept. of Select Committee on Finance 1817* (HC 410 pp. 184–8 (1817) iv, 206–10); order in council 10 Feb. 1818 (PC 2/200 pp. 81–2).

[81] Order in council 17 Jan. 1822 (PC 2/204 pp. 14–23).   [82] Adm. 12/215, 23 Oct. 1823.

[83] Adm. 12/245, 15 Sept. 1827; Barrow, *Autobiography*, 341.

[84] Order in council 23 June 1824 (PC 2/205 pp. 501–2).

[85] For early references to the First Lord's private office, see Adm. 12/154, 13 Feb. 1812; Adm. 12/160, 22 Feb. 1813; Adm. 12/222, 17 June 1824. The Messenger was appointed in 1804 (SPB, iii f. 18).

[86] Order in council 23 June 1824 (PC 2/205 pp. 501–2).

[87] For the reforms of 1832 and the duties of the junior Lords, see Vesey Hamilton, *Naval Administration*, 22–4; Murray, Admiralty, xxiii, 19–25; Barrow, *Autobiography*, 417; J. H. Briggs, *Naval Administrations 1827–92* (London 1897), 33–4.   [88] 2 Will. IV, c 40, s 1.

were taken in the direction of a permanent division of work amongst the various members of the Admiralty Board. During Sir James Graham's period of office as First Lord (1830–4) each junior Lord was made responsible for a specific area of naval administration. This arrangement was linked with the general reform of the naval departments which took place in 1832. This involved the abolition of the Navy and Victualling Boards and the transfer of their functions to five principal officers of the Navy, the Surveyor, the Accountant General, the Storekeeper General, the Controller of the Victualling and Transport Service and the Physician, whose activities were placed generally under the supervision of the Admiralty Board and specifically under the direction of a particular junior Lord. The former staffs of the Navy and Victualling Boards were placed under the authority of the five principal officers who conducted their business from Somerset House. These officials were thus both physically and administratively distinct from the Admiralty establishment in Whitehall and have not been included in these lists.

The reforms of 1832 prompted a review of the clerical establishment of the Admiralty which was fixed in that year at thirty-one, composed of one Chief, six First Class (or Senior), nine Second Class and fifteen Third Class Clerks.[89] In April 1837 the superintendence of the business relating to mail packets was transferred from the Post Office to the Admiralty; as a result one First Class, one Second Class and three Third Class Clerks were added. In June of the same year it was recognised that, due to the increase in the establishment, it was taking Clerks an excessively long time to reach the maximum salary for their grade; increases in the increments for the First and Second Classes were therefore authorised.[90]

In February 1841 another Clerk was added to the second class in order to provide assistance for the Controller of Steam Machinery.[91] In the following May the office of Reader was placed on a new footing. This important post, which involved being present at meetings of the Board, had previously been filled by one of the Clerks who received an additional allowance from the contingent fund. It was now provided that the Reader should, immediately on appointment, receive the maximum salary appropriate to his grade together with an allowance of £100.[92]

In 1842 the increasing amount of work falling upon the office, in particular that caused by the correspondence arising from the control of the slave trade, the supervision of the packet service and the introduction of steam machinery into ships, necessitated the appointment of an additional Second Class Clerk to the establishment which was fixed at one Chief Clerk, seven First Class, eleven Second Class and eighteen Third Class Clerks.[93] A further Third Class Clerk was added in 1847 to strengthen the steam department.[94]

[89] Order in council 1 Aug. 1832 (PC 2/213 pp. 495–9).

[90] Orders in council 5 April and 21 June 1837 (PC 2/219 pp. 151–2, 313–14).

[91] Order in council 11 Feb. 1841 (PC 2/223 pp. 77–8). The Controller of Steam Machinery, who had been appointed in 1837, was under the authority of the Admiralty but did not himself form part of the establishment in Whitehall. [92] Order in council 8 May 1841 (PC 2/223 pp. 230–2).

[93] Order in council 2 Nov. 1842 (PC 2/224 pp. 759–60). On this occasion the First Secretary, S. Herbert, wrote a minute stressing that the Board would in future be guided by considerations of merit in making promotions from one class to another, while the Second Secretary, J. Barrow, defended the system of promotion by seniority in these circumstances, expressing the view that 'rejection may in some instances be found expedient, but selection never' (Adm. 1/5519, minutes of 24 Oct. and 10 Nov. 1842).

[94] Adm. 12/474, 7 Dec. 1846; order in council 27 Feb. 1847 (PC 2/230 p. 150). For the organisation of the steam department generally, see order in council 24 April 1847 (ibid. pp. 316–17).

In 1853 it was decided that the clerical duties associated with the Naval Coast Volunteers should be undertaken by the Admiralty. This decision prompted a general review of the establishment. The increasing amount of work, in particular that arising from the department's responsibilities for steam machinery, the contract packet service and the dockyard brigades, had for some time made it necessary to employ Extra Clerks. These Clerks, whose position was defined in 1841, were usually five in number. They held their posts on a permanent tenure and were promoted to the establishment as vacancies occurred. It was recognised that their status was anomalous and in conflict with the concept of a fixed establishment authorised by order in council. Since, however, the loss of their services would bring about serious inconvenience, the only satisfactory solution to the problem was to increase the establishment. The Treasury approved the addition of two First Class and six Third Class Clerks, thus bringing the total clerical staff to forty-seven, consisting of one Chief, nine First Class, twelve Second Class and twenty-five Third Class Clerks.[95]

In 1854 the extra work occasioned by the Crimean War led to the appointment of an additional First Class Clerk and three further Third Class Clerks.[96] In March 1855 it was recognised that the many alterations that had been made to the establishment in the course of the years had resulted in a considerable change in the relative proportions of the various classes of Clerks. In particular it was felt that the more senior Clerks in the third class were inadequately remunerated and required an increase of salary so that more encouragement could be held out to them. Accordingly the third class was divided into two sections, the first consisting of twelve Clerks with salaries ranging from £250 to £350 and the second consisting of sixteen Clerks with salaries ranging from £100 to £150.[97] Following the order in council of May 1855 arrangements were made for all those nominated to places on the establishment to be examined by the Civil Service Commissioners.[98]

In October 1855 the Board, after considering the reports of the investigations made by Sir Stafford Northcote and Sir Charles Trevelyan into the organisation of various public departments, approached the Treasury with the suggestion that a similar enquiry should be undertaken into the Admiralty establishment in Whitehall. The Treasury concurred and nominated the Hon. H. B. W. Brand, one of its junior Lords, to serve with Captain Milne, one of the Naval Lords, and Phinn, the Second Secretary of the Admiralty as a committee for the purpose. The committee never actually made a report but it gathered a great deal of valuable evidence from various Admiralty officials about the organisation and functioning of the office.[99] Conflicting opinions were expressed about the value of a system of promotion based upon merit rather than seniority. Witnesses admitted that, in spite of the terms of the order in council of 1816, there had been only one case since that date in which a Clerk had been passed over for promotion.[100] A number of changes were put forward during the proceedings of the committee, some of which were ultimately adopted. These included the appointment of a Librarian and the discontinuance of the system whereby Clerks on the establishment were entrusted with the preparation of the digests and indexes of Admiralty records and the introduction of a distinct class of Writers to undertake this

[95] Adm. 12/383, Lord Minto's minute of 28 Aug. 1841; order in council 29 Dec. 1853 (PC 2/238 pp. 466-8). [96] Order in council 7 April 1854 (PC 2/239 p. 337).
[97] Order in council 31 March 1855 (PC 2/241 p. 368).
[98] Adm. 12/602, 25 Oct. 1855. [99] Adm. 1/5660.
[100] For Barrow's view on promotion see n. 93.

work. The proposal that the duties of the Chief Clerk should be revised and his office associated with that of Assistant Secretary was not adopted until after the period covered by these lists.

Even after the end of the Crimean War it proved possible to make only relatively modest reductions in the establishment. The number of Third Class (Second Section) Clerks was gradually reduced, reaching eleven in 1859 and nine in 1862. However, from 1855 to 1866 it proved necessary to employ a body of Temporary Clerks who, despite their name, soon became accepted as a permanent feature of the office. Between 1861 and 1866 all new recruits to the establishment were selected from amongst the Temporary Clerks. In 1862 the additional work arising from the increased size of the naval force now maintained in commission and also from the measures that had been introduced to secure an adequate reserve of seamen led to the appointment of a further First Class Clerk. At the same time a Librarian was added to the establishment to take charge of the Admiralty Library which contained in the region of 25,000 books and was increasing at the rate of about 500 annually.[101]

In 1863 it was recognised that the increase in the size of the fleet and the introduction of iron ships into the navy had created more additional work for the department than it was able to undertake satisfactorily with its existing staff. The appointment of an additional Second Class Clerk was therefore authorised. At the same time the work of the Record Branch of the Admiralty was reorganised. As already noted it had previously been the practice for Clerks on the ordinary establishment to undertake the duties of registering, digesting and indexing papers. The decision was now made to entrust these tasks to a distinct grade of Writers specifically recruited for the purpose. Authority was given for the appointment of two Digest Writers with salaries ranging from £200 to £350 and two Index Writers with salaries ranging from £100 to £250. It was understood that the Writers would remain quite distinct from the ordinary establishment. Following these changes the permanent clerical staff of the Admiralty was fixed at one Chief, eleven First Class, thirteen Second Class and twenty-three Third Class Clerks, and four Writers.[102]

In January 1866 the Temporary Clerks were dispensed with and replaced by a new class of Temporary Writers who were to have no claim to be placed on the establishment.[103] In December 1866 a further revision of the clerical staff was made necessary as a result of the additional work caused by changes in the construction and armament of the fleet and the transfer to the Admiralty of the management of the estates of Greenwich Hospital. Authority was given for the appointment of an additional Second Class Clerk and three additional Third Class Clerks. The clerical establishment was thereupon fixed at fifty-one, consisting of one Chief, eleven First Class (or Senior), fourteen Second Class, twelve Third Class (First Section) and thirteen Third Class (Second Section) Clerks.[104] In 1867 the financial prospects of the Clerks were improved as a result of an increase in the size of the annual increments appropriate to the various grades.[105] Later in the same year the office of one of the First Class Clerks was dispensed with.[106]

[101] HC 44 pp. 12–13, 16–17 (1888) lxxx, 16–17, 20–1; order in council 26 April 1862 (PC 2/255 pp. 361–2). [102] Order in council 9 Jan. 1863 (PC 2/257 pp. 213–14).
[103] Adm. 12/778, 10 Jan. 1866; Adm. 12/828, 15 Jan. 1869. Temporary Writers have not been included in these lists.
[104] Minute of Lord C. E. Paget 27 April 1866 (Adm. 2/778); order in council 28 Dec. 1866 (PC 2/264 pp. 998–9). [105] Order in council 2 Feb. 1867 (PC 2/265 pp. 158–9).
[106] Adm. 12/794, 3 April 1867.

Following the appointment of Childers as First Lord of the Admiralty in December 1868 important changes were introduced into naval administration generally. It was provided that the office of Second Naval Lord (or Third Lord) of the Admiralty should be combined with that of Comptroller of the Navy.[107] This change heralded a process of rationalisation and consolidation of naval administration generally. In particular it prompted a review of the staff of the Admiralty proper and that of the Comptroller. A departmental committee was set up in June 1869 consisting of Sir S. Robinson, the Third Lord and Comptroller of the Navy, Trevelyan, the Civil Lord and Lushington, the Second Secretary, which conducted a detailed enquiry into the departments. The committee noted that considerable reforms had already taken place. At the beginning of 1869 the work of the department apart from that concerned with the Record Office had been distributed amongst nine branches known as the military, naval, commission, warrant, legal, miscellaneous, pension, establishment and steam branches. In April the legal and miscellaneous and the commission and warrant branches were united and the business of the steam branch largely transferred to the Comptroller's department. The number of branches was thus effectively reduced to six. The committee recommended that the establishment branch should be broken up and the work of the department concentrated in five branches with the titles military, naval, commission and warrant, legal and miscellaneous and pension. The committee urged that no one should be finally placed permanently on the establishment until he had served three years on probation and it also approved a minute of 2 January 1869 according to which promotions in the department were to rest with the Permanent (or Second) Secretary subject to the approval of the First Lord.[108]

The recommendations of the committee were carried into effect by a minute of 4 January 1870. The Chief Clerk was confirmed in his position as the head of the clerical establishment. The number of First Class Clerks was fixed at six, five of whom were to preside over the five branches into which the business of the department was divided, while the remaining Clerk in the class was to have charge of the Record Office. The rest of the clerical staff was divided into twelve Clerks of the second class and eighteen of the third class. Four Digest Writers and thirteen other Writers were also to be employed.[109] This minute governed the structure of the office at the end of the year 1870, the terminal point for the period covered by these lists.

[107] These changes were embodied in an order in council of 14 Jan. 1869 (Vesey Hamilton, *Naval Administration*, 189–91). The title of Comptroller of the Navy had been revived in 1860 and conferred upon the Surveyor of the Navy, one of the Principal Officers appointed at the time of the reorganisation of Admiralty administration in 1832.
[108] Adm. 116/8.
[109] Adm. 12/846, 4 Jan. 1870.

Lord High Admiral and Commissioners of the Admiralty 1660-1870

The powers and functions of the Admiralty were vested in the office of Lord High Admiral throughout the period except for the years 1684–9 when they were exercised directly by the crown.[1] The office was held by individuals during the years 1660–73, 1702–9 and 1827–8; at other times it was placed in commission. Appointments were made by letters patent under the great seal.[2] Except in the case of the Duke of York who was appointed for life, tenure was during pleasure.

Between 1673 and 1679 the Board was composed of between twelve and sixteen Privy Counsellors who served without salaries. In 1673 provision was made for the holders of the offices of Lord Chancellor (or Lord Keeper), Lord Treasurer and Lord Privy Seal to be *ex officio* members.[3] This arrangement was extended to include the Secretaries of State in the following year.[4] In 1679 a smaller number of paid Commissioners were substituted who were not necessarily members of the Council. The number of Commissioners was fixed in principle at seven although between 1679 and 1718 it fell on occasion to six or to five. From 1683 to 1684 there were seven paid Commissioners and one supernumerary Commissioner who served without salary. Between 1718 and 1822 the Board was invariably composed of seven Commissioners. In the latter year the number was reduced to five.[5] It was increased to six in 1832 but reduced again to five in 1868.

Although the standing of all the Commissioners was in theory the same, the First Commissioner or First Lord exercised an ascendancy over his colleagues from an early date.[6] Until the early nineteenth century it was not unusual for the First Lord to be a naval officer; after 1806 the only naval officer to occupy the post was the Duke of Northumberland (1852).[7] During the eighteenth century it was usual for at least

[1] For the office of Lord High Admiral and the Admiralty Board generally, see James and Shaw, *Admiralty Administration*, 10–24, 172–80; Ehrman, *Navy*, 186–98, 651–6; Corbett MS, iv pp. 1–25; D. A. Baugh, *British Naval Administration in the Age of Walpole* (Princeton 1965), 61–81; *Rept. of Select Committee on Board of Admiralty 1861* (HC 438 pp. 1–792 (1861) v, 1–808); Murray, Admiralty, xxiii, 19–25.

[2] It was also the practice for the Lord High Admiral to be declared in Council. The ceremony preceded the issue of the letters patent in the case of the Earl of Pembroke (PC 2/78 p. 303, 18 Jan. 1702; PC 2/82 p. 205, 25 Nov. 1708) and followed it in the cases of Prince George (PC 2/79 p. 129, 21 May 1702) and the Duke of Clarence (PC 2/208, 10 May 1827).

[3] Commission of 9 July 1673 (Adm. 2/1736 pp. 31–4).

[4] Commission of 31 Oct. 1674 (C 66/3164).

[5] *Parliamentary Debates*, 2nd ser., vi, cols. 866–82. In the same year it was enacted that, when the number of Commissioners was less than six, the quorum should be reduced from three to two (3 Geo. IV, c 19).

[6] Leake, although named first in the Admiralty commission between 1710 and 1712, 'declined to be First Commissioner' (S. Martin Leake, *The Life of Sir John Leake*, ed. G. Callender ii (Navy Records Soc., liii, 1920), 344–5). See also *Queen Anne's Navy*, ed. R. D. Merriman (Navy Records Soc., ciii 1961), 3–4.

[7] HC 235 pp. 1–3 (1876) xlv, 571–3.

one of the junior Commissioners to be a naval officer; occasionally the number rose to three. Between 1804 and 1822 there were invariably three junior 'Naval' Lords.[8] The number fell to two in the latter year when the membership of the Board was reduced to five. Barham was apparently the earliest First Lord to introduce a settled arrangement for the distribution of duties amongst the members of the Board. In 1805 he assigned specific functions to each of the Naval Lords, described as 'Professional' Lords, while leaving to the 'Civil' Lords the routine business of signing documents.[9] This arrangement was revised and given greater definition during Graham's period of office as First Lord (1830–4) when, following the abolition of the Navy and Victualling Boards, the work of the Admiralty Board was reorganised and each of its members given particular responsibility for areas of naval administration.[10] From 1830 it was fixed in principle that, apart from the First Lord, there should be four Naval Lords; a Civil Lord was added in 1832. This arrangement was subject to minor variations. In 1834–5 there were three Naval and two Civil Lords while in 1852–3 and again in 1866 there were five Naval Lords and no Civil Lord. In 1868 the number of Naval Lords was reduced to three and the office of second Naval Lord (or Third Lord) was combined with that of Comptroller of the Navy.[11] Originally all the Commissioners of the Admiralty were entitled to sit in the House of Commons; in 1832 the number so entitled was reduced to five.[12]

Substantial perquisites were attached to the office of Lord High Admiral. The Duke of York was the last occupant of the office to receive these for his personal use. Both the Earl of Pembroke and Prince George surrendered their rights to the crown. In the case of the Duke of Clarence the perquisites were specifically reserved to the crown in the patent of appointment; when the office was in commission they were invariably so reserved.[13] With the exception of the Duke of Clarence each Lord High Admiral was granted a patent salary payable at the Exchequer. The Duke of York received 200 marks and the Earl of Pembroke and Prince George 300 marks.[14] In addition Pembroke was granted £5000 from Admiralty perquisites in recognition of his brief period of service as Lord High Admiral in 1702.[15] On his reappointment in 1708 he was accorded £7000 a year payable by the Treasurer of the Navy in addition to his patent salary.[16] The salary of the Duke of Clarence as Lord High Admiral was £5000.[17]

From 1679 the salaries of the Admiralty Commissioners were fixed at £1000 each payable by the Treasurer of the Navy.[18] Originally the First Lord received the same as the others. In 1699 an attempt was made to increase his remuneration in view of

[8] The use of the term 'Sea Lord' was not officially authorised until 1904 (Murray, Admiralty, xxiii, 23).

[9] Adm. 3/256, minute of May 1805 printed in Letters and Papers of Charles, Lord Barham, ed. J. K. Laughton, iii (Navy Records Soc., xxxix, 1911), 76–8. The editor has imported into the printed text the term 'Sea Lord' which is not to be found in the original. See also Murray, Admiralty, xxiv, 347–8.

[10] Barrow, Autobiography, 417; J. H. Briggs, Naval Administrations 1827–92 (London 1897), 33–4; Vesey Hamilton, Naval Administration, 22–4. In the alphabetical list of officials the designations 'Naval' and 'Civil' Lord have been applied to the Commissioners only from 1830.

[11] Order in council 14 Jan. 1869 (Vesey Hamilton, Naval Administration, 189–91).

[12] 2 Will. IV, c 40, s 1.

[13] Corbett MS, v pp. 113–14; HCA 50/7 ff. 154–5; CTB, xviii, 316; letters patent to Clarence 2 May 1827 (C 66/4319).

[14] Letters patent to York 29 Jan. 1661 (C 66/2932), to Pembroke 26 Jan. 1702 (C 66/3422) and 29 Nov. 1708 (C 66/3466), to Prince George 20 May 1702 (C 66/3424) and 28 June 1707 (C 66/3462).

[15] CTB, xvii, 323.   [16] CTB, xxiii, 106; SPB, xiv f. 1.

[17] Order in council 30 June 1827 (PC 2/208 p. 306).   [18] CTB, vi, 81.

his special responsibilities but was unsuccessful.[19] The earliest First Lord to be granted an additional salary appears to have been Orford (1709–10) who received £2000 from an unknown source. Strafford (1712–14) was granted the same amount paid by the Treasurer of the Navy out of money arising from the sale of old stores.[20] However, Orford received only the basic Commissioner's salary of £1000 during his period of service as First Lord from 1714 to 1717. It was not until the appointment of Berkeley in 1717 that it became the invariable practice for each First Lord to be granted the additional salary of £2000. At first this sum was carried on the ordinary establishment but from 1718 to 1806 it was again paid out of old stores money.[21] In 1806 the First Lord was provided with a salary of £5000 on the ordinary establishment.[22] In 1831 this was reduced to £4500.[23] In addition to their salaries some of the Admiralty Commissioners were entitled to official residences and various other allowances.[24] In 1869 their remuneration was fixed as follows: First Lord £4500 a year with a residence, First and Second Naval Lords £1500 a year with residences, Third Naval Lord £1000 a year with a residence and Civil Lord £1000 a year without a residence.[25]

In the following list the letter (N) after the name of a Commissioner indicates that he was a naval officer.

LIST OF APPOINTMENTS

1661	29 Jan.[26]	York, Duke of (C 66/2932).
1673	9 July	Rupert, Prince; Shaftesbury, Earl of; Osborne, Viscount; Anglesey, Earl of; Buckingham, Duke of; Monmouth, Duke of; Lauderdale, Duke of; Ormond, Duke of; Arlington, Earl of; Carteret, Sir G.; Coventry, Hon. H.; Seymour, E. (Adm. 2/1736 pp. 31–4).
1674	31 Oct.	Rupert, Prince; Finch, Lord; Danby, Earl of; Anglesey, Earl of; Monmouth, Duke of; Lauderdale, Duke of; Ormond, Duke of; Arlington, Earl of; Carteret, Sir G.; Coventry, Hon. H.; Williamson, Sir J.; Seymour, E. (C 66/3164).
1677	26 Sept.	Rupert, Prince; Finch, Lord; Danby, Earl of; Anglesey, Earl of; Monmouth, Duke of; Lauderdale, Duke of; Ormond, Duke of; Ossory, Earl of; Arlington, Earl of; Craven, Earl of; Carteret, Sir G.; Coventry, Hon. H.; Williamson, Sir J.; Ernle, Sir J.; Chicheley, Sir T.; Seymour, E. (C 66/3194).

[19] *CTB*, xiv, 100, 400–1.

[20] *CTB*, xxvi, 527; *CTB*, xxvii, 3, 84; SPB, i f. 44; BL Add. MS 31144 ff. 371–2 cited by G. S. Holmes, *British Politics in the Age of Anne* (London 1967), 137.

[21] SPB, i ff. 44, 48; *CTB*, xxxi, 314; *CTB*, xxxii, 305; Corbett MS, iv p. 16.

[22] Royal warrant 27 June 1806 (T 52/90 pp. 369–70); SPB, iii f. 2; Corbett MS, iv p. 16.

[23] *Rept. of Select Committee on Reduction of Salaries 1831* (HC 322 p. 8 (1830–1) iii, 452); TM 15 April 1831 (HC 375 p. 3 (1830–1) vii, 495).

[24] *3rd Rept. on Fees*, 108–9; order in council 15 Jan. 1800 (HC 138 p. 12 (1816) xiii, 180). When such residences were not available an additional allowance of £200 a year was provided (HC 5 p. 5 (1843) xxxi, 307).

[25] Order in council 14 Jan. 1869 (Vesey Hamilton, *Naval Administration*, 189–91).

[26] The date of the letters patent issued after the Restoration; in fact York acted as Lord High Admiral from the Restoration, presumably by virtue of a grant made about 1649 (James and Shaw, Admiralty Administration, 19 n. 4).

1679	14 May	Capel, Hon. Sir H.; Finch, Hon. D.; Lee, Sir T.; Winch, Sir H.; Meres, Sir T.; Vaughan, E.; Hales, E. (C 66/3210).
1681	19 Feb.	Finch, Hon. D.; Winch, Sir H.; Meres, Sir T.; Hales, E.; Brouncker, Viscount; Littleton, Sir T. (C 66/3217).
1682	20 Jan.	Finch, Lord; Winch, Sir H.; Meres, Sir T.; Hales, E.; Brouncker, Viscount; Savile, H.; Chicheley, Sir J. (N) (C 66/3225).
1683	22 Aug.	Nottingham, Earl of; Winch, Sir H.; Meres, Sir T.; Hales, E.; Brouncker, Viscount; Savile, H.; Chicheley, Sir J. (N); Herbert, A. (N) (*supernumerary*) (C 66/3237).
1684	17 April[27]	Nottingham, Earl of; Winch, Sir H.; Meres, Sir T.; Hales, Sir E.; Savile, H.; Chicheley, Sir J. (N); Herbert, A. (N); Vaughan, Lord (*supernumerary*) (C 66/3245).
1689	8 March	Herbert, A. (N); Carbery, Earl of; Warton, Sir M.; Lee, Sir T.; Chicheley, Sir J. (N); Lowther, Sir J.; Sacheverell, W. (C 66/3325).
1690	20 Jan.	Pembroke, Earl of; Carbery, Earl of; Lee, Sir T.; Lowther, Sir J.; Chicheley, Sir J. (N) (C 66/3332).
1690	5 June	Pembroke, Earl of; Carbery, Earl of; Lee, Sir T.; Lowther, Sir J.; Russell, E. (N); Onslow, Sir R.; Priestman, H. (N) (C 66/3334).
1691	23 Jan.	Pembroke, Earl of; Lee, Sir T.; Lowther, Sir J.; Onslow, Sir R.; Priestman, H. (N); Falkland, Viscount; Austen, R. (C 66/3339).
1691	16 Nov.	Pembroke, Earl of; Lowther, Sir J.; Onslow, Sir R.; Priestman, H. (N); Falkland, Viscount; Austen, R.; Rich, Sir R. (C 66/3347).
1692	10 March	Cornwallis, Lord; Lowther, Sir J.; Onslow, Sir R.; Priestman, H. (N); Falkland, Viscount; Austen, R.; Rich, Sir R. (C 66/3350).
1693	15 April	Falkland, Viscount; Lowther, Sir J.; Priestman, H. (N); Austen, R.; Rich, Sir R.; Killigrew, H. (N); Delaval, Sir R. (N) (C 66/3364).
1694	2 May	Russell, E. (N); Lowther, Sir J.; Priestman, H. (N); Austen, R.; Rich, Sir R.; Rooke, Sir G. (N); Houblon, Sir J. (C 66/3368).
1696	24 Feb.	Russell, E. (N); Priestman, H. (N); Austen, R.; Rich, Sir R.; Rooke, Sir G. (N); Houblon, Sir J.; Kendall, J. (C 66/3385).
1697	5 June	Orford, Earl of (N); Priestman, H. (N); Rich, Sir R.; Rooke, Sir G. (N); Houblon, Sir J.; Kendall, J.; Wharton, Hon. G. (C 66/3395).
1699	31 May	Bridgwater, Earl of; Haversham, Lord; Rich, Sir R.; Rooke, Sir G. (N); Mitchell, Sir D. (N) (C 66/3413).
1699	28 Oct.	Bridgwater, Earl of; Haversham, Lord; Rooke, Sir G. (N); Mitchell, Sir D. (N); Churchill, G. (N) (C 66/3410).
1701	4 April	Pembroke, Earl of; Haversham, Lord; Rooke, Sir G. (N); Mitchell, Sir D. (N); Churchill, G. (N) (Adm. 7/726 pp. 1–19).
1702	26 Jan.	Pembroke, Earl of (C 66/3422).
1702	20 May	George, Prince (C 66/3424).
1707	28 June	George, Prince[28] (C 66/3462).

[27] Commission revoked by letters patent 19 May 1684 (C 66/3245).
[28] Reappointed following the union with Scotland.

1708   29 Nov.   Pembroke, Earl of (C 66/3466).

1709   8 Nov.   Orford, Earl of (N); Leake, Sir J. (N); Byng, Sir G. (N); Dodington, G.; Methuen, P. (C 66/3471).

1710   4 Oct.   Leake, Sir J. (N);[29] Byng, Sir G. (N); Dodington, G.; Methuen, P.; Drake, Sir W.; Aislabie, J. (C 66/3474).

1710   20 Dec.   Leake, Sir J. (N);[29] Byng, Sir G. (N); Drake, Sir W.; Aislabie, J.; Wishart, Sir J. (N); Clarke, G. (C 66/3476).

1712   30 Sept.   Strafford, Earl of; Leake, Sir J. (N); Byng, Sir G. (N); Drake, Sir W.; Aislabie, J.; Wishart, Sir J. (N); Clarke, G. (C 66/3486).

1714   19 Jan.   Strafford, Earl of; Leake, Sir J. (N); Drake, Sir W.; Aislabie, J.; Wishart, Sir J. (N); Clarke, G. (C 66/3494).

1714   9 April   Strafford, Earl of; Leake, Sir J. (N); Drake, Sir W.; Wishart, Sir J. (N); Clarke, G.; Beaumont, Sir G. (C 66/3495).

1714   14 Oct.   Orford, Earl of (N); Byng, Sir G. (N); Dodington, G.; Jennings, Sir J. (N); Turner, Sir C.; Stanyan, A.; Baillie, G. (C 66/3508).

1717   16 April   Berkeley, Earl of (N); Aylmer, M. (N); Byng, Sir G. (N); Cockburn, J.; Chetwynd, W. R. (C 66/3519).

1718   19 March   Berkeley, Earl of (N); Byng, Sir G. (N); Jennings, Sir J. (N); Cockburn, J.; Chetwynd, W. R.; Norris, Sir J. (N); Wager, Sir C. (N) (C 66/3523).

1721   30 Sept.   Berkeley, Earl of (N); Jennings, Sir J. (N); Cockburn, J.; Chetwynd, W. R.; Norris, Sir J. (N); Wager, Sir C. (N); Pulteney, D. (C 66/3546).

1725   3 June   Berkeley, Earl of (N); Jennings, Sir J. (N); Cockburn, J.; Chetwynd, W. R.; Norris, Sir J. (N); Wager, Sir C. (N); Oxenden, Sir G. (C 66/3557).

1727   1 June   Berkeley, Earl of (N); Cockburn, J.; Chetwynd, W. R.; Norris, Sir J. (N); Wager, Sir C. (N); Oxenden, Sir G.; Lyttelton, Sir T. (C 66/3565).

1727   2 Aug.   Torrington, Viscount (N); Cockburn, J.; Norris, Sir J. (N); Wager, Sir C. (N); Lyttelton, Sir T.; Malpas, Viscount; Molyneux, S. (C 66/3566).

1728   1 June   Torrington, Viscount (N); Cockburn, J.; Norris, Sir J. (N); Wager, Sir C. (N); Lyttelton, Sir T.; Malpas, Viscount; Yonge, Sir W. (C 66/3571).

1729   19 May   Torrington, Viscount (N); Cockburn, J.; Norris, Sir J. (N); Wager, Sir C. (N); Lyttelton, Sir T.; Yonge, Sir W.; Hamilton, Lord A. (N) (C 66/3577).

1730   13 May   Torrington, Viscount (N); Cockburn, J.; Wager, Sir C. (N); Lyttelton, Sir T.; Hamilton, Lord A. (N); Frankland, Sir T.; Winnington, T. (C 66/3580).

1732   15 June   Torrington, Viscount (N); Wager, Sir C. (N); Lyttelton, Sir T.; Hamilton, Lord A. (N); Frankland, Sir T.; Winnington, T.; Clutterbuck, T. (C 66/3587).

1733   21 June   Wager, Sir C. (N); Lyttelton, Sir T.; Hamilton, Lord A. (N); Frankland, Sir T.; Winnington, T.; Clutterbuck, T.; Powlett, Lord H. (C 66/3590).

[29] Not 'First Lord'. See p. 18 n. 6.

1736	22 May	Wager, Sir C. (N); Lyttelton, Sir T.; Hamilton, Lord A. (N); Frankland, Sir T.; Clutterbuck, T.; Powlett, Lord H. (N); Campbell, J. (C 66/3596).
1738	13 March	Wager, Sir C. (N); Lyttelton, Sir T.; Frankland, Sir T.; Clutterbuck, T.; Powlett, Lord H. (N); Campbell, J.; Beauclerk, Lord V. (N) (C 66/3598).
1741	5 May	Wager, Sir C. (N); Frankland, Sir T.; Powlett, Lord H. (N); Campbell, J.; Beauclerk, Lord V. (N); Glenorchy, Lord; Thompson, E. (C 66/3604).
1742	19 March	Winchilsea, Earl of; Cockburn, J.; Hamilton, Lord A. (N); Baltimore, Lord; Cavendish, P. (N); Lee, G.; Trevor, J. (C 66/3608).
1743	13 Dec.	Winchilsea, Earl of; Cockburn, J.; Hamilton, Lord A. (N); Baltimore, Lord; Lee, G.; Hardy, Sir C. (N); Phillipson, J. (C 66/3613).
1744	27 Dec.	Bedford, Duke of; Sandwich, Earl of; Hamilton, Lord A. (N); Beauclerk, Lord V. (N); Baltimore, Lord; Anson, G. (N); Grenville, G. (C 66/3615).
1745	25 April	Bedford, Duke of; Sandwich, Earl of; Hamilton, Lord A. (N); Beauclerk, Lord V. (N); Anson, G. (N); Grenville, G.; Legge, Hon. H. (C 66/3616).
1746	25 Feb.	Bedford, Duke of; Sandwich, Earl of; Beauclerk, Lord V. (N); Anson, G. (N); Grenville, G.; Legge, Hon. H.; Barrington, Viscount (C 66/3618).
1746	27 June	Bedford, Duke of; Sandwich, Earl of; Beauclerk, Lord V. (N); Anson, G. (N); Grenville, G.; Barrington, Viscount; Duncannon, Viscount (C 66/3619).
1747	23 June	Bedford, Duke of; Sandwich, Earl of; Beauclerk, Lord V. (N); Anson, G. (N); Barrington, Viscount; Duncannon, Viscount; Ellis, W. (C 66/3622).
1748	26 Feb.	Sandwich, Earl of; Beauclerk, Lord V. (N); Anson, Lord (N); Barrington, Viscount; Duncannon, Viscount; Ellis, W.; Stanhope, Hon. J. (C 66/3624).
1748	24 Dec.	Sandwich, Earl of; Beauclerk, Lord V. (N); Anson, Lord (N); Barrington, Viscount; Duncannon, Viscount; Ellis, W.; Villiers, Hon. T. (C 66/3625).
1749	18 Nov.	Sandwich, Earl of; Anson, Lord (N); Barrington, Viscount; Duncannon, Viscount; Ellis, W.; Villiers, Hon. T.; Trentham, Viscount (C 66/3628).
1751	22 June	Anson, Lord (N); Barrington, Viscount; Duncannon, Viscount; Ellis, W.; Villiers, Hon. T.; Rowley, W. (N); Boscawen, Hon. E. (N) (C 66/3633).
1754	9 April	Anson, Lord (N); Duncannon, Viscount; Ellis, W.; Villiers, Hon. T.; Rowley, Sir W. (N); Boscawen, Hon. E. (N); Townshend, Hon. C. (C 66/3643).
1755	29 Dec.	Anson, Lord (N); Duncannon, Viscount; Villiers, Hon. T.; Rowley, Sir W. (N); Boscawen, Hon. E. (N); Bateman, Viscount; Edgcumbe, Hon. R. (C 66/3650).

1756	17 Nov.	Temple, Earl; Boscawen, Hon. E. (N); West, T. (N); Pitt, J.; Hay, G.; Hunter, T. O.; Elliot, G. (C 66/3654).
1756	13 Dec.	Temple, Earl; Boscawen, Hon. E. (N); West, T. (N); Hay, G.; Hunter, T. O.; Elliot, G.; Forbes, Hon. J. (N) (C 66/3655).
1757	6 April	Winchilsea, Earl of; Rowley, Sir W. (N); Boscawen, Hon. E. (N); Elliot, G.; Carysfort, Lord; Mostyn, S. (N); Sandys, Hon. E. (C 66/3657).
1757	2 July	Anson, Lord (N); Boscawen, Hon. E. (N); West, T. (N); Hay, G.; Hunter, T. O.; Elliot, G.; Forbes, Hon. J. (N) (C 66/3658).
1757	26 Sept.	Anson, Lord (N); Boscawen, Hon. E. (N); Hay, G.; Hunter, T. O.; Elliot, G.; Forbes, Hon. J. (N); Stanley, H. (ibid.).
1761	19 March	Anson, Lord (N); Hay, G.; Hunter, T. O.; Forbes, Hon. J. (N); Stanley, H.; Villiers, Viscount; Pelham, T. (C 66/3674).
1762	17 June	Halifax, Earl of; Hay, G.; Hunter, T. O.; Forbes, Hon. J. (N); Stanley, H.; Villiers, Viscount; Pelham, T. (C 66/3684).
1762	18 Oct.	Grenville, Hon. G.; Hay, G.; Hunter, T. O.; Forbes, Hon. J. (N); Stanley, H.; Villiers, Viscount; Pelham, T. (C 66/3686).
1763	1 Jan.	Grenville, Hon. G.; Hay, G.; Hunter, T. O.; Forbes, Hon. J. (N); Stanley, H.; Carysfort, Lord; Harris, J. (ibid.).
1763	20 April	Sandwich, Earl of; Hay, G.; Stanley, H.; Carysfort, Lord; Howe, Viscount (N); Digby, Lord; Pitt, T. (C 66/3687).
1763	16 Sept.	Egmont, Earl of; Hay, G.; Stanley, H.; Carysfort, Lord; Howe, Viscount (N); Digby, Lord; Pitt, T. (C 66/3692).
1765	31 July	Egmont, Earl of; Pitt, T.; Saunders, Sir C. (N); Keppel, Hon. A. (N); Townshend, C.; Meredith, Sir W.; Buller, J. (C 66/3702).
1765	21 Dec.	Egmont, Earl of; Saunders, Sir C. (N); Keppel, Hon. A. (N); Townshend, C.; Meredith, Sir W.; Buller, J.; Yorke, Hon. J. (C 66/3704).
1766	15 Sept.	Saunders, Sir C. (N); Keppel, Hon. A. (N); Townshend, C.; Meredith, Sir W.; Buller, J.; Palmerston, Viscount; Yonge, Sir G. (C 66/3708).
1766	11 Dec.	Hawke, Sir E. (N); Townshend, C.; Buller, J.; Palmerston, Viscount; Yonge, Sir G.; Brett, Sir P. (N); Jenkinson, C. (C 66/3710).
1768	8 March	Hawke, Sir E. (N); Townshend, C.; Buller, J.; Palmerston, Viscount; Yonge, Sir G.; Brett, Sir P. (N); Spencer, Lord C. (C 66/3716).
1770	28 Feb.	Hawke, Sir E.; Buller, J.; Palmerston, Viscount; Spencer, Lord C.; Lisburne, Viscount; Holburne, F. (N); Fox, Hon. C. J. (C 66/3725).
1771	12 Jan.	Sandwich, Earl of; Buller, J.; Palmerston, Viscount; Spencer, Lord C.; Lisburne, Viscount; Holburne, F. (N); Fox, Hon. C. J. (C 66/3729).
1771	2 Feb.	Sandwich, Earl of; Buller, J.; Palmerston, Viscount; Spencer, Lord C.; Lisburne, Viscount; Fox, Hon. C. J.; Hervey, Hon. A. J. (N) (C 66/3730).

1772 6 May — Sandwich, Earl of; Buller, J.; Palmerston, Viscount; Spencer, Lord C.; Lisburne, Viscount; Hervey, Hon. A. J. (N); Bradshaw, T. (C 66/3736).

1774 30 Dec. — Sandwich, Earl of; Buller, J.; Palmerston, Viscount; Spencer, Lord C.; Lisburne, Viscount; Hervey, Hon. A. J. (N); Penton, H. (C 66/3752).

1775 12 April — Sandwich, Earl of; Buller, J.; Palmerston, Viscount; Spencer, Lord C.; Lisburne, Viscount; Penton, H.; Palliser, Sir H. (N) (C 66/3753).

1777 15 Dec. — Sandwich, Earl of; Buller, J.; Spencer, Lord C.; Lisburne, Earl of; Penton, H.; Palliser, Sir H. (N); Mulgrave, Lord (C 66/3767).

1779 23 April — Sandwich, Earl of; Buller, J.; Spencer, Lord C.; Lisburne, Earl of; Penton, H.; Mulgrave, Lord; Man, R. (N) (C 66/3774).

1779 16 July — Sandwich, Earl of; Buller, J.; Lisburne, Earl of; Penton, H.; Mulgrave, Lord; Man, R. (N); Gascoyne, B. (C 66/3775).

1780 22 Sept. — Sandwich, Earl of; Lisburne, Earl of; Penton, H.; Mulgrave, Lord; Gascoyne, B.; Greville, Hon. C. F.; Darby, G. (N) (C/66 3781).

1782 1 April — Keppel, Hon. A. (N); Harland, Sir R. (N); Pigot, H. (N); Duncannon, Viscount; Townshend, Hon. J.; Brett, C.; Hopkins, R. (C 66/3792).

1782 18 July — Keppel, Viscount (N); Harland, Sir R. (N); Pigot, H. (N); Brett, C.; Hopkins, R.; Pratt, Hon. J. J.; Aubrey, J. (C 66/3797).

1783 30 Jan. — Howe, Viscount (N); Pigot, H. (N); Brett, C.; Hopkins, R.; Pratt, Hon. J. J.; Aubrey, J.; Leveson Gower, Hon. J. (N) (C 66/3800).

1783 10 April — Keppel, Viscount (N); Pigot, H. (N); Duncannon, Viscount; Townshend, Hon. J.; Lindsay, Sir J. (N); Jolliffe, W.; Keene, W. (C 66/3803).

1783 31 Dec. — Howe, Viscount (N); Brett, C.; Pratt, Hon. J. J.; Leveson Gower, Hon. J. (N); Apsley, Lord; Perceval, Hon. C. G.; Heywood, J. M. (C 66/3809).

1784 2 April — Howe, Viscount (N); Brett, C.; Hopkins, R.; Pratt, Hon. J. J.; Leveson Gower, Hon. J. (N); Apsley, Lord; Perceval, Hon. C. G. (C 66/3812).

1788 16 July — Chatham, Earl of; Hopkins, R.; Bayham, Viscount; Leveson Gower, Hon. J. (N); Apsley, Lord; Arden, Lord; Hood, Lord (N) (C 66/3840).

1789 12 Aug. — Chatham, Earl of; Hopkins, R.; Arden, Lord; Hood, Lord (N); Drake, Sir F. S. (N); Belgrave, Viscount; Townshend, Hon. J. T. (C 66/3850).

1790 19 Jan. — Chatham, Earl of; Hopkins, R.; Arden, Lord; Hood, Lord (N); Belgrave, Viscount; Townshend, Hon. J. T.; Gardner, A. (N) (C 66/3854).

1791 27 June — Chatham, Earl of; Arden, Lord; Hood, Lord (N); Townshend, Hon. J. T.; Gardner, A. (N); Smyth, J.; Pybus, C. S. (C 66/3868).

1793	26 April	Chatham, Earl of; Arden, Lord; Hood, Lord (N); Gardner, A. (N); Smyth, J.; Pybus, C. S.; Affleck, P. (N) (C 66/3890).
1794	12 May	Chatham, Earl of; Arden, Lord; Hood, Lord (N); Gardner, A. (N); Pybus, C. S.; Affleck, P. (N); Middleton, Sir C. (N) (C 66/3901).
1794	19 Dec.	Spencer, Earl; Arden, Lord; Hood, Lord (N); Gardner, Sir A. (N); Pybus, C. S.; Affleck, P. (N); Middleton, Sir C. (N) (C 66/3908).
1795	7 March	Spencer, Earl; Arden, Lord; Pybus, C. S.; Middleton, Sir C. (N); Seymour, Lord H.; Stephens, P.; Gambier, J. (N) (C 66/3910).
1795	20 Nov.	Spencer, Earl; Arden, Lord; Pybus, C. S.; Seymour, Lord H.; Stephens, Sir P.; Gambier, J. (N); Young, W. (N) (C 66/3918).
1797	25 July	Spencer, Earl; Arden, Lord; Seymour, Lord H.; Stephens, Sir P.; Gambier, J. (N); Young, W. (N); Wallace, T. (C 66/3941).
1798	10 Sept.	Spencer, Earl; Arden, Lord; Stephens, Sir P.; Gambier, J. (N); Young, W. (N); Wallace, T.; Man, R. (N) (C 66/3951).
1800	10 July	Spencer, Earl; Arden, Lord; Stephens, Sir P.; Gambier, J. (N); Young, W. (N); Man, R. (N); Eliot, Hon. W. (C 66/3975).
1801	19 Feb.	St. Vincent, Earl of (N); Stephens, Sir P.; Eliot, Hon. W.; Troubridge, Sir T. (N); Adams, J.; Markham, J. (N); Garthshore, W. (C 66/3985).
1804	17 Jan.	St. Vincent, Earl of (N); Stephens, Sir P.; Troubridge, Sir T. (N); Adams, J.; Markham, J. (N); Lemon, J.; Burrard Neale, Sir H. (N) (C 66/4023).
1804	15 May	Melville, Viscount; Stephens, Sir P.; Gambier, J. (N); Burrard Neale, Sir H. (N); Colpoys, Sir J. (N); Patton, P. (N); Dickenson, W. (C 66/4025).
1804	13 Sept.	Melville, Viscount; Stephens, Sir P.; Gambier, J. (N); Colpoys, Sir J. (N); Patton, P. (N); Dickenson, W.; Nepean, Sir E. (C 66/4029).
1805	2 May	Barham, Lord (N); Stephens, Sir P.; Gambier, J. (N); Patton, P. (N); Dickenson, W.; Nepean, Sir E.; Garlies, Lord (N) (C 66/4038).
1806	10 Feb.	Grey, Hon. C.; Stephens, Sir P.; Markham, J. (N); Pole, Sir C. M. (N); Burrard Neale, Sir H. (N); Russell, Lord W.; Kensington, Lord (C 66/4049).
1806	29 Sept.	Grenville, T.; Stephens, Sir P.; Markham, J. (N); Pole, Sir C. M. (N); Burrard Neale, Sir H. (N); Russell, Lord W.; Kensington, Lord (C 66/4057).
1806	23 Oct.	Grenville, T.; Markham, J. (N); Burrard Neale, Sir H. (N); Russell, Lord W.; Kensington, Lord; Fremantle, T. F. (N); Frankland, W. (C 66/4058).
1807	6 April	Mulgrave, Lord; Gambier, J. (N); Bickerton, Sir R. (N); Johnstone Hope, W. (N); Ward, R.; Palmerston, Viscount; Buller, J. (C 66/4064).
1808	9 May	Mulgrave, Lord; Bickerton, Sir R. (N); Johnstone Hope, W. (N); Ward, R.; Palmerston, Viscount; Buller, J.; Domett, W. (N) (C 66/4077).

1809 30 March   Mulgrave, Lord; Bickerton, Sir R. (N); Ward, R.; Palmerston, Viscount; Buller, J.; Domett, W. (N); Moorsom, R. (N) (C 66/4088).

1809 24 Nov.   Mulgrave, Lord; Bickerton, Sir R. (N); Ward, R.; Buller, J.; Domett, W. (N); Moorsom, R. (N); Lowther, Viscount (C 66/4095).

1810 4 May   Yorke, C. P.; Bickerton, Sir R. (N); Ward, R.; Buller, J.; Domett, W. (N); Moorsom, R. (N); Lowther, Viscount (C 66/4101).

1810 3 July   Yorke, C. P.; Bickerton, Sir R. (N); Ward, R.; Buller, J.; Domett, W. (N); Yorke, Sir J. S. (N); Robinson, Hon. F. J. (C 66/4103).

1811 17 June   Yorke, C. P.; Bickerton, Sir R. (N); Buller, J.; Domett, W. (N); Yorke, Sir J. S. (N); Robinson, Hon. F. J.; Walpole, Lord (C 66/4113).

1812 25 March   Melville, Viscount; Domett, W. (N); Yorke, Sir J. S. (N); Robinson, Hon. F. J.; Walpole, Lord; Dundas, W.; Johnstone Hope, G. (N) (C 66/4121).

1812 5 Oct.   Melville, Viscount; Domett, W. (N); Yorke, Sir J. S. (N); Dundas, W.; Johnstone Hope, G. (N); Warrender, Sir G.; Osborn, J. (C 66/4127).

1813 18 May   Melville, Viscount; Domett, W. (N); Yorke, Sir J. S. (N); Dundas, W.; Warrender, Sir G.; Osborn, J.; Paulet, Lord H. (N) (C 66/4137).

1813 23 Oct.   Melville, Viscount; Yorke, Sir J. S. (N); Dundas, W.; Johnstone Hope, G. (N); Warrender, Sir G.; Osborn, J.; Paulet, Lord H. (N) (C 66/4141).

1814 23 Aug.   Melville, Viscount; Yorke, Sir J. S. (N); Johnstone Hope, G. (N); Warrender, Sir G.; Osborn, J.; Paulet, Lord H. (N); Blachford, B. P. (C 66/4153).

1816 24 May   Melville, Viscount; Yorke, Sir J. S. (N); Johnstone Hope, G. (N); Warrender, Sir G.; Osborn, J.; Moore, Sir G. (N); Worcester, Marquess of (C 66/4176).

1818 2 April   Melville, Viscount; Warrender, Sir G.; Osborn, J.; Moore, Sir G. (N); Worcester, Marquess of; Cockburn, Sir G. (N); Hotham, Hon. Sir H. (N) (C 66/4196).

1819 15 March   Melville, Viscount; Warrender, Sir G.; Osborn, Sir J.; Moore, Sir G. (N); Cockburn, Sir G. (N); Hotham, Hon. Sir H. (N); Clerk, Sir G. (C 66/4209).

1820 13 March   Melville, Viscount; Johnstone Hope, Sir W. (N); Warrender, Sir G.; Osborn, Sir J.; Cockburn, Sir G. (N); Hotham, Hon. Sir H. (N); Clerk, Sir G. (C 66/4218).

1822 8 Feb.   Melville, Viscount; Johnstone Hope, Sir W. (N); Osborn, Sir J.; Cockburn, Sir G. (N); Hotham, Hon. Sir H. (N); Clerk, Sir G.; Douglas, W. R. K. (C 66/4242).

1822 23 March   Melville, Viscount; Johnstone Hope, Sir W. (N); Osborn, Sir J.; Cockburn, Sir G. (N); Clerk, Sir G. (C 66/4244).

1824 16 Feb.   Melville, Viscount; Johnstone Hope, Sir W. (N); Cockburn, Sir G. (N); Clerk, Sir G.; Douglas, W. R. K. (C 66/4267).

1827	2 May	Clarence, Duke of (C 66/4319).
1828	19 Sept.	Melville, Viscount; Cockburn, Sir G. (N); Hotham, Hon. Sir H. (N); Clerk, Sir G.; Brecknock, Earl of (C 66/4343).
1829	15 July	Melville, Viscount; Cockburn, Sir G. (N); Hotham, Hon. Sir H. (N); Clerk, Sir G.; Castlereagh, Viscount (C 66/4353).
1830	31 July	Melville, Viscount; Cockburn, Sir G. (N); Hotham, Hon. Sir H. (N); Castlereagh, Viscount; Ross, C. (C 66/4366).
1830	25 Nov.	Graham, Sir J. R. G.; Hardy, Sir T. M. (N); Dundas, Hon. G. H. L. (N); Brooke Pechell, Sir S. J. (N); Barrington, Hon. G. (N) (C 66/4375).
1832	8 June	Graham, Sir J. R. G.; Hardy, Sir T. M. (N); Dundas, Hon. G. H. L. (N); Brooke Pechell, Sir S. J. (N); Barrington, Hon. G. (N); Labouchere, H. (C 66/4407).
1833	13 April	Graham, Sir J. R. G.; Hardy, Sir T. M. (N); Dundas, Hon. G. H. L. (N); Brooke Pechell, Sir S. J. (N); Labouchere, H.; Berkeley, Hon. M. F. F. (N) (C 66/4418).
1834	11 June	Auckland, Lord; Hardy, Sir T. M. (N); Dundas, Hon. G. H. L. (N); Brooke Pechell, Sir S. J. (N); Labouchere, H.; Berkeley, Hon. M. F. F. (N) (C 66/4436).
1834	1 Aug.	Auckland, Lord; Dundas, Hon. G. H. L. (N); Parker, Sir W. (N); Brooke Pechell, Sir S. J. (N); Labouchere, H.; Berkeley, Hon. M. F. F. (N) (C 66/4439).
1834	1 Nov.	Auckland, Lord; Adam, C. (N); Parker, Sir W. (N); Brooke Pechell, Sir S. J. (N); Labouchere, H.; Berkeley, Hon. M. F. F. (N) (C 66/4444).
1834	23 Dec.	de Grey, Earl; Cockburn, Sir G. (N); Beresford, Sir J. P. (N); Rowley, Sir C. (N); Ashley, Lord; Fitzgerald, M. (C 66/4447).
1835	25 April	Auckland, Lord; Adam, C. (N); Parker, Sir W. (N); Elliot, Hon. G. (N); Troubridge, Sir E. T. (N); Dalmeny, Lord (C 66/4455).
1835	19 Sept.	Minto, Earl of; Adam, Sir C. (N); Parker, Sir W. (N); Elliot, Hon. G. (N); Troubridge, Sir E. T. (N); Dalmeny, Lord (C 66/4462).
1837	22 July	Minto, Earl of; Adam, Sir C. (N); Parker, Sir W. (N); Troubridge, Sir E. T. (N); Dalmeny, Lord; Berkeley, Hon. M. F. F. (N) (C 66/4507).
1839	5 March	Minto, Earl of; Adam, Sir C. (N); Parker, Sir W. (N); Troubridge, Sir E. T. (N); Brooke Pechell, Sir S. J. (N); Dalmeny, Lord (C 66/4560).
1841	25 June	Minto, Earl of; Adam, Sir C. (N); Troubridge, Sir E. T. (N); Brooke Pechell, Sir S. J. (N); Dalmeny, Lord; Deans Dundas, J. W. (N) (C 66/4632).
1841	8 Sept.	Haddington, Earl of; Cockburn, Sir G. (N); Gage, Sir W. H. (N); Seymour, Sir G. F. (N); Gordon, Hon. W. (N); Lowry Corry, Hon. H. T. (C 66/4638).
1844	22 May	Haddington, Earl of; Cockburn, Sir G. (N); Gage, Sir W. H. (N); Bowles, W. (N); Gordon, Hon. W. (N); Lowry Corry, Hon. H. T. (C 66/4714).

1845	12 Feb.	Haddington, Earl of; Cockburn, Sir G. (N); Gage, Sir W. H. (N); Bowles, W. (N); Gordon, Hon. W. (N); Fitzroy, Hon. H. (C 66/4735).
1846	13 Jan.	Ellenborough, Earl of; Cockburn, Sir G. (N); Gage, Sir W. H. (N); Bowles, W. (N); Gordon, Hon. W. (N); Fitzroy, Hon. H. (C 66/4768).
1846	17 Feb.	Ellenborough, Earl of; Cockburn, Sir G. (N); Gage, Sir W. H. (N); Bowles, W. (N); Fitzroy, Hon. H.; Rous, Hon. H. J. (N) (C 66/4771).
1846	13 July	Auckland, Earl of; Parker, Sir W. (N); Deans Dundas, J. W. (N); Berkeley, Hon. M. F. F. (N); Hay, Lord J. (N); Cowper, Hon. W. F. (C 66/4785).
1846	24 July	Auckland, Earl of; Adam, Sir C. (N); Deans Dundas, J. W. (N); Berkeley, Hon. M. F. F. (N); Hay, Lord J. (N); Cowper, Hon. W. F. (C 66/4787).
1847	20 July	Auckland, Earl of; Deans Dundas, J. W. (N); Prescott, H. (N); Berkeley, Hon. M. F. F. (N); Hay, Lord J. (N); Cowper, Hon. W. F. (C 66/4819).
1847	23 Dec.	Auckland, Earl of; Deans Dundas, J. W. (N); Berkeley, Hon. M. F. F. (N); Hay, Lord J. (N); Cowper, Hon. W. F.; Milne, A. (N) (C 66/4831).
1849	18 Jan.	Baring, Sir F. T.; Deans Dundas, J. W. (N); Berkeley, Hon. M. F. F. (N); Hay, Lord J. (N); Cowper, Hon. W. F.; Milne, A. (N) (C66/4856).
1850	9 Feb.	Baring, Sir F. T.; Deans Dundas, J. W. (N); Berkeley, Hon. M. F. F. (N); Stewart, H. (N); Milne, A. (N); Cowper, Hon. W. F. (C 66/4891).
1852	13 Feb.	Baring, Sir F. T.; Berkeley, Hon. M. F. F. (N); Stewart, H. (N); Stirling, Sir J. (N); Milne, A. (N); Cowper, Hon. W. F. (C66/4954).
1852	2 March	Northumberland, Duke of (N); Parker, H. (N); Hornby, P. (N); Herbert, Sir T. (N); Duncombe, Hon. A. (N); Milne, A. (N) (C 66/4956).
1853	5 Jan.	Graham, Sir J. R. G.; Parker, H. (N); Berkeley, Hon. M. F. F. (N); Saunders Dundas, Hon. R. (N); Milne, A. (N); Cowper, Hon. W. F. (C 66/4980).
1854	3 June	Graham, Sir J. R. G.; Berkeley, Hon. M. F. F. (N); Saunders Dundas, Hon. R. (N); Richards, P. (N); Milne, A. (N); Cowper, Hon. W. F. (C 66/4985).
1855	8 March	Wood, Sir C.; Berkeley, Hon. M. F. F. (N); Eden, H. (N); Richards, P. (N); Milne, A. (N) (C 66/4988).
1855	14 March	Wood, Sir C.; Berkeley, Hon. M. F. F. (N); Eden, H. (N); Richards, P. (N); Milne, A. (N); Peel, Sir R. (ibid.).
1857	2 April	Wood, Sir C.; Berkeley, Hon. Sir M. F. F. (N); Saunders Dundas, Hon. Sir R. (N); Eden, H. (N); Milne, A. (N); Peel, Sir R. (C 66/4997).
1857	30 May	Wood, Sir C.; Berkeley, Hon. Sir M. F. F. (N); Saunders Dundas, Hon. Sir R. (N); Eden, H. (N); Milne, A. (N); Baring, T. G. (ibid.).

1857   24 Nov.   Wood, Sir C.; Saunders Dundas, Hon. Sir R. (N); Eden, H. (N); Milne, A. (N); Pelham, Hon. F. T. (N); Baring, T. G. (C 66/4999).

1858   8 March   Pakington, Sir J. S.; Martin, W. F. (N); Saunders Dundas, Hon. Sir R. (N); Milne, A. (N); Drummond, Hon. J. R. (N); Lovaine, Lord (C 66/5000).

1859   28 Jan.   Pakington, Sir J. S.; Martin, W. F. (N); Saunders Dundas, Hon. Sir R. (N); Milne, Sir A. (N); Carnegie, Hon. S. T. (N); Lovaine, Lord (C 66/5003).

1859   11 March   Pakington, Sir J. S.; Martin, W. F. (N); Saunders Dundas, Hon. Sir R. (N); Milne, Sir A. (N); Carnegie, Hon. S. T. (N); Lygon, Hon. F. (ibid.).

1859   23 April   Pakington, Sir J. S.; Martin, W. F. (N); Saunders Dundas, Hon. Sir R. (N); Leeke, Sir H. J. (N); Milne, Sir A. (N); Lygon, Hon. F. (C 66/5004).

1859   28 June   Somerset, Duke of; Saunders Dundas, Hon. Sir R. (N); Pelham, Hon. F. T. (N); Eden, C. (N); Frederick, C. (N); Whitbread, S. (C 66/5005).

1861   15 June   Somerset, Duke of; Grey, Hon. Sir F. W. (N); Eden, C. (N); Frederick, C. (N); Drummond, Hon. J. R. (N); Whitbread, S. (C 66/5009).

1863   27 March   Somerset, Duke of; Grey, Hon. Sir F. W. (N); Eden, C. (N); Frederick, C. (N); Drummond, Hon. J. R. (N); Hartington, Marquess of (C 66/5016).

1863   5 May   Somerset, Duke of: Grey, Hon. Sir F. W. (N); Eden, C. (N); Frederick, C. (N); Drummond, Hon. J. R. (N); Stansfeld, J. (ibid.).

1864   22 April   Somerset, Duke of; Grey, Hon. Sir F. W. (N); Eden, C. (N); Frederick, C. (N); Drummond, Hon. J. R. (N); Childers, H. C. E. (C 66/5018).

1865   25 March   Somerset, Duke of; Grey, Hon. Sir F. W. (N); Eden, C. (N); Fanshawe, E. G. (N); Drummond, Hon. J. R. (N); Childers, H. C. E. (C 66/5021).

1866   23 Jan.   Somerset, Duke of; Grey, Hon. Sir F. W. (N); Eden, C. (N); Fanshawe, E. G. (N); Drummond, Hon. J. R. (N); Fenwick, H. (C 66/5024).

1866   10 April   Somerset, Duke of; Grey, Hon. Sir F. W. (N); Eden, C. (N); Fanshawe, E. G. (N); Drummond, Hon. J. R. (N); Hay, Lord J. (N) (C 66/5025).

1866   9 May   Somerset, Duke of; Grey, Hon. Sir F. W. (N); Eden, C. (N); Fanshawe, E. G. (N); Hay, Lord J. (N); Shaw Lefevre, G. J. (ibid.).

1866   13 July   Pakington, Sir J. S.; Milne, Sir A. (N); Dacres, Sir S. C. (N); Seymour, G. H. (N); Dalrymple Hay, Sir J. C. (N); Du Cane, C. (C 66/5026).

1867   8 March   Lowry Corry, Hon. H. T.; Milne, Sir A. (N); Dacres, Sir S. C. (N); Seymour, G. H. (N); Dalrymple Hay, Sir J. C. (N); Du Cane, C. (C 66/5030).

1868	3 Sept.	Lowry Corry, Hon. H. T.; Milne, Sir A. (N); Dacres, Sir S. C. (N); Seymour, G. H. (N); Dalrymple Hay, Sir J. C. (N); Stanley, Hon. F. A. (C 66/5035).
1868	18 Dec.	Childers, H. C. E.; Dacres, Sir S. C. (N); Robinson, Sir R. S. (N); Hay, Lord J. (N); Trevelyan, G. O. (C 66/5037).
1870	12 July	Childers, H. C. E.; Dacres, Sir S. C. (N); Robinson, Sir R. S. (N); Hay, Lord J. (N); Camperdown, Earl of (C 66/5044).

Members of the Council of the
Lord High Admiral 1702-8; 1827-8

In the cases of Prince George (1702–8) and the Duke of Clarence (1827–8) provision was made for the appointment of a Council to assist and advise the Lord High Admiral in the conduct of the business of the office. In 1702 Prince George was authorised to appoint a Council consisting of not more than five Members who were to hold office during his pleasure; in 1704 the limit was raised to seven.[1] At first there were three naval officers amongst the Members; after 1704 there were usually five. In May 1827 the Duke of Clarence was authorised to appoint a Council of not more than four Members to hold office during his pleasure; in July of the same year the right of appointment was transferred from the Lord High Admiral to the crown.[2] This Council was composed of two naval and two civil Members. The salaries of the Members of both Councils were fixed at £1000.[3]

In the following list the letter (N) after the name of a Member indicates that he was a naval officer.

LISTS OF APPOINTMENTS

COUNCIL OF PRINCE GEORGE

1702	22 May	Rooke, Sir G. (N); Mitchell, Sir D. (N); Churchill, G. (N); Hill, R. (Adm. 6/7).
1703	29 March	Rooke, Sir G. (N); Mitchell, Sir D. (N); Churchill, G. (N); Hill, R.; Brydges, Hon. J. (ibid.).
1704	30 April	Rooke, Sir G. (N); Mitchell, Sir D. (N); Churchill, G. (N); Hill, R.; Brydges, Hon. J.; Paget, Hon. H. (Adm. 7/726 p. 58).
1704	26 Dec.[4]	Rooke, Sir G. (N); Mitchell, Sir D. (N); Churchill, G. (N); Hill, R.; Brydges, Hon. J.; Paget, Hon. H.; Shovell, Sir C. (N) (Adm. 3/20, 26 Dec. 1704).
1705	11 June[5]	Mitchell, Sir D. (N); Churchill, G. (N); Hill, R.; Paget, Hon. H.; Shovell, Sir C. (N); Walpole, R. (AO 1/1725/147).
1706	8 Feb.	Mitchell, Sir D. (N); Churchill, G. (N); Hill, R.; Paget, Hon. H.; Shovell, Sir C. (N); Walpole, R.; Fairborne, Sir S. (N) (Adm. 7/726 p. 58).

---

[1] Letters patent to Prince George 20 May 1702 (C 66/3424), 10 June 1704 (C 66/3445), 28 June 1707 (C 66/3462); D. B. Smith, 'The Lord High Admiral's Council', *Mariner's Mirror*, xvii (1931), 181–2.

[2] Letters patent to Duke of Clarence, 2 May 1827 (C 66/4319); 7 & 8 Geo. IV, c 65, s 4.

[3] SPB, i f. 1; order in council 10 May 1827 (PC 2/208 pp. 229–30).

[4] Warrant not traced; appointment dated approximately from Admiralty minutes.

[5] Warrant not traced; appointment dated approximately from declared accounts, Treasurer of Navy.

1707	28 June[6]	Mitchell, Sir D. (N); Churchill, G. (N); Hill, R.; Paget, Hon. H.; Shovell, Sir C. (N); Walpole, R.; Fairborne, Sir S. (N) (Adm. 6/9 f. 78).
1708	19 April	Wemyss, Earl of (N); Churchill, G. (N); Hill, R.; Paget, Hon. H.; Fairborne, Sir S. (N); Leake, Sir J. (N) (ibid. f. 155).
1708	20 June	Wemyss, Earl of (N); Churchill, G. (N); Hill, R.; Paget, Hon. H.; Leake, Sir J. (N); Wishart, Sir J. (N); Fairfax, R. (N) (ibid. f. 171).

COUNCIL OF THE DUKE OF CLARENCE

1827	2 May	Johnstone Hope, Sir W. (N); Cockburn, Sir G. (N); Douglas, W. R. K.; Denison, J. E. (SPB, xiv f. 1).
1828	4 Feb.	Johnstone Hope, Sir W. (N); Cockburn, Sir G. (N); Clerk, Sir G.; Brecknock, Earl of (ibid.).
1828	12 March	Cockburn, Sir G. (N); Clerk, Sir G.; Brecknock, Earl of; Owen, Sir E. W. C. R. (N) (ibid.).

[6] Reappointed following the union with Scotland.

Secretaries 1660-1870

The Secretary was the senior official of the Admiralty.[1] During the years 1684-9, when the powers and functions of the department were exercised directly by the crown, the Secretary was appointed by the crown by letters patent under the great seal with the title 'Secretary for the Affairs of the Admiralty'.[2] At other times he was designated simply 'Secretary' and was appointed by the Lord High Admiral or the Admiralty Board.[3] The office was held singly until 1694 when two joint Secretaries were appointed.[4] The office of one of the joint Secretaries was dispensed with in 1698 but revived in 1702. It was again dispensed with in 1705 when the office of Deputy Secretary was created.[5] Except during the years 1741-2 no joint Secretary was appointed thereafter.[6] In 1746 the additional business arising from the war led to the appointment of a Second Secretary who became sole Secretary on the death of his colleague in 1751.[7] In 1759 similar considerations again gave rise to the appointment of a Second Secretary who also became sole Secretary on the death of his colleague in 1763.[8] It was not until 1783 that the office of Second Secretary was established on a permanent basis.[9]

From Burchett's period of office (1694-1742) until the early nineteenth century it was the general rule for the Secretaries to be members of the House of Commons but to enjoy nevertheless a secure tenure which was largely unaffected by political changes.[10] However, in 1804 and again in 1806 Second Secretaries were displaced on political grounds. From 1807 it was accepted that the office of First Secretary should be held by a member of the Commons and that its tenure should be subject to the same considerations as that of other political members of the administration. From the same period it was understood that the office of Second Secretary should be non-parliamentary and held on a permanent tenure.[11] Nevertheless it was not until the end of the period covered by these lists that the terms First and Second Secretary began to be superseded by those of Parliamentary and Permanent Secretary.[12]

---

[1] For these offices generally, see Corbett MS, xiii pp. 180-94; James and Shaw, Admiralty Administration, 166-71, 182-3; G. F. James, 'Josiah Burchett, Secretary to the Lords Commissioners of the Admiralty 1695-1742', *Mariner's Mirror*, xxiii (1937), 477-97; F. B. Wickwire, 'Admiralty Secretaries and the British Civil Service', *Huntington Library Quarterly*, xxviii (1964-5), 235-54.

[2] Letters patent 10 June 1684 (C 66/3245).

[3] In 1673 and 1694 the crown took an active interest in the appointment of the Secretary. See *A Descriptive Catalogue of the Naval Manuscripts in the Pepysian Library*, ed. J. R. Tanner ii (Navy Records Soc., xxvii, 1904), 1; Ehrman, *Navy*, 558 n.

[4] Adm. 2/16 p. 414. Phineas Bowles had urged the appointment of a second Secretary in 1690 (Ehrman, *Navy*, 657-61). [5] SPB, i f. 1; Adm. 6/8 f. 201.

[6] PC 2/96 pp. 442, 447-8, 455. [7] Adm. 3/55, 1 Aug. 1746.

[8] Adm. 3/67, 16 Oct. 1759. [9] Adm. 3/96, 13 Jan. 1783.

[10] *3rd Rept. on Fees*, 102. [11] Barrow, *Autobiography*, 254-5, 291-2, 298-9. See also p. 11.

[12] On his appointment in 1869 Lushington was described as 'Permanent or Second Secretary' (Adm. 12/828, 29 June 1869). In the departmental estimates the terms 'Financial' and 'Permanent' were substituted for 'First' and 'Second' Secretaries in 1868 (HC 7 p. 13 (1867-8) xlv, 13; HC 10 p. 14 (1868-9) xxxviii, 14).

Between 1660 and 1664 the Secretary was entirely dependent on fees for his remuneration. In the latter year a salary of £500, payable by the Treasurer of the Navy, was made available by the crown in consideration of the abolition of certain of these fees.[13] In the case of the office of Secretary for the Affairs of the Admiralty (1684–9) it was provided that, when the fees arising from the issue of passes fell short of £2000 a year, the difference should be made up from public funds.[14] In 1694 the salary of the Secretary was fixed at £800 on the general abolition of the fees. A second salary of the same amount was provided while joint Secretaries were serving.[15] Burchett enjoyed, as Secretary, an additional allowance of £200 from the contingent fund while Prince George was Lord High Admiral.[16] In 1717 the fees were restored and in the following year provision was made for the Secretary to receive half the product for his own use.[17] On the formation of the Marine Department in 1755 the Secretary or First Secretary became its Secretary *ex officio* and was accorded a salary of £300 as such payable by the Paymaster of Marines. He also received all the fees arising in the Marine Department.[18] In 1800 the various forms of remuneration received by the First Secretary were replaced by a single salary of £3000, with an additional allowance of £1000 in time of war.[19] In 1815 the distinction between war and peace salaries was abolished and the salary of the First Secretary fixed permanently at the war level of £4000.[20] It was, however, reduced again to £3000 in 1818.[21] In 1831 it was fixed at £2000 with provision for an increase to £2500 after five years' service.[22]

The salary of the Second Secretary varied. On his appointment in August 1746 Clevland was granted £600 which was increased to £800 in the following October.[23] Stephens was also appointed at £600 in 1759, his salary being raised to £800 in 1761.[24] When the office was established on a permanent basis in 1783 the salary was fixed at £600, being raised to £800 in 1790.[25] From 1783 the Second Secretary was also Second Secretary of the Marine Department and received as such £200 payable by the Paymaster of Marines.[26] In addition to these salaries the Second Secretary also enjoyed a proportion of the office fees, his share being calculated on the basis of the Chief Clerk's salary of £400.[27] In 1800 the various forms of remuneration received

---

[13] Letters of privy seal to Coventry 6 Sept. 1664 (MS Rawlinson A 185 f. 451). The grants of salaries to successive Secretaries were usually embodied in letters of privy seal until 1689.

[14] Warrant 7 Aug. 1687 (MS Rawlinson A 177 f. 131).

[15] Ehrman, *Navy*, 662–3.

[16] Subsequently Burchett received the arrears of this allowance from the death of Prince George in 1708 until the end of the war in 1713 (PC 2/86 pp. 13, 26; Adm. 3/31, 5 Aug. 1717).

[17] Order in council 31 July 1717 (PC 2/86 pp. 13, 26, 482); Adm. 3/31, 8 July 1718; *3rd Rept. on Fees*, 96. While he was joint Secretary 1741–2 Corbett enjoyed half the Secretary's share of the fees in addition to the fees which he had previously been accorded as Deputy Secretary Adm. 3/45, 2 Dec. 1741 and 23 Feb. 1742).

[18] Adm. 2/1152 pp. 134–5; *3rd Rept. on Fees*, 97, 107, 116.

[19] Order in council 15 Jan. 1800 (HC 138 p. 2 (1816) xiii, 170).

[20] Order in council 21 June 1815 (HC 125 p. 1 (1816) xiii, 167).

[21] Order in council 10 Feb. 1818 (PC 2/212 pp. 34–5).

[22] *Rept. of Select Committee on Reduction of Salaries 1831* (HC 322 p. 8 (1830–1) iii, 452); TM 15 April 1831 (HC 375 p. 3 (1830–1) vii, 495).

[23] Adm. 3/55, 1 Aug. and 14 Oct. 1746.

[24] Adm. 3/67, 16 Oct. 1759; Adm. 3/68, 9 June 1761.

[25] Adm. 3/96, 13 Jan. 1783; Adm. 3/107, 19 May 1790.

[26] Adm. 3/96, 13 Jan. 1783; *3rd Rept. on Fees*, 97, 108.

[27] Adm. 3/55, 1 Aug. 1746; Adm. 3/67, 16 Oct. 1759; *3rd Rept. on Fees*, 108.

by the Second Secretary were replaced by a single salary of £1500, with an additional allowance of £500 in time of war.[28] In 1815 the salary was fixed permanently at the war level of £2000.[29] It was reduced again to £1500 in 1818.[30] In 1831 it was fixed at £1000 with provision for an increase to £1500 after five years' service.[31] Baillie Hamilton was appointed on this basis in 1845 but was, in the event, allowed the increased salary from 1848.[32] His successors were each appointed at £1500 until the end of the period.

LISTS OF APPOINTMENTS

SECRETARIES AND FIRST SECRETARIES

1660	July	Coventry, Hon. W.	1807	24 June	Wellesley Pole, Hon. W.
1667	Sept.	Wren, M.			
1672	July	Werden, Sir J.	1809	12 Oct.	Croker, J. W.
1673	June	Pepys, S.	1830	29 Nov.	Elliot, Hon. G.
1679	May	Hayter, T.	1834	24 Dec.	Dawson, G. R.
1680	Feb.	Brisbane, J.	1835	27 April	Wood, C.
1684	May	Pepys, S.	1839	4 Oct.	More O'Ferrall, R.
1689	March	Bowles, P.	1841	9 June	Parker, J.
1690	Jan.	Southerne, J.	1841	10 Sept.	Herbert, Hon. S.
1694	Aug.	Bridgeman, W.	1845	13 Feb.	Lowry Corry, Hon. H. T.
1694	26 Sept.	Bridgeman, W. / Burchett, J.	1846	13 July	Ward, H. G.
1698	24 June	Burchett, J.	1849	21 May	Parker, J.
1702	20 May	Burchett, J. / Clarke, G.	1852	3 March	O'Brien Stafford, S. A.
1705	25 Oct.	Burchett, J.	1853	6 Jan.	Osborne, R. B.
1741	29 April	Burchett, J. / Corbett, T.	1858	9 March	Lowry Corry, Hon. H. T.
1742	14 Oct.	Corbett, T.	1859	30 June	Paget, Lord C. E.
1751	30 April	Cleveland, J.	1866	30 April	Baring, Hon. T. G.
1763	18 June	Stephens, P.	1866	16 July	Gordon Lennox, Lord H.
1795	3 March	Nepean, E.			
1804	21 Jan.	Marsden, W.	1868	22 Dec.	Baxter, W. E.

SECOND SECRETARY

1746	1 Aug.	Cleveland, J.	1795	3 March	Marsden, W.
1759	16 Oct.	Stephens, P.	1804	21 Jan.	Tucker, B.
			1804	22 May	Barrow, J.
1783	13 Jan.	Ibbetson, J.	1806	10 Feb.	Tucker, B.

[28] Order in council 15 Jan. 1800 (HC 138 p. 2 (1816) xiii, 170).
[29] Order in council 21 June 1815 (HC 125 p. 1 (1816) xiii, 167).
[30] Order in council 10 Feb. 1818 (PC 2/212 pp. 34-5).
[31] *Rept. of Select Committee on Reduction of Salaries 1831* (HC 322 p. 8 (1830-1) iii, 452); TM 15 April 1831 (HC 375 p. 3 (1830-1) vii, 495).
[32] Adm. 12/442, 22 March 1845; Adm. 12/474, 26 Nov. 1847.

1807	9 April	Barrow, J.	1855	22 May	Phinn, T.
1845	28 Jan.	Baillie Hamilton, W. A.	1857	7 May	Romaine, W. G.
			1869	29 June	Lushington, V.

Deputy Secretary 1705-83

The office of Deputy Secretary, to which appointments were made by Admiralty commission, was filled only on an intermittent basis until 1764. Created in 1705,[1] it was left vacant from 1714 to 1728. Thereafter it was the usual practice to promote the Chief Clerk to the position at times when the Secretary was acting alone. The office was left vacant between 1741 and 1744, between 1746 and 1756 and between 1759 and 1764. Between 1764 and 1783 it was filled continuously. It was abolished in the latter year when the then Deputy Secretary was promoted to the position of Second Secretary.[2]

The salary attached to the office was £500, an addition of £100 being made in time of war.[3] Jackson and Ibbetson also occupied the position of senior Clerk or Deputy Secretary in the Marine Department with a salary of £200 payable by the Paymaster of Marines.[4] The share of the fees enjoyed by the Deputy Secretary was calculated on the basis of a salary of £400 as Chief Clerk.[5]

LIST OF APPOINTMENTS

1705	15 Nov.	Fawler, J.
1728	27 July	Corbett, T.
1744	17 Nov.	Osborn, R.
1756	15 June	Milnes, J.
1764	28 June	Fearne, C.
1766	11 Nov.	Jackson, G.
1782	12 June	Ibbetson, J.

[1] Adm. 6/8 f. 201.   [2] Adm. 3/96, 13 Jan. 1783.
[3] Adm. 3/21, 19 Nov. 1705; SPB, i f. 42; Adm. 3/37, 27 July 1728; Adm. 3/49, 17 Nov. 1744; Adm. 3/64, 15 June 1756; SPB, v f. 5.
[4] *3rd Rept. on Fees*, 116-17.   [5] ibid. 108.

Clerks 1660–1800

Before 1694 little is known of the Clerks of the Admiralty. Their appointment, tenure and remuneration were matters within the discretion of successive Secretaries. For Pepys' two periods of office as Secretary between 1673 and 1679 and between 1684 and 1689 it is possible to form some idea of the identity of the Clerks serving in the office; for other periods very little information is available.[1]

In 1694 the fees of the office, out of which the remuneration of the Clerks had been found, were abolished and provision was made for six salaried Clerks, apart from the Chief Clerks, each of whom was to receive £80 a year payable by the Treasurer of the Navy.[2] From this date the identity and periods of service of the Clerks can be accurately determined. Frequent changes in the number of the Clerks and the size of their salaries occurred in the following years. In 1698 the number was again fixed at six, four at £80 and two at £40.[3] In 1703 a new establishment was authorised consisting of nine Clerks, one at £150, one at £100, two at £80, three at £70 and two at £60.[4] From 1705 until the end of the war in 1713 between four and five Clerks, sometimes known as 'extra Clerks' were also employed with salaries of £50.[5]

In 1712 the establishment was fixed at eight Clerks, two at £120, one at £90, two at £80, two at £70 and one at £60, together with four others at £50.[6] At the end of the war in 1713 the clerical staff was reduced to six, two at £100, two at £80 and two at £60.[7] Finally in 1715 it was fixed at seven with salaries of £200, £150, £120, £100, £80, £70 and £60.[8] Following the reintroduction of the fees in 1717 provision was made for the established Clerks to receive shares in half the product in proportion to the size of their respective salaries.[9] Apart from the fact that the Clerk with the salary of £200 was detached from the rest and given special responsibilities as Chief Clerk in 1783, the establishment of 1715 continued in force until 1800 when the remaining six Clerks were appointed to the new grade of Senior Clerk.[10]

LIST OF APPOINTMENTS

1660	Southerne, J.	1679	Pett, S.
1673	Hewer, W.	1684	Atkins, S.[11]
1673	Walbanke, J.		⎰Walbanke, R.
1677	Atkins, S.	By 1687	⎱Burchett, J.
	⎰Lewis, –		⎱Skinner, P.
By 1678	⎨Lawrence, –	1689	Pett, S.[11]
	⎱Roberts, –	1689	Burchett, J.[11]

[1] See pp. 1–2. [2] Adm. 2/16 p. 414. [3] Adm. 2/179 p. 26. [4] Adm. 2/183 pp. 189–90, 218.
[5] Adm. 2/184 p. 582; AO 1/1725/147–AO 1/1729/155. [6] Adm. 2/191 p. 98; AO 1/1729/154.
[7] Adm. 2/191 pp. 417–18; AO 1/1729/155. [8] Adm. 2/193 pp. 127–8.
[9] Adm. 3/31, 8 July 1718; Adm. 3/55, 1 Aug. 1746; *3rd Rept. on Fees*, 96–7.
[10] Adm. 3/96, 13 Jan. 1783; order in council 15 Jan. 1800 (HC 138 p. 3 (1816) xiii, 171).
[11] Reappointed.

By 1694	Gibbs, T.	1709	Fisher, W.
	Halford, E.	1710	Sherer, R.
	Saunders, S.	1711	Hinsom, T.
	Parmiter, T. P.	1711	Melmerby, T.
	Warren, T.	1713	Newson, J.[11]
	Baston, T.	1715 17 Jan.	Corbett, T.
1694	Bradley, S.	1715 17 Jan.	Hawes, T.
1694–5	Pett, P.	1715 17 Jan.	Edwards, J.
1695	Gordon, G.	1715 17 Jan.	Hinsom, T.[11]
1695–6	Whittaker, T.	1715 17 Jan.	Westcomb, G.
1697	Russell, P.	1716 7 June	Osborn, R.
1697	Williams, J.	1716 29 Aug.	Ram, A.
1698	Hutchinson, C.	1717 11 Feb.	Kirkpatrick, J.
1698	Rich, N.	1717 21 June	Young, W.
1699	Gordon, G.[11]	1721 10 Oct.	Varney, J.
1699	Coling, R.	1723 22 March	Bird, W.
1699	Drake, J.	1725 29 July	Milnes, J.
1700	Halford, E.[11]	1725 20 Sept.	Borrodale, J. A.
1700	Bradley, S.[11]	1727 11 Aug.	Atkins, W.
1700	Dod, J.	1727 4 Nov.	Burchett, G. A.
1700–1	Crosfield, R.	1728 19 Dec.	Troughton, J.
1701	Gibbs, T.[11]	1738 7 Nov.	Fearne, C.
1702	Golding, R.	1742 14 Oct.	Phillips, E.
1702	Oldner, J.	1743 18 June	Blanckley, T. R.
1702	Cole, E.	1751 6 April	Stephens, P.
1702–3	Lynn, F.	1751 2 May	Corbett, J.
1703–4	Bowles, B.	1753 5 May	Clevland, J.
1704	Oakes, L.	1753 6 June	Alcock, J.
1704–5	Regins, W.	1759 16 Oct.	Ibbetson, J.
1704–5	Nicholas, G.	1761 31 July	Hastings, H.
1704–5	Honywood, E.	1763 4 July	Parker, H.
1704–5	Pelham, K.	1766 12 Nov.	Fearne, T. W.
1705	Barnett, P.	1768 5 Oct.	Bryer, W.
1706	Cooper, G.	1773 25 Aug.	Wright, C.
1706–7	Budgett, J.	1777 28 March	Belson, J.
1707	Pembroke, W.	1777 22 Dec.	Barkham, S. D.
1708	Crickett, P.	1782 12 June	Robinson, R.
1708	Bennet, T.	1790 18 Jan.	Gimber, W.
1708	Walker, G.	1790 13 March	Kite, T.
1708	Allen, C.	1795 16 June	Gascoigne, W.
1708	Newson, J.	1795 16 June	Pearce, W.
1709	Reynolds, J.	1799 11 March	Hollinworth, M.
1709	Pack, J.		

[11] Reappointed.

Chief Clerks c. 1694-1870

Provision was made for two Chief Clerks, sometimes known as 'First' Clerks, in the establishment of 1694, each with a salary of £200.[1] The number was reduced to one in 1696 on Burt's departure from office. The salary of his colleague, Fawler, was then increased to £250. It was further increased to £400 in 1703.[2] On Fawler's promotion to the position of Deputy Secretary in 1705, Burt returned to the office and succeeded him as Chief Clerk with a salary of £300 which was reduced to £200 at the peace of 1713. In 1715 it was increased to £400 which remained the salary of the Chief Clerk until 1783.[3]

Between 1728 and 1783 the office was not filled on a regular basis, appointments being made only when the Secretary was acting without the assistance of a joint Secretary, a Second Secretary or a Deputy Secretary: 1742-4, 1751-6 and 1763-4. At other times during this period the senior established Clerk received a salary of £200 as opposed to £400. When a Deputy Secretary was serving he apparently undertook the duties of the Chief Clerk. During the time that the post of Second Secretary was occupied (1746-51 and 1759-63) it appears that the senior established clerk had a rather greater measure of responsibility than he had at other times.[4]

In 1783 the office of Chief Clerk was established on a permanent basis with a basic salary of £200 together with fees and a variety of allowances.[5] In 1800 a consolidated salary of £800 was provided with an additional £150 as Receiver of Fees and Paymaster of Contingencies in time of war.[6] In 1807 the remuneration was fixed at £900 in time of peace and at £1000, together with the Paymaster's allowance of £150, in time of war.[7] In 1815 the war allowances were made permanent and the salary was fixed at £1150.[8] It was reduced to £1000 in 1832.[9] In 1867 provision was made for the salary to rise by annual increments of £50 to £1100.[10]

LIST OF APPOINTMENTS

By 1694	Fawler, J.	1694	Burt, E.

[1] Adm. 2/16 p. 414. For a conjectural account of the earlier holders of the office of Chief Clerk, see p. 2.   [2] SPB, i f. 20; Adm. 2/183 pp. 189-90, 317.

[3] Adm. 2/185 p. 205; Adm. 2/191 pp. 417-18; Adm. 2/193 pp. 127-8.

[4] The senior established Clerks during these periods were: Ram (1746-51), Milnes (April-May 1751) and Fearne (1759-63). That Fearne was accorded a relatively important position in the office is clear from the list of distribution of duties of 26 Oct. 1759 (G. F. James, 'The Admiralty Establishment 1759', BIHR, xvi (1938-9), 24-7). See also Adm. 3/67, 16 Oct. 1759 where Fearne is in fact called 'Chief Clerk'.

[5] Adm. 3/96, 13 Jan. 1783; 3rd Rept. on Fees, 97-8.

[6] Order in council 15 Jan. 1800 (HC 138 pp. 2-3 (1816) xiii, 170-1).

[7] Order in council 28 Oct. 1807 (PC 2/174 pp. 284-6).

[8] Order in council 21 June 1815 (HC 125 p. 1 (1816) xiii, 167); Adm. 12/178, 27 June 1816.

[9] Adm. 12/284, 14 May 1832; order in council 1 Aug. 1832 (PC 2/213 pp. 495-9).

[10] Order in council 2 Feb. 1867 (PC 2/265 pp. 158-9).

1705	19 Nov.	Burt, E.[11]		1807	28 Sept.	Kite, T.
1723	15 March	Corbett, T.		1813	1 July	Pearce, W.
1742	14 Oct.	Hawes, T.		1819	21 Aug.	Dyer, J.
1743	18 June	Osborn, R.		1832	14 May	Amedroz, H. F.
				1849	5 Jan.	Hay, J. H.
1751	2 May	Milnes, J.		1853	18 Nov.	Dyer, J. J.
1763	4 July	Fearne, C.		1857	21 March	Pennell, C. H.
				1865	13 July	Briggs, J. H.
1783	13 Jan.	Parker, H.		1870	31 March	Wolley, T.
1795	16 June	Wright, C.				

[11] Reappointed.

Extra Clerks c. 1721–1816

Clerks, sometimes described as 'Extra Clerks', were employed in the Admiralty office at salaries of £50 between 1705 and 1713. However, their status does not appear to have been very clearly defined at this period and it is impossible to distinguish them satisfactorily from the other Clerks, particularly as they all received their salaries in the same manner from the Treasurer of the Navy. Their appointments have, therefore, been included in the list of Clerks 1660–1800.

Between 1715 and 1800 the number of established Clerks was fixed at seven and during this period the Extra Clerks were clearly differentiated from them. Little is known of their identity or periods of service before 1740. At first they appear to have been employed as writers without salary.[1] From 1738 it was the practice for them to receive £50 a year from the contingent fund.[2] In 1740, when they were five in number, their salaries were transferred to the ordinary estimate for the navy and made payable by the Treasurer of the Navy.[3] From this period the details of their careers can be accurately established. The number of Extra Clerks fluctuated according to whether conditions of peace or war prevailed.[4] On occasion Clerks who had been discharged at the end of a period of war were re-engaged at a later date. Vacancies on the establishment were almost invariably filled by the promotion of Extra Clerks.

In 1786 the Extra Clerks numbered eleven, each receiving a salary of £50.[5] In 1790 provision was made for ten, four with salaries of £110, three with salaries of £100 and three with salaries of £90.[6] In 1800 the existing Extra Clerks were recruited into the new grade of Junior Clerk, while provision was made for a further seven Extra Clerks, three at £100 a year and four at £90 a year, whose salaries were to be increased by a fifth in time of war.[7] In 1807 new salary arrangements were introduced as follows: for under three years' service £90, for three to five years' service £110, for five to seven years' service £120 and for more than seven years' service £140, again with the addition of a fifth in time of war.[8] In 1815 the war salaries were made permanent.[9] The grade was abolished in 1816.[10]

LIST OF APPOINTMENTS

By 1721	Varney, J.	By 1738	Fearne, C.
By 1728	Troughton, J.	1738 7 Nov.	Berkeley, L. S.

[1] Adm. 3/32, 10 Oct. 1721; Adm. 3/37, 19 Dec. 1728; Adm. 3/43, 30 May 1738.
[2] Adm. 3/43, 30 May and 7 Nov. 1738, 25 Sept. 1739.
[3] Adm. 3/44, 13 Nov. 1740; SPB, vi f. 7.   [4] Adm. 3/48, 31 Aug. 1744.
[5] 3rd Rept. on Fees, 95, 98.   [6] Adm. 3/107, 24 May 1790.
[7] Order in council 15 Jan. 1800 (HC 138 pp. 3–4 (1816) xiii, 171–2).
[8] Order in council 28 Oct. 1807 (PC 2/174 pp. 284–6).
[9] Order in council 21 June 1815 (HC 125 p. 1 (1816) xiii, 167).
[10] Order in council 30 Jan. 1816 (HC 139 pp. 1–12 (1816) xiii, 183–94).

1739	25 Sept.	Phillips, E.
By 1740		Vanbrugh, E.
		Blanckley, T. R.
		Alcock, J.
1741	29 April	Sewell, T.
1741	30 Nov.	Cox, W.
1742	12 Feb.	Guion, D.
1742	14 Oct.	Davies, W.
1743	18 June	Fawcett, W.
1744	31 Aug.	Bere, J.
1744	31 Aug.	Graydon, R.
1744	31 Aug.	Lawes, T.
1744	12 Oct.	Hopwood, T.
1744	17 Nov.	French, G.
1745	26 Feb.	Hastings, H.
1745	21 Dec.	Jones, R.
1745	21 Dec.	Lloyd, J.
1746	5 April	Harris, J.
1746	13 June	Oakes, T.
1746	10 Nov.	Corbett, J.
1747	24 June	Hickes, W.
1747	4 Sept.	Howison, T.
1748	23 Feb.	Bowers, R.
1748	23 Feb.	Noble, T.
1749	6 June	Corbett, J.[11]
1751	2 May	Howison, T.[11]
1751	10 Dec.	Cleveland, J.
1752	21 Nov.	Parker, H.
1753	5 May	Bell, T.
1753	11 June	Bullock, D.
1755	8 Feb.	Hastings, H.[11]
1755	8 Feb.	Ibbetson, J.
1755	6 May	Bryer, W.
1755	22 Dec.	Fouace, C.
1756	22 March	Cooke, G. A.
1756	17 Aug.	Webster, W. C.
1756	14 Dec.	Powdick, J.
1757	21 Jan.	Wright, C.
1757	24 Feb.	Ward, E.
1757	21 March	Dancer, F.
1757	17 Nov.	Palairet, E. J.
1759	1 Jan.	Pollock, W.
1759	1 March	Belson, J.
1759	16 April	Davie, C.
1759	18 Oct.	Jeafryson, S.
1760	6 May	Irish, T.
1761	21 Jan.	Fearne, T. W.
1761	25 Sept.	Reynolds, J. E.
1762	19 Aug.	Howard, C.
1764	4 May	Belson, J.[11]
1764	8 Dec.	Morrison, J.
1766	24 June	Howe, P.
1766	26 Nov.	Willett, A. S.
1767	2 Dec.	Sayer, V.
1769	16 March	Barkham, S. D.
1770	11 Sept.	Robinson, R.
1771	22 Feb.	Gimber, W.
1771	9 March	Bindley, J.
1773	25 Aug.	Smith, N.
1776	26 Jan.	Spriggs, C.
1776	12 April	Dale, R.
1777	8 April	Kite, T.
1777	8 April	Gascoigne, W.
1778	18 May	Freshfield, J.
1778	8 July	Brisbane, T.
1778	19 Aug.	Pearce, W.
1779	6 April	Hollinworth, M.
1780	22 April	Edwards, J.
1780	12 June	Maxwell, R.
1780	28 Aug.	Banes, E.
1780	10 Nov.	Perigal, J.
1782	14 Feb.	Maxwell, B.
1782	20 March	King, T.
1782	25 March	Raymond, A. M.
1787	8 May	Braithwaite, T.
1787	9 Oct.	King, T.[11]
1787	9 Oct.	Raymond, A. M.[11]
1787	9 Oct.	Marsh, R.
1787	27 Oct.	Wright, H.
1790	18 Jan.	Reynolds, W.
1790	13 March	Losack, R.
1793	12 March	Dyer, J.
1793	25 April	Moss, S.
1794	20 Sept.	Cutforth, J.
1795	19 June	Barker, J. D.
1795	19 June	Keltie, R.
1795	19 June	Hollinworth, T.
1795	19 June	Riley, R.
1795	19 June	Sayer, C.
1796	13 Aug.	Hawdon, G.
1796	14 Nov.	Thurtle, S.
1797	25 July	Sedgwick, C.
1799	10 Jan.	Amedroz, H. F.
1799	25 Jan.	Martin, R.

[11] Reappointed.

1799	25 Jan.	Fisher, J.		1807	12 Feb.	Tupper. C, C.
1799	12 March	Cowcher, W. P.		1807	25 April	Nesbitt, W.
1800	19 Dec.	Darch, T.		1807	5 May	Hay, J. H.
1801	16 Feb.	Evans, J.		1807	26 Aug.	Allen, T. C.
1801	16 Feb.	Greaves, R.		1807	26 Aug.	Creswell, W.
1804	3 May	Shepherd, G.		1807	26 Aug.	Scott, G.
1804	3 May	Smith, C.		1807	26 Aug.	Gibson, J.
1804	3 May	Bedford, H.		1807	26 Aug.	Nicholas, H.
1804	3 May	Wilder, F.		1807	28 Sept.	Mountain, W. J.
1804	3 May	Stables, J.		1807	28 Sept.	Forster, T. R.
1804	3 May	Spence, J.		1808	30 Jan.	Croasdaile, R.
1804	3 May	Barnes, M.		1809	4 Sept.	Barker, G. R.
1804	3 May	Innes, J. W.		1809	6 Sept.	Rouse, J.
1804	15 June	Moss, H.		1811	15 March	Biggs, L. J.
1804	15 June	Randall, R.		1811	15 March	Holworthy, C. D.
1805	8 June	Barker, F. E.		1811	15 March	Templeman, G.
1805	28 Aug.	Brodie, A.		1812	5 Feb.	Houghton, G. R.
1805	9 Sept.	Spence, J.[11]		1813	17 July	Ryland, F.
1805	9 Sept.	Clifton, M. W.		1814	30 July	Miller, J.
1806	15 April	Mends, M. B.		1815	18 Jan.	Hardman, J.

[11] Reappointed.

Senior Clerks 1800-16

This grade was created in 1800 when it was provided that there should be six Senior Clerks.[1] The number was increased to seven in 1809 when the office of Senior Clerk in the Marine Department was fully incorporated into the ordinary establishment.[2] There was a further increase to nine in 1811.[3] The grade was abolished in 1816.[4]

In 1800 the salaries of the Senior Clerks were fixed at £500, £450, £400, £400, £350 and £300.[5] In 1807 new salary arrangements were introduced as follows: for seven to ten years' service £380, for ten to fifteen years' service £400, for fifteen to twenty years' service £500, for twenty to twenty-five years' service £550 and for twenty-five years' service or longer £600. These sums were increased to £420, £450, £600, £650 and £750 respectively in time of war.[6] In 1815 the war salaries were made permanent.[7]

LIST OF APPOINTMENTS

1800	7 Feb.	Robinson, R.	1804	3 May	Wright, H.
1800	7 Feb.	Gimber, W.	1807	30 April	Reynolds, W.
1800	7 Feb.	Kite, T.	1807	26 Aug.	Dyer, J.
1800	7 Feb.	Gascoigne, W.	1809	4 Sept.	Sayer, C.
1800	7 Feb.	Pearce, W.	1811	15 March	Thurtle, S.
1800	7 Feb.	Hollinworth, M.	1811	15 March	Amedroz, H. F.
1801	12 Feb.	Banes, E.	1813	1 July	Fisher, J.
1804	3 May	Raymond, A. M.	1814	30 July	Evans, J.

Junior Clerks 1800-16

This grade was created in 1800 when it was provided that there should be ten Junior Clerks.[8] The number was increased to eleven in 1809 when the office of Junior Clerk in the Marine Department was fully incorporated into the ordinary establishment.[9]

[1] Order in council 15 Jan. 1800 (HC 138 pp. 3-4 (1816) xiii, 171-2).
[2] Admiralty order 6 Sept. 1809 (SPB, xii ff. 13-14).
[3] Order in council 14 March 1811 (PC 2/192 pp. 98-100).
[4] Order in council 30 Jan. 1816 (HC 139 pp. 1-12 (1816) xiii, 183-94).
[5] Order in council 15 Jan. 1800 (HC 138 pp. 3-4 (1816) xiii, 171-2).
[6] Order in council 28 Oct. 1807 (PC 2/174 pp. 284-6).
[7] Order in council 21 June 1815 (HC 125 p. 1 (1816) xiii, 167).
[8] Order in council 15 Jan. 1800 (HC 138 pp. 3-4 (1816) xiii, 171-2).
[9] Admiralty order 6 Sept. 1809 (SPB, xii ff. 13-14).

There was a further increase to twelve in 1811.[10] The grade was abolished in 1816.[11]

In 1800 the salary of the first Junior Clerk was fixed at £250, the salaries of the next two at £200, those of the next three at £175 and those of the remaining four at £150.[12] In 1807 new salary arrangements were introduced as follows: for under five years' service £150, for five to seven years' service £200, for seven to ten years' service £280, for ten to fifteen years' service £380 and for fifteen years' service or longer £400. These sums were increased to £190, £240, £320, £420 and £450 respectively in time of war.[13] In 1815 the war salaries were made permanent.[14]

LIST OF APPOINTMENTS

1800	11 April	Banes, E.	1804	3 May	Darch, T.
1800	11 April	Raymond, A. M.	1804	3 May	Evans, J.
1800	11 April	Wright, H.	1806	15 April	Shepherd, G.
1800	11 April	Reynolds, W.	1807	30 April	Bedford, H.
1800	11 April	Dyer, J.	1807	26 Aug.	Barnes, M.
1800	19 Dec.	Hollinworth, T.	1807	28 Sept.	Innes, J. W.
1800	19 Dec.	Riley, R.	1809	4 Sept.	Randall, R.
1800	19 Dec.	Sayer, C.	1809	6 Sept.	Barker, F. E.
1800	19 Dec.	Thurtle, S.	1811	15 March	Clifton, M. W.
1800	19 Dec.	Barker, J. D.	1811	15 March	Mends, M. B.
1801	12 Feb.	Martin, R.	1811	15 March	Tupper, C. C.
1802	11 June	Amedroz, H. F.	1813	1 July	Hay, J. H.
1803	28 March	Cowcher, W. P.	1814	30 July	Nesbitt, W.
1803	30 June	Fisher, J.			

[10] Order in council 14 March 1811 (PC 2/192 pp. 98–100).
[11] Order in council 30 Jan. 1816 (HC 139 pp. 1–12 (1816) xiii, 183–94).
[12] Order in council 15 Jan. 1800 (HC 138 pp. 3–4 (1816) xiii, 171–2).
[13] Order in council 28 Oct. 1807 (PC 2/174 pp. 284–6).
[14] Order in council 21 June 1815 (HC 125 p. 1 (1816) xiii, 167).

Supernumerary Clerks 1811–16

Between 1811 and 1816 up to six Supernumerary Clerks were employed by the Admiralty on a temporary basis, receiving pay at the rate of £2 2s a week.[1]

LIST OF APPOINTMENTS

1811	26 Dec.	Hardman, J.	1812	7 July	Alves, W.
1811	26 Dec.	Walker, M.	1812	30 Sept.	Murray, J.
1811	26 Dec.	Wall, W.	1812	26 Dec.	Clifton, J. B.
1811	26 Dec.	Hay, E.	1813	2 Feb.	Caley, R.
1812	26 March	Garner, J.	1813	26 Dec.	Miller, J.
1812	26 March	Ellis, N.			

[1] SPB, xii ff. 45–6.

First Class Clerks 1816-70

This grade was created in 1816 when it was provided that there should be eight First Class Clerks.[1] The number was reduced to six in 1821 when two of the clerkships were left vacant.[2] One of these vacancies was filled in 1829.[3] In 1832 the number of First Class Clerks was fixed at six.[4] It was increased to seven in 1837,[5] to nine in 1853,[6] to ten in 1854[7] and to eleven in 1862.[8] One of the clerkships was left vacant in 1867 and four more during the course of 1869. In 1870 the number of First Class Clerks was established at six.[9]

In 1816 the salary scale attached to the grade was fixed at £600 rising by annual increments of £10 to £850.[10] The amount of the annual increment was increased to £25 in 1837.[11] In 1867 the scale was fixed at £650 rising by annual increments of £25 to £900.[12]

LIST OF APPOINTMENTS

1816	5 Feb.	Dyer, J.	1833	25 May	Mountain, W. J.
1816	5 Feb.	Riley, R.	1834	15 Dec.	Houghton, G. R.
1816	5 Feb.	Sayer, C.	1837	5 April	Croker, T. C.
1816	5 Feb.	Thurtle, S.	1838	20 April	Dyer, J. J.
1816	5 Feb.	Amedroz, H. F.	1841	26 Aug.	Worth, G.
1816	5 Feb.	Evans, J.	1844	4 May	Barrow, J.
1816	5 Feb.	Finlaison, J.	1847	24 May	Pennell, C. H.
1816	5 Feb.	Darch, T.	1847	8 Oct.	Evans, R. S.
1819	21 Aug.	Clifton, M. W.	1849	9 Jan.	Briggs, J. H.
1822	22 Jan.	Innes, J. W.	1850	4 June	Jesse, J. H.
1826	2 June	Bedford, H.	1853	18 Nov.	Houghton, J. H. N.
1829	2 June	Hay, J. H.	1853	30 Dec.	Wolley, H.
1832	14 May	Rouse, J.	1853	30 Dec.	Clifton, W.
1832	14 May	Biggs, L. J.	1854	12 April	Wolley, T.

[1] Order in council 30 Jan. 1816 (HC 139 pp. 1–12 (1816) xiii, 183–94). In spite of the fact that 'First Class Clerk' was their official title, members of this grade were described as 'Senior Clerks' in the *Navy Lists* throughout the period.
[2] SPB, xiii ff. 017–18; order in council 17 Jan. 1822 (PC 2/204 pp. 14–23).
[3] SPB, xiv f. 5; Adm. 12/261, 2 June 1829.
[4] Adm. 12/284, 14 May 1832; order in council 1 Aug. 1832 (PC 2/213 pp. 495–9).
[5] Order in council 5 April 1837 (PC 2/219 pp. 151–2).
[6] Order in council 29 Dec. 1853 (PC 2/238 pp. 466–8).
[7] Order in council 7 April 1854 (PC 2/239 p. 337).
[8] Order in council 26 April 1862 (PC 2/255 pp. 361–2).
[9] Adm. 12/784, 3 April 1867; Adm. 12/846, 4 Jan. 1870.
[10] Order in council 30 Jan. 1816 (HC 139 pp. 1–12 (1816) xiii, 183–94).
[11] Order in council 21 June 1837 (PC 2/219 pp. 313–14).
[12] Order in council 2 Feb. 1867 (PC 2/265 pp. 158–9).

1854	16 Aug.	Giffard, E.	1862	10 March	James, T.
1855	22 Feb.	Midlane, M. W.	1865	13 July	Hay, J. H.
1857	21 March	Giffard, E.[13]	1867	7 Oct.	Innes, A. W.
1857		Amedroz, H. F.	1867	21 Oct.	Bell, R.
1857	1 April	Jackson, J. (*acting*)	1870	31 March	Kennedy, C. S.
1858	7 April	Jackson, J.	1870	31 March	Kempe, C. N.
1861	18 July	Evans, W. F.			

[13] Reappointed.

Second Class Clerks 1816-70

This grade was created in 1816 when provision was made for eleven Second Class Clerks.[1] In fact only seven were then appointed.[2] The number was reduced to six in 1821 when one of the clerkships was left vacant.[3] A seventh Second Class Clerk was again appointed in May 1832 and the number was fixed at nine when the establishment was revised in August of that year.[4] There were increases to ten in 1837,[5] to eleven in 1841,[6] to twelve in 1842,[7] to thirteen in 1863[8] and to fourteen in 1866.[9] During the years 1847-50, 1855-7 and 1859-66 there were also either one or two acting Second Class Clerks. The number of Second Class Clerks was fixed at twelve in 1870.[10]

In 1816 the salary scale attached to the grade was fixed at £400 rising by annual increments of £10 to £600.[11] In 1822 this was reduced to £350 rising by annual increments of £10 to £550.[12] The amount of the annual increment was increased to £15 in 1837[13] and to £20 in 1867.[14]

LIST OF APPOINTMENTS

1816	5 Feb.	Shepherd, G.	1824	5 June	Mountain, W. J.
1816	5 Feb.	Bedford, H.	1824	17 June	Houghton, G. R.
1816	5 Feb.	Innes, J. W.	1826	2 June	Miller, J.
1816	5 Feb.	Barker, F. E.	1829	2 June	Barker, G. R.
1816	5 Feb.	Clifton, M. W.	1831	10 Feb.	Ryland, F.
1816	5 Feb.	Mends, M. B.	1832	14 May	Croker, T. C.
1816	5 Feb.	Hay, J. H.	1832	14 May	Dyer, J. J.
1819	21 Aug.	Creswell, W.	1832	14 May	Worth, G.
1821	17 July	Rouse, J.	1832	20 July	Barrow, J.
1821	17 July	Biggs, L. J.	1833	21 Jan.	Pennell, C. H.
1822	22 Jan.	Biggs, L. J.[15]	1833	2 May	Evans, R. S.

[1] Order in council 30 Jan. 1816 (HC 139 pp. 1-12 (1816) xiii, 183-94).
[2] SPB, xiii ff. 019-20.
[3] ibid.; order in council 17 Jan. 1822 (PC 2/204 pp. 14-23).
[4] Adm. 12/284, 14 May 1832; order in council 1 Aug. 1832 (PC 2/213 pp. 495-9).
[5] Order in council 5 April 1837 (PC 2/219 pp. 151-2).
[6] Order in council 11 Feb. 1841 (PC 2/223 pp. 77-8).
[7] Order in council 2 Nov. 1842 (PC 2/224 pp. 759-60).
[8] Order in council 9 Jan. 1863 (PC 2/257 pp. 213-14).
[9] Order in council 28 Dec. 1866 (PC 2/264 pp. 998-9).
[10] Adm. 12/846, 4 Jan. 1870.
[11] Order in council 30 Jan. 1816 (HC 139 pp. 1-12 (1816) xiii, 183-94).
[12] Order in council 17 Jan. 1822 (PC 2/204 pp. 14-23).
[13] Order in council 21 June 1837 (PC 2/219 pp. 313-14).
[14] Order in council 2 Feb. 1867 (PC 2/265 pp. 158-9).
[15] Reappointed.

1833	25 May	Clifton, F.		1861	18 July	Pennell, H. C.
1834	15 Dec.	Briggs, J. H.				(*acting*)
1835	28 March	Jesse, J. H.		1861–2		Kempe, C. N.
1837	5 April	Middleton, A.		1861–2		Pennell, H. C.
1837	5 April	Houghton, J. H. N.		1861–2		Swainson, E. N.
1838	20 April	Wolley, H.				(*acting*)
1841	17 Feb.	Clifton, W.		1861–2		Fonblanque, B. A.
1841	13 March	Wolley, T.				(*acting*)
1841	26 Aug.	Giffard, E.		1862		West, A. E.
1842	7 Nov.	Midlane, M. W.		1862		Swainson, E. N.
1844	4 May	Jackson, J.		1862		Noel, J. G. (*acting*)
1846	25 July	Amedroz, H. F.		1865	13 July	Fonblanque, B. A.
1847	24 May	Evans, W. F.		1865	13 July	Scott, J. (*acting*)
1847	8 Oct.	Baylee, H. W.		1865	21 Nov.	Noel, J. G.
1847	9 Oct.	Hamilton, R. W.		1865	21 Nov.	Callander, R. J.
		(*acting*)				(*acting*)
1849	9 Jan.	Hamilton, R. W.		1865		Scott, J.
1849	9 Jan.	James, T. (*acting*)		1865		Senior, J. (*acting*)
1850	4 June	James, T.		1866	22 Jan.	Callander, R. J.
1850	4 June	Hay, J. H.		1866	22 Jan.	Spalding, A. F. M.
1853	18 Nov.	Piers, O. B.				(*acting*)
1853	30 Dec.	O'Reilly, C. W.		1866	8 Feb.	Senior, J.
1853	30 Dec.	Sheridan, J.		1866	8 Feb.	Carroll, H. A.
1854	12 April	Innes, A. W.				(*acting*)
1854	16 Aug.	Bell, R.		1866	28 Sept.	Spalding, A. F. M.
1854	19 Oct.	Proby, C. J.		1866	28 Sept.	Dundas, H. (*acting*)
1855	22 Feb.	Grant, T. G.		1866	9 Oct.	Dundas, H.
1855	15 Dec.	Graves, F. (*acting*)		1866	9 Oct.	Anderson, N. R.
1856–7		Piers, O. B.[15]				(*acting*)
1856–7		Graves, F.		1866	6 Nov.	Anderson, N. R.
1858	27 Jan.	Perrier, J.		1866	6 Nov.	Whish, G. C.
1858	14 Oct.	Locker, F.				(*acting*)
1859	21 Feb.	Paris, J. R. (*acting*)		1867	8 May	Gordon, F. F.
1859	1 June	Paris, J. R.		1867	7 Oct.	Domvile, H. W.
1859	15 June	Kennedy, C. S.		1867	21 Oct.	Miller, J. V.
1859	27 Aug.	Drummond, W.		1868	27 Oct.	Dormer, Hon. H. F.
		(*acting*)		1870	31 March	Macgregor, E.
1861	18 July	Drummond, W.		1870	31 March	de Vismes, A. M.
1861	18 July	Kempe, C. N.		1870	31 March	Awdry, R. D.
		(*acting*)				

[15] Reappointed.

Third Class Clerks 1816–55

This grade was created in 1816 when provision was made for fourteen Third Class Clerks.[1] In fact only thirteen were then appointed.[2] The number was reduced to twelve in 1821 when one of the clerkships was left vacant.[3] It was fixed at fifteen in 1832,[4] being increased to eighteen in 1837,[5] to nineteen in 1847,[6] to twenty-five in 1853[7] and to twenty-eight in 1854.[8] In 1855 the grade was divided into First and Second Sections.[9]

In 1816 the salary scale attached to the grade was £150 rising by annual increments of £10 to £400.[10] In 1822 it was reduced to £100 rising by annual increments of £10 to £350.[11]

LIST OF APPOINTMENTS

1816	5 Feb.	Creswell, W.	1824	10 May	Halsted, W. A.
1816	5 Feb.	Gibson, J.	1824	5 June	Montgomery, W. V.
1816	5 Feb.	Mountain, W. J.	1824	6 Nov.	Worth, G.
1816	5 Feb.	Croasdaile, R.	1824	17 Nov.	Barrow, J.
1816	5 Feb.	Barker, G. R.	1825	4 July	Pennell, C. H.
1816	5 Feb.	Rouse, J.	1826	7 Aug.	Walker, E. A.
1816	5 Feb.	Biggs, L. J.	1827	1 Jan.	Evans, R. S.
1816	5 Feb.	Holworthy, C. D.	1827	1 Jan.	Clifton, F.
1816	5 Feb.	Templeman, G.	1827	19 April	Briggs, J. H.
1816	5 Feb.	Houghton, G. R.	1827	1 Sept.	Giffard, J. W.
1816	5 Feb.	Ryland, F.	1827	1 Nov.	Lawes, E.
1816	5 Feb.	Miller, J.	1829	26 Oct.	Jesse, J. H.
1816	5 Feb.	Hardman, J.	1830	29 June	Middleton, A.
1818	6 May	Alves, W.	1831	10 Feb.	Sheridan, F. C.
1819	21 Aug.	Croker, T. C.	1832	14 May	Drinkwater, E.
1820	15 April	Miller, W.	1832	14 May	Houghton, J. H. N.
1821	24 Dec.	Biggs, L. J.[12]	1832	11 June	Whiffen, J.
1822	22 Jan.	Dyer, J. J.	1832	11 June	Warren, E. C.
1824	23 Feb.	Barrow, G.	1832	11 June	Seppings, N. L.

[1] Order in council 30 Jan. 1816 (HC 139 pp. 1–12 (1816) xiii, 183–94).
[2] SPB, xiii ff. 021–2.
[3] ibid.; order in council 17 Jan. 1822 (PC 2/204 pp. 14–23).
[4] Order in council 14 May 1832 (PC 2/213 pp. 495–9).
[5] Order in council 5 April 1837 (PC 2/219 pp. 151–2).
[6] Order in council 27 Feb. 1847 (PC 2/230 p. 150).
[7] Order in council 29 Dec. 1853 (PC 2/238 pp. 466–8).
[8] Order in council 7 April 1854 (PC 2/239 p. 337).
[9] Order in council 31 March 1855 (PC 2/241 p. 368).
[10] Order in council 30 Jan. 1816 (HC 139 pp. 1–12 (1816) xiii, 183–94).
[11] Order in council 17 Jan. 1822 (PC 2/204 pp. 14–23).
[12] Transferred from the second class on the reduction of the establishment.

1832	11 June	Wolley, H.
1832	11 June	Gardner, F. C.
1832	11 June	Clifton, W.
1832	14 June	Graham, W. C.
1832	19 June	Evans, W. F.
1832	19 June	Saul, J.
1832	27 July	Hore, H. F.
1833	19 Jan.	Sheridan, C. K.
1833	21 Jan.	Barrow, P.
1833	3 May	Wolley, T.
1833	30 May	Montgomery, A.
1833	12 July	Giffard, E.
1833	30 Sept.	Midlane, M. W.
1834	17 Oct.	Jackson, J.
1834	15 Dec.	Amedroz, H. F.
1835	28 March	Evans, W. F.[13]
1836	21 March	Elliot, G. J.
1836	13 May	Bell, W. H.
1836	27 Oct.	Bunter, E. J.
1837	19 April	Baylee, H. W.
1837	20 April	Bell, J. C.
1837	1 May	Hamilton, R. W.
1837	1 May	Price, T.
1837	4 May	James, T.
1837	5 May	Hay, J. H.
1837	24 May	Piers, O. B.
1837	13 Oct.	Rutherford, T. L.
1838	25 April	O'Reilly, C. W.
1840	22 Aug.	Sheridan, J.
1840	31 Oct.	Forrest, W.
1840	5 Nov.	Innes, A. W.
1841	2 Feb.	Bell, R.
1841	17 Feb.	Roney, C. P.
1841	13 March	Proby, C. J.
1841	13 March	Grant, T. G.
1841	26 Aug.	Graves, F.
1842	11 Nov.	Perrier, J.
1842	12 Nov.	Locker, F.
1844	10 May	Jones, R. M.
1844	17 Dec.	Gilly, W. O. S.
1846	22 July	Miller, W. C.
1847	27 Feb.	Bedford, H. C. G.
1847	24 May	Chetwynd Stapylton, H. E.
1847	8 Oct.	Paris, J. R.
1847	9 Oct.	Currie, C. (*acting*)
1848	15 March	Braddyll, C. (*acting*)
1849	9 Jan.	Braddyll, C.
1849	9 Jan.	Cooper, A. P. (*acting*)
1850	4 June	Malleson, E.
1850	4 June	Berkeley, C. P. F.
1850	1 Oct.	Kennedy, C. S.
1853	18 Nov.	Ward, S.
1853	30 Dec.	Drummond, W.
1853	30 Dec.	Kempe, C. N.
1853	30 Dec.	Pennell, H. C.
1853	30 Dec.	Alderson, F. J.
1853	30 Dec.	West, A. E.
1853	30 Dec.	Cooper, A. P.[13]
1853	30 Dec.	Swainson, E. N.
1853	30 Dec.	Fonblanque, B. A.
1854	13 April	Noel, J. G.
1854	13 April	Scott, J.
1854	13 April	Callander, R. J.
1854	12 May	Buckley, A.
1854	16 Aug.	Moreton, Hon. W. P.
1854	16 Nov.	Senior, J.
1855	22 Feb.	Eliot, Hon. H. C.
1855	24 Feb.	Spalding, A. F. M.
1855	22 March	Cooke, C. E. S.

[13] Reappointed.

Third Class (First Section) Clerks
1855-70

This grade was created in 1855 when the number of Clerks in the first section of the third class was fixed in principle at twelve.[1] There were minor variations in the following years when there were frequently either one or two Clerks serving in an acting capacity. In 1866 the number of Third Class (First Section) Clerks was again fixed at twelve.[2]

In 1855 the salary scale attached to the grade was £250 rising by annual increments of £10 to £350.[3] In 1867 the size of the annual increment was increased to £15.[4]

LIST OF APPOINTMENTS

1855	31 March	Graves, F.	1859	21 Feb.	Callander, R. J. (acting)
1855	31 March	Perrier, J.			
1855	31 March	Locker, F.	1859	1 June	Callander, R. J.
1855	31 March	Jones, R. M.	1859	15 June	Buckley, A.
1855	31 March	Gilly, W. O. S.	1859	27 Aug.	Senior, J.
1855	31 March	Miller, W. C.	1859	27 Aug.	Spalding, A. F. M. (acting)
1855	31 March	Bedford, H. C. G.			
1855	31 March	Chetwynd Stapylton, H. E.	1861	18 July	Spalding, A. F. M.
			1861	18 July	Cooke, C. E. S. (acting)
1855	31 March	Paris, J. R.			
1855	31 March	Braddyll, C.	1861-2		Cooke, C. E. S.
1855	31 March	Berkeley, C. P. F.	1861-2		Carroll, H. A.
1855	31 March	Kennedy, C. S.	1861-2		Dundas, H. (acting)
1855	15 Dec.	Drummond, W. (acting)	1861-2		Anderson, N. R. (acting)
1856	15 March	Drummond, W.	1862		Whish, G. C. (acting)
1856	15 March	Kempe, C. N. (acting)	1862		Dundas, H.
1857	18 April	Pennell, H. C.	1862		Anderson, N. R.
1857	18 April	West, A. E.	1862		Gordon, F. F. (acting)
1857	14 Dec.	Swainson, E. N.			
1858	29 Jan.	Fonblanque, B. A.	1862		Domvile, H. W. (acting)
1858	4 Sept.	Noel, J. G.			
1858	14 Oct.	Scott, J.	1864	2 Jan.	Whish, G. C.

[1] Order in council 31 March 1855 (PC 2/241 p. 368).
[2] Order in council 28 Dec. 1866 (PC 2/264 pp. 998-9).
[3] Order in council 31 March 1855 (PC 2/241 p. 368).
[4] Order in council 2 Feb. 1867 (PC 2/265 pp. 158-9).

1865	26 April	Gordon, F. F.	1866	9 Oct.	Knox, A. E. E.
1865	26 April	Miller, J. V. (*acting*)	1866	9 Oct.	Wilson, H. J. C. (*acting*)
1865	13 July	Domvile, H. W.	1866	6 Nov.	Wilson, H. J. C.
1865	13 July	Dormer, Hon. H. F. (*acting*)	1866	6 Nov.	Brodrick, Hon. H.
1865		Miller, J. V.	1866	6 Nov.	Carmichael, J. M. (*acting*)
1865	21 Nov.	Daniell, S. W. (*acting*)	1867	7 May	Whish, G. C.[5]
			1867		Carmichael, J. M.
1865		Dormer, Hon. H. F.	1867	7 Oct.	Jeffreys, M. D.
1865		Macgregor, E. (*acting*)	1867	21 Oct.	Gambier, J. W. M.
			1868	14 Aug.	Vansittart Neale, H. J.
1866	22 Jan.	Daniell, S. W.			
1866	22 Jan.	de Vismes, A. M. (*acting*)	1868	27 Oct.	Primrose, E. M.
			1869	2 Dec.	Caulfield, M. P. F.
1866	8 Feb.	Macgregor, E.	1869	2 Dec.	Thomas, C. I.
1866	8 Feb.	Awdry, R. D. (*acting*)	1870	31 March	Yorke, H. F. R.
			1870	31 March	Hodgson, T. H.
1866	28 Sept.	Awdry, R. D.	1870	31 March	Birch, C. C.
1866	28 Sept.	Knox, A. E. E. (*acting*)			

[5] Reverted to the rank of Third Class (First Section) Clerk following the Board's refusal to confirm him as a Second Class Clerk.

Third Class (Second Section) Clerks
1855-70

This grade was created in 1855 when the number of Clerks in the second section of the third class was fixed in principle at sixteen.[1] In fact there were considerable variations in the number serving in the following years. Between 1859 and 1862 there were usually eleven and between 1862 and 1866 nine Clerks in the grade.[2] In 1866 the number was fixed at thirteen.[3] In 1870 it was reduced to eleven.[4]

In 1855 the salary scale attached to the grade was £100 rising by annual increments of £10 to £250.[5]

LIST OF APPOINTMENTS

1855	31 March	Drummond, W.	1858	11 Aug.	Whish, G. C.
1855	31 March	Kempe, C. N.	1858	29 Oct.	Domvile, H. W.
1855	31 March	Pennell, H. C.	1858	23 Nov.	Miller, J. V.
1855	31 March	Alderson, F. J.	1859	19 April	Balfour, A. (acting)
1855	31 March	West, A. E.	1859	1 June	Balfour, A.
1855	31 March	Cooper, A. P.	1859	29 June	Seymour, W. R.
1855	31 March	Swainson, E. N.	1859	17 Aug.	Dormer, Hon. H. F.
1855	31 March	Fonblanque, B. A.	1861	26 Aug.	Daniell, S. W.
1855	31 March	Noel, J. G.	1861	2 Sept.	Willes, J. W. S.
1855	31 March	Scott, J.	1862	16 Jan.	Macgregor, E.
1855	31 March	Callander, R. J.	1862	27 Feb.	de Vismes, A. M.
1855	31 March	Buckley, A.	1862	27 Feb.	Awdry, R. D.
1855	31 March	Moreton, Hon. W. P.	1862	15 July	Knox, A. E. E.
			1862	11 Nov.	Wilson, H. J. C.
1855	31 March	Senior, J.	1863	5 June	Brodrick, H.
1855	31 March	Spalding, A. F. M.	1865	12 May	Carmichael, J. M.
1855	31 March	Cooke, C. E. S.	1865	24 July	Jeffreys, M. D.
1855	18 Dec.	Cator, F. H. (acting)	1865	13 Dec.	Gambier, J. W. M.
			1865	13 Dec.	Vansittart Neale, H. J.
1856	17 June	Carroll, H. A.			
1858	12 Jan.	Phipps, P. W.	1866	1 Feb.	Primrose, E. M.
1858	6 Feb.	Dundas, H.	1866	17 Feb.	Caulfield, M. P. F.
1858	7 July	Anderson, N. R.	1866	18 May	Thomas, C. I.
1858	20 July	Gordon, F. F.	1866	27 Sept.	Yorke, H. F. R.

[1] Order in council 31 March 1855 (PC 2/241 p. 368).
[2] Adm. 12/634, 24 Jan. 1857; *Navy Lists*.
[3] Order in council 28 Dec. 1866 (PC 2/264 pp. 998-9).
[4] Adm. 12/846, 4 Jan. 1870; *Navy List*.
[5] Order in council 31 March 1855 (PC 2/241 p. 368).

1866	22 Oct.	Birch, C. C.	1867	10 Dec.	Maude, C. J.
1866	24 Oct.	Hodgson, T. H.	1867	10 Dec.	Dacres, S. L.
1866	22 Dec.	Lambert, G. T.	1868	4 Nov.	Dalrymple Hay,
1866	22 Dec.	Macgregor, A.			W. A.
1866	22 Dec.	Daly, J. F.	1868	11 Dec.	Stuart, H. N.
1866	22 Dec.	Giffard, J. H.			

Extra Clerks 1841–53

Between 1841 and 1853 permanent Extra Clerks were engaged by the Admiralty to supplement the ordinary establishment. The number employed fluctuated according to the pressure of business and never exceeded six.[1]

LIST OF APPOINTMENTS

1841	1 April	Graves, F.	1845	7 June	Paris, J. R.
1841	5 April	Elliot, A. P. C.	1846	28 May	Currie, C.
1841	22 May	Perrier, J.	1846	22 June	Braddyll, C.
1841	31 Aug.	Lomas, T.	1846	22 July	Cooper, A. P.
1841	28 Oct.	Miller, W. C.	1847	4 Feb.	Malleson, E.
1841	2 Nov.	Gilly, W. O. S.	1847	5 May	Berkeley, C. P. F.
1842	8 Oct.	Locker, F.	1847	29 May	Kennedy, C. S.
1842	12 Nov.	Jones, R. M.	1847	8 Oct.	Ward, S.
1842	12 Nov.	Bedford, H. C. G.	1847	Oct.	Drummond, W.
1844	17 Dec.	Chetwynd Stapylton, H. E.	1848	15 March	Osborne, F. G. G.
1845	14 Jan.	Jackson, R. H. S.	1852	1 May	Noel, J. G.

[1] Adm. 12/383, 25 Jan., 1 May and 28 Aug. 1841; Adm. 12/570, 4 Feb. 1853.

Temporary Clerks 1855-66

Between 1855 and 1866 up to six Temporary Clerks were employed by the Admiralty at £2 2s a week.[1]

LIST OF APPOINTMENTS

1855	17 May	Baker, J.	1861	23 March	Awdry, R. D.
1855	17 May	Lambert, A.	1861	29 Nov.	Knox, A. E. E.
1855	17 May	McCann, T.	1862	20 Jan.	Wilson, H. J. C.
1855	30 Oct.	Cator, F.	1862	20 Jan.	Brodrick, H.
1855	18 Dec.	Carroll, H. A.	1862	10 April	Carmichael, J. M.
1857	24 Oct.	Smith, –	1862	10 April	Jeffreys, M. D.
1858	17 March	Daunt, R.	1862	11 April	Gambier, J. W. M.
1858	23 June	Breaks, –	1862	4 Aug.	Vansittart Neale,
1858	29 July	Halifax, H. F.			H. J.
1858	24 Sept.	Clifton, W. C.	1862	11 Nov.	Primrose, E. M.
1859	4 April	de Vismes, A. M.	1863	25 June	Caulfield, M. P. F.
1859	17 Sept.	Spencer, A. L.	1865	14 June	Thomas, C. I.
1859	21 Sept.	Willes, J. W. S.	1865	4 Sept.	Yorke, H. F. R.
1860	26 June	Daniell, S. W.	1866	26 Jan.	Hodgson, T. H.
1860	13 Aug.	Macgregor, E.	1866	12 Feb.	Birch, C. C.

[1] HC 44 pp. 12–13, 16–17 (1888) lxxx, 16–17, 20–1; Adm. 12/778, 18 Oct. and 3 Dec. 1866.

Writers 1863-70

In 1863 provision was made for two permanent Digest Writers with salaries of £200 rising by annual increments of £10 to £350 and for two permanent Index Writers with salaries of £100 rising by annual increments of £10 to £250.[1]

LIST OF APPOINTMENTS

DIGEST WRITERS

1863	9 Jan.	Baker, J.	1863	9 Jan.	Abbot, T. C.

INDEX WRITERS

1863	9 Jan.	Smith, W.	1863	9 Jan.	Pickard, J. J.

Clerk of the Journals 1738-41

This office was created in 1738, the duties of its holder being to inspect and make abstracts from captains' journals. The salary was £200.[2] It was discontinued as a distinct appointment in 1741 when provision was made for the duties to be carried out by one of the Extra Clerks in the office.[3]

APPOINTMENT

1738   8 Dec.   Gashry, F.

[1] Order in council 9 Jan. 1863 (PC 2/257 pp. 213-14).
[2] Adm. 3/43, 29 Sept. 1738; order in council 30 Nov. 1738 (PC 2/95 pp. 21-3, 33).
[3] Adm. 3/44, 7 March 1741; order in council 27 April 1741 (PC 2/96 pp. 447-8, 455).

Translator 1755-1869

In 1745 an Extra Clerk was granted an additional allowance of £20 for acting as Translator of the French Language.[1] In 1755 the office of Translator of the French Language was established on a permanent basis with a salary of £100, payable by the Treasurer of the Navy.[2] In 1781 an allowance of £30 a year out of the contingent fund was given to an Extra Clerk, R. Maxwell, for acting as Translator of Spanish papers.[3] This allowance ceased in 1784 when Maxwell was appointed Translator of French and Spanish Languages with the established allowance of £100.[4] In 1787 Maxwell was replaced as French Translator by Braithwaite who was given the allowance of £100 while Maxwell himself resumed his former position of Translator of Spanish papers with an allowance of £50 from the contingent fund.[5] In 1788 the appointment of Braithwaite was rescinded and Maxwell became the only Translator.[6] In 1795 his allowance was increased to £100.[7] In 1800 the office of Translator of French and Spanish Languages was included in the establishment with a salary of £100.[8] The office was discontinued in 1869.[9]

LIST OF APPOINTMENTS

1755	22 Dec.	Fouace, C.	1788	18 June	Maxwell, R.
1776	5 March	Bindley, J.	1800	11 April	Amedroz, H. F.
1784	12 Feb.	Maxwell, R.	1845	22 April	Amedroz, H. F.
1787	8 May	Braithwaite, T.			

[1] Adm. 3/50, 18 June 1745.
[2] SPB, vii f. 7.
[3] Adm. 17/7.
[4] Adm. 3/99, 12 Feb. 1784.
[5] Adm. 3/103, 8 May 1787; Adm. 17/7.
[6] Adm. 3/104, 18 June 1788.
[7] *17th Rept. on Finance*, 335.
[8] Order in council 15 Jan. 1800 (HC 138 p. 3 (1816) xiii, 171).
[9] HC 10 p. 14 (1868–9) xxxviii, 14; HC 4 pp. 14–15 (1870) xliv, 14–15.

Keeper of Records 1809-16

This office was created in 1809 with a salary of £500.[1] In 1812 an additional allowance of £50 a year was made available to the Keeper of the Records in consideration of his acting as Librarian.[2] The office ceased to exist in 1816 when it was provided that the duties should be undertaken by one of the First Class Clerks.[3]

APPOINTMENT

1809   21 Aug.   Finlaison, J.

Reader 1841-70

The position of Reader or Reading Clerk may have had its origin in an order made in 1739 which laid down that 'One of the Clerks be appointed to receive and read to the Board once a week the petitions of persons who apply in order to their being answered'.[4] In 1795 an allowance of £150 out of the contingent fund was made available for the Clerk acting as Reader.[5] In 1816 it was provided that the Reader should occupy one of the first class clerkships.[6] In 1834 an additional allowance of £100 was made available.[7] It was not until 1841 that the position of Reader was made an established office. Provision was then made for the Clerk who held it automatically to receive the maximum salary of his class with an additional allowance of £100.[8]

LIST OF APPOINTMENTS

1841	18 June	Briggs, J. H.	1866	27 Sept.	Miller, J. V.
1865	13 July	Carroll, H. A.			

[1] Order in council 16 Aug. 1809 (PC 2/182 pp. 474-6).
[2] Adm. 12/154, 22 July 1812.
[3] Order in council 30 Jan. 1816 (HC 139 p. 5 (1816) xiii, 187).
[4] Adm. 3/43, 23 April 1739. See also the duties allocated to Clevland in 1759 (*BIHR*, xvi (1938-9), 26).
[5] *17th Rept. on Finance*, 335.
[6] Order in council 30 Jan. 1816 (HC 139 pp. 1-12 (1816) xiii, 183-94).
[7] Adm. 12/298, 3 June 1834.
[8] Order in council 8 May 1841 (PC 2/223 pp. 230-2); J. H. Briggs, *Naval Administrations 1827-92* (London 1897), 65.

Librarian 1862-70

This office, which had existed on a temporary basis for the previous six years, was placed on the establishment in 1862 with a salary of £150 rising by annual increments of £10 to £250.[1]

APPOINTMENT

1862   26 April   Thorburn, R.

[1] Adm. 12/698, 11 Jan. 1862; order in council 26 April 1862 (PC 2/255 p. 362).

Private Secretary to First Lord
and Lord High Admiral 1800-70

The office of Secretary or Private Secretary to the First Lord (or Lord High Admiral) was first included in the establishment in 1800 when a salary of £300 was made available for its holder.[1] In 1824 it was provided that, in those cases in which the Private Secretary was not in receipt of any other emolument from the crown, the salary should begin at £500 and rise by annual increments of £10 to £600.[2] No salary was paid to those Private Secretaries who were members of the House of Commons.[3]

LIST OF APPOINTMENTS

Spencer	1794–1801	1800	7 Feb.	Harrison, J.
St. Vincent	1801–4	1801	17 April	Tucker, B.
		1802	5 Jan.	Parker, G.
Melville	1804–5	1804	12 July	Budge, W.
Barham	1805–6	1805	8 May	Thomson, J. D.
Grey	1806	1806	14 March	Grant, H.
Grenville	1806–7	1806	3 Oct.	Golding, E.
Mulgrave	1807–10	1807	29 June	Moorsom, R.
		1809	19 April	O'Brien, Lord E.
Yorke	1810–12	1810	7 May	Edgcumbe, F.
Melville	1812–27	1812	22 June	Hay, R. W.
		1823	3 April	Baillie Hamilton, G.
Clarence	1827–8	1827	13 Sept.	Spencer, Hon. R. C.
Melville	1828–30	1828	4 Oct.	Saunders Dundas, Hon. R.
Graham	1830–4	1830	29 Nov.	Briggs, J. T.
		1830	11 Dec.	Stewart, E.
		1831	26 May	Graham, G.
Auckland	1834	1834	16 June	Gipps, G.
de Grey	1834–5	1834	31 Dec.	Cole, J. G.
Auckland	1835	1835	27 April	Gipps, G.
		1835	22 June	Grey, Hon. F. W.
Minto	1835–41	1835	23 Sept.	Tufnell, H.
		1839		Melgund, Viscount (*acting*)
		1841	27 April	Christie, W. D.
Haddington	1841–6	1841	10 Sept.	Baillie Hamilton, W. A.
		1845	29 Jan.	Saunders Dundas, Hon. R.

[1] Order in council 15 Jan. 1800 (HC 138 p. 3 (1816) xiii, 171).
[2] Order in council 23 June 1824 (PC 2/205 pp. 501–2).
[3] Adm. 12/344, 23 Oct. 1838.

Ellenborough	1846	1846	16 Jan.	Law, Hon. H. S.
Auckland	1846–9	1846	13 July	Eden, H.
		1848	13 Nov.	Eden, C.
Baring	1849–52	1849	16 Jan.	Eden, C.
Northumberland	1852–3	1852	3 March	Pelham, Hon. F. T.
Graham	1853–5	1853	6 Jan.	O'Brien, H. H. D.
Wood	1855–8	1855	8 March	Baring, T. G.
		1857	1 May	Drummond, Hon. J. R.
Pakington	1858–9	1858	13 March	Murray, H. H.
Somerset	1859–66	1859	4 July	Moore, J.
		1862	24 Nov.	Ryder, A. P.
		1863	27 April	Hall, R.
		1866	20 March	Campbell, F. A.
Pakington	1866–7	1866	16 July	Pakington, J. S.
Lowry Corry	1867–8	1867	9 March	Brandreth, T.
Childers	1868	1868	22 Dec.	Seymour, F. B. P.
		1870	16 July	Scudamore Stanhope, C. S.

Private Secretary to First Secretary
1812-70

Provision was made for an annual allowance to be paid to the Clerk acting as Private Clerk or Private Secretary to the First Secretary in 1812.[1] The post was briefly discontinued in 1821–2.[2] Beginning at £50, the allowance was increased to £100 in 1844 and to £150 in 1866.[3]

LIST OF APPOINTMENTS

Croker	1809–30	1812	5 Feb.	Biggs, L. J.
		1822	22 Jan.	Mountain, W. J.
		1826	2 June	Ryland, F.
Elliot	1830–4	1831	10 Feb.	Dyer, J. J.
		1832	31 May	Pennell, C. H.
		1832	18 Aug.	Drinkwater, E.
Dawson	1834–5	1835	15 Jan.	Giffard, E.
Wood	1835–9	1835	28 April	Houghton, J. H. N.
		1837	11 April	Clifton, W.
More O'Ferrall	1839–41	1839		Clifton, W.
		1841	17 Feb.	Wolley, T.
		1841	13 March	Roney, C. P.
Parker	1841	1841	9 June	Roney, C. P.
Herbert	1841–5	1841	29 Sept.	Piers, O. B.
Lowry Corry	1845–6	1845		Piers, O. B.
Ward	1846–9	1846	13 July	O'Reilly, C. W.
		1848	14 June	James, T.
Parker	1849–52	1849	21 May	Ward, S.
O'Brien Stafford	1852–3	1852	3 March	Grant, T. G.
Osborne	1853–8	1853	6 Jan.	Chetwynd Stapylton, H. E.
		1857	13 March	Kempe, C. N.
Lowry Corry	1858–9	1858	9 March	Callander, R. J.
Paget	1859–66	1859	30 June	Kempe, C. N.
Baring	1866	1866	30 April	Kempe, C. N.
Gordon Lennox	1866–8	1866	17 July	Kempe, C. N.
Baxter	1868	1869	14 Jan.	Awdry, R. D.

[1] Adm. 12/154, 5 Feb. 1812.   [2] SPB, xiii ff. 019–20.
[3] Adm. 12/426, 21 Nov. 1844; Adm. 12/778, 23 Oct. 1866.

Private Secretary to Second Secretary
1812–70

Provision was made for an annual allowance of £50 to be paid to the Clerk acting as Private Clerk or Private Secretary to the Second Secretary in 1812.[1] The post was discontinued in 1821 but revived in 1845.[2]

LIST OF APPOINTMENTS

Barrow	1807–45	1812	5 Feb.	Gibson, J.
Baillie Hamilton	1845–55	1845	29 Jan.	Graves, F.
Phinn	1855–7	1855	18 June	Graves, F.
		1857	16 March	Swainson, E. N.
Romaine	1857–69	1857	9 May	Swainson, E. N.
		1862		Miller, J. V.
		1865	17 Aug.	Awdry, R. D.
		1866	15 Oct.	Vansittart Neale, H. J.
Lushington	1869	1869	2 July	Vansittart Neale, H. J.

[1] Adm. 12/154, 5 Feb. 1812.
[2] SPB, xiii ff. 019–20; Barrow, *Autobiography*, 273 n.; Adm. 12/442, 29 Jan. 1845.

Head Messenger 1666-1870

This office, whose holder was originally known simply as the Messenger or the Messenger and Doorkeeper, is traceable to the year 1666 when a salary of £20 was attached to it.[1] The salary was raised to £30 in 1668 and to £50 in 1694.[2] In 1782 an additional allowance was provided to compensate the Head Messenger for the loss of his apartments in the Admiralty.[3] In 1800 the salary was fixed at £120 and increased to £280 in 1808.[4] It was reduced to £250 in 1820 and to £200 in 1859.[5]

LIST OF APPOINTMENTS

1666		Harris, A.	1781	10 Feb.	Millman, W.
1682		Marratt, R.	1820	24 Jan.	Nye, J. M.
1698		Baker, J.	1841	26 July	Lilburn, G.
1708		Bennet, L.	1841	10 Aug.	Laplume, G. P.
1733	8 Oct.	Doody, H.	1854		Sivewright, G.
1763	30 Sept.	Collett, J.	1864	17 Feb.	Winter, N.
1768	21 April	Cooke, W.			

[1] AO 1/1711/106.
[2] AO 1/1711/107; AO 1/1720/135.
[3] SPB, v f. 26. See also *3rd Rept. on Fees*, 118–19.
[4] Orders in council 15 Jan. 1800 (HC 138 p. 4 (1816) xiii, 172); 20 Jan. 1808 (PC 2/175 p. 326).
[5] SPB, xiii f. 027; order in council 12 April 1859 (PC 2/249 pp. 264–6).

Messengers, Extra Messengers and Board Room Messengers c. 1694-1870

Provision was made for two Servants to the Head Messenger, each with a salary of £25, in the establishment of 1694.[1] In the course of time they came to be known as Assistant Messengers or simply as Messengers. One of the offices was left vacant between 1698 and 1710. In 1711 a distinction was made between the First and Second Messengers, the latter usually being promoted to the senior post when it fell vacant. The salary of the First Messenger was then fixed at £30; that of the Second at £20. In 1717 these sums were raised to £40 and £30 respectively.[2] Between 1756 and 1760 there was an additional Messenger with a salary of £30.[3] In 1800 the salaries of the two Messengers were fixed at £60 and £50.[4] That of the First Messenger was raised to £80 in 1804; that of the Second to £70 in April 1806.[5]

In 1795 two Extra Messengers were appointed with salaries of £30 which were raised to £40 in 1800.[6] In September 1806 the four offices were consolidated into a single class and designated Board Room Messengers to distinguish them from the distinct class of Hall Messengers.[7] One of the offices was left vacant between 1816 and 1827. The salary provided in 1806 was £100 which was raised to £150 in 1811.[8] In 1831 the Messengers were placed on a daily pay of 9s 7d. In 1840 they were once again given salaries of £150. In 1859 it was provided that the two senior Messengers should receive £150 and the two junior £120.[9] A fifth Board Room Messenger was appointed in 1868.[10]

LISTS OF APPOINTMENTS

MESSENGERS

By 1694	{ Burrows, J.	1714	17 Sept.	Nicholls, T.
	{ Claridge, T.	1715	9 Nov.	Gould, J.
1696	Golding, E.	1716	7 June	Pell, W.
1697	Thompson, W.	1717	26 July	Rogers, J.
1705	Bennet, L.	1729	3 Oct.	Woolley, J.
		1734	25 Feb.	Gough, J.
1708	Wright, G.	1738	8 Dec.	Gough, B.
1709-10	Owen, P.	1748	5 Aug.	Collett, J.
1711	Elliston, R.	1751	31 July	Tranter, T.

[1] SPB, ii ff. 20, 50-1.   [2] SPB, i f. 20.   [3] SPB, vii f. 22.
[4] Order in council 15 Jan. 1800 (HC 138 p. 4 (1816) xiii, 172).   [5] SPB, iii f. 17.
[6] SPB, viii f. 43; order in council 15 Jan. 1800 (HC 138 p. 4 (1816) xiii, 172).
[7] SPB, iii f. 18; Adm. 12/160, 18 May 1813. Information about Hall Messengers is not sufficient to make their listing possible.
[8] SPB, iii f. 17; SPB, xii f. 64.
[9] Orders in council 10 Nov. 1840 (PC 2/222 pp. 543-6), 12 April 1859 (PC 2/249 pp. 264-6).
[10] Adm. 12/810, 28 May and 5 Aug. 1868; order in council 29 April 1869 (PC 2/269 pp. 526-7).

1756	5 June	Cooke, W.	1781	7 Nov.	Hill, J.
1756	5 June	Hutchinson, R.	1788	24 June	Potts, R.
1763	30 Sept.	Butler, T.	1792	6 Aug.	Powell, J.
1768	26 April	Haysom, J.	1798	20 Feb.	Eastwood, J.
1777	27 March	Downing, W.	1799	26 Nov.	Klyne, J.
1778	4 July	Man, J.	1806	26 April	Woolley, J.

Extra Messengers

1795	13 Aug.	Winchester, J.	1804	28 Jan.	Nye, J. J.
1795	13 Aug.	Evans, E.	1806	26 April	Lilburn, G.
1800	11 April	Woolley, J.			

Board Room Messengers

1806	24 Sept.	Klyne, J.	1841	24 Aug.	Chown, W.
1806	24 Sept.	Woolley, J.	1845	7 April	Groves, J.
1806	24 Sept.	Nye, J. J.	1846	28 Aug.	Giles, J.
1806	24 Sept.	Lilburn, G.	1850	19 June	Priest, C.
1813	19 May	Heald, W.	1854		Winter, N.
1820	24 Jan.	Metcalf, J.	1860	23 Sept.	Ives, G.
1820	1 April	Laplume, G. P.	1864	17 Feb.	Styan, W.
1820	27 May	Christie, J.	1864	23 April	Wild, A.
1827	27 April	Haynes, J.	1867	28 Oct.	Ansell, J.
1828	25 March	Powell, C.	1868	29 July	Weaver, J. F.
1833	15 Jan.	Sivewright, C.	1868	5 Aug.	Roberts, J.

Porter 1676-1870

A Porter with a salary of £20 was attached to the Admiralty between 1676 and 1678 and between 1686 and 1689.[1] Provision was made for a Porter with a salary of £30 in the establishment of 1694.[2] The salary was raised to £50 in 1800.[3] In 1832 the remuneration was fixed at 10s 3d a day. A salary of £160 was substituted in 1840.[4]

LIST OF APPOINTMENTS

1676		Harris, J.	1756	5 June	Collett, J.
1686		Barsley, E.	1763	30 Sept.	Cooke, W.
1688		Gaspy, J.	1768	21 April	Hutchinson, R.
			1786	23 Dec.	Housen, G.
By 1694		Hartwell, M.	1804	2 May	Morris, J.
1694-5		Baker, J.	1806	2 May	Newbegin, J.
1698	20 Sept.	Thompson, W.	1817	4 Nov.	Fetter, G. P.
1714	17 Sept.	Elliston, R.	1820	1 April	Nutland, J.
1731	30 April	Elliston, G.	1837	3 Feb.	Cox, H.
1732	3 April	Elliston, R.[5]	1846	11 June	Guy, J.
1732	5 July	Mears, J.	1862	2 April	Carter, T.

[1] AO 1/1715/120; AO 1/1717/127; AO 1/1719/132.
[2] SPB, ii ff. 50-1.
[3] Order in council 15 Jan. 1800 (HC 138 p. 4 (1816) xiii, 172).
[4] Order in council 10 Nov. 1840 (PC 2/222 pp. 543-6).
[5] Reappointed.

Watchmen c. 1694-1832

Provision was made for a Watchman with a salary of £20 in the establishment of 1694.[1] Salaries of £27 for two further Watchmen were made available in 1705.[2] The salaries of all three Watchmen were fixed at £18 in 1713, at £20 in 1728 and at £25 in 1800.[3] In 1800 it was arranged that one of the Watchmen should act as Extra Porter with an additional allowance of £40. This was raised to £50 in 1807.[4] The office of one of the Watchmen was discontinued in 1821. In 1832 the remaining two Watchmen appear to have been absorbed into the class of Hall Messengers.[5]

LIST OF APPOINTMENTS

By 1694		Mason, G.	1773	14 Jan.	Downing, W.
1698		Buck, T.	1773	10 April	Allpuss, R.
1699		Lindsey, J.	1777	8 April	Man, J.
1704-5		Pratt, B.	1778	4 July	Millman, W.
1704-5		Waldron, R.	1781	10 Feb.	Scott, T.
1719	27 Oct.	Blasedale, A.	1784	11 Feb.	Winchester, C.
1720	7 April	Kettlewell, J.	1786	29 Sept.	Potts, R.
1720	30 Sept.	Mears, H.	1788	24 June	Crockford, J.
1732	5 July	Jefferson, T.	1791	16 July	Sandford, T.
1742	28 June	Pearce, J.	1800	11 Jan.	Munday, J.
1742	4 Nov.	Spike, A.	1801	19 Aug.	Smith, J.
1748	3 June	White, W.	1801	19 Aug.	Legatt, J.
1751	21 March	Chirm, T.	1812	14 Jan.	Barlow, J.
1754	25 Dec.	Hutchinson, R.	1822	6 May	Taylor, J.
1761	16 Feb.	Spike, S.	1825	30 March	Legatt, R.
1768	26 Dec.	Merryam, J.			

[1] SPB, ii ff. 50-1.
[2] Adm. 2/184 p. 582.
[3] SPB, i f. 20; SPB, iv f. 20; order in council 15 Jan. 1800 (HC 138 p. 4 (1816) xiii, 172).
[4] SPB, iii ff. 18-19.
[5] SPB, xiii ff. 029-30; order in council 10 Nov. 1840 (PC 2/222 pp. 543-6).

Housekeeper c. 1697–1800

The salary of £40 attached to this office was originally paid out of the contingent fund. The identity of its holders can be ascertained only after 1697 from which date the salary was transferred to the ordinary establishment.[1] The office had become a sinecure by 1786.[2] It was abolished in 1800.[3]

LIST OF APPOINTMENTS

By 1697		Baker, M.	1727	14 Sept.	Holland, E.
1708		Halsey, S.	1739	24 Oct.	Fisher, S.
1713		Bennet, A.	1740	15 March	Perchard, R.
1727	3 Jan.	Head, E.	1752	13 May	Bell, E.

[1] SPB, i f. 20.
[2] *3rd Rept. on Fees*, 119.
[3] Order in council 15 Jan. 1800 (HC 138 p. 4 (1816) xiii, 172).

Necessary Woman (Housekeeper)
c. 1694-1865

Provision was made for a Cleaner or Necessary Woman in the establishment of 1694. The salary, originally £20, was raised to £25 in 1755, to £30 in 1779 and to £35 in 1782.[1] By 1786 the Necessary Woman had apparently assumed responsibility for the duties of the office of Housekeeper which had become a sinecure.[2] The salary was fixed at £60 in 1796 and raised to £100 in 1800 on the abolition of the office of Housekeeper.[3] From 1832 the Necessary Woman was officially designated Housekeeper.[4] The office was abolished in 1865 when provision was made for the duties to be carried out by the wife of one of the Messengers with an annual allowance of £65.[5]

LIST OF APPOINTMENTS

By 1694		Buck, E.	1775	3 Aug.	Butler, E.
1706		Lindsey, A.	1794	27 March	Hill, E.
1720	27 April	Lindsey, M.	1816	15 May	Robinson, A.
1722	17 Aug.	Roberts, M.	1823	26 March	Blackie, H.
1729	19 Dec.	Clack, C.	1832	14 March	Smith, S.
1762	15 April	Clack, J.	1851	28 May	Blount, L. A.
1767	26 May	Reynolds, E.			

[1] Adm. 2/16 p. 414; SPB, ii ff. 50-1; SPB, vii f. 23; SPB, v f. 27.
[2] *3rd Rept. on Fees*, 119.
[3] SPB, viii f. 45; order in council 15 Jan. 1800 (HC 138 p. 4 (1816) xiii, 172).
[4] SPB, xiv f. 12.
[5] Adm. 12/762, 26 Jan. 1865.

Gardener c. 1700-1827

The salary attached to this office was originally paid out of the contingent fund. Its holders can be identified only after 1700 when payment was transferred to the ordinary establishment.[1] The office was abolished in 1827.[2] The salary, originally £30, was raised to £40 in 1705. It was reduced to £20 in 1723 but raised once again to £30 in 1733.[3] An additional allowance of £30 in lieu of a house was provided in 1791.[4]

LIST OF APPOINTMENTS

By 1700		Cooke, F.	1741	12 March	Tucker, J.
1716	10 April	{ Cooke, F.	1786	27 Feb.	Combe, D.
		{ Cooke, J.	1812	11 Aug.	Kitchen, W.
1717	19 June	Cooke, J.			

Inspector of Repairs 1731-1800

This office was created in 1731 when it was provided that the Surveyor of Works of the Victualling Office should undertake similar duties for the Admiralty. The salary was fixed at £30. The office was abolished in 1800.[5]

LIST OF APPOINTMENTS

1731	1 April	Glanville, B.	1785	30 Sept.	Cockerell, S. P.
1774	8 Aug.	Arrow, J.			

[1] SPB, i f. 10.
[2] SPB, xiv f. 12.
[3] SPB, i f. 10; SPB, iv f. 20.
[4] SPB, viii f. 44.
[5] Adm. 3/39, 1 April 1731; order in council 15 Jan. 1800 (HC 138 p. 4 (1816) xiii, 172).

Hydrographer 1795-1870

This office was created in 1795 and was invariably held by a naval officer. The salary was originally £500.[1] In 1838 the remuneration was increased to £800 which included an allowance of £300 for a house.[2] In 1865 the salary was fixed at £1000 in addition to half pay.[3] The office was filled on a temporary basis between 1823 and 1829.

LIST OF APPOINTMENTS

1795	13 Aug.	Dalrymple, A.	1827	1 Nov.	Parry, W. E.[4]
1808	28 May	Hurd, T.	1829	19 May	Beaufort, F.
1823	8 Dec.	Parry, W. E.[4]	1855	25 Jan.	Washington, J.
1825	22 Nov.	Parry, W. E.[4]	1863	19 Sept.	Richards, G. H.

Inspector of Telegraphs 1796-1816

This office was created in 1796 with a salary of £500.[5] It was dispensed with in 1816 following the termination of the war.[6]

APPOINTMENT

1796   23 April   Roebuck, G.

[1] Order in council 12 Aug. 1795 (PC 2/144 pp. 51-3).
[2] HC 101 p. 14 (1838) xxxvii, 188.
[3] Order in council 29 Nov. 1865 (PC 2/262 p. 739).
[4] Temporary appointment.
[5] SPB, ix f. 11; *17th Rept. on Finance*, 329.
[6] Adm. 12/178, 9 March 1816; SPB, xii ff. 55-6.

Counsel 1673–1870

This office, to which appointments were made by Admiralty warrant, was created in 1673.[1] Originally it was attached to the Navy Board only. It was not until 1696 that the Counsel was formally deputed to act for the Admiralty as well.[2] However, in the interests of continuity the earlier holders of the office have been included in these lists. The office was discontinued in 1679, as a result of the decision to retrench naval expenditure, but was revived in 1685.[3] Until 1696 the Counsel was empowered to appoint a Solicitor with a salary of £5.[4] The salary of the Counsel which was originally £20, was raised to £100 in 1703.[5] From 1824 the office was held concurrently with that of Judge Advocate of the Fleet.

LIST OF APPOINTMENTS

1673		Wright, R.	1757	15 Feb.	Hussey, R.
1685	4 July	Porter, C.	1770	28 March	Cust, F.
1686	23 April	Killingworth, W.	1791	12 Dec.	Brodrick, Hon. T.
1696	14 Sept.	Lechmere, T.	1795	16 Jan.	Perceval, Hon. S.
1703	18 Feb.	Ettrick, W.	1801	20 Feb.	Jervis, T.
1708	8 Dec.	Phipps, C.	1824	9 Feb.	Twiss, H.
1709	19 Nov.	Townsend, G.	1828	2 June	Shepherd, H. J.
1711	11 June	Ettrick, W.[6]	1845	7 Feb.	Godson, R.
1715	18 Jan.	Townsend, G.[6]	1849	5 Sept.	Crowder, R. B.
1726	4 Oct.	Baynes, J.	1854	17 April	Phinn, T.
1737	1 March	Hunter, J.	1855	6 June	Atherton, W.
1742	1 March	Clarke, C.	1859	16 Dec.	Collier, R. P.
1743	9 Feb.	Legge, Hon. H.	1863	12 Nov.	Phinn, T.[6]
1747	5 June	Jervis, S.	1866	5 Nov.	Huddleston, J. W.

[1] Corbett MS, v p. 140; AO 1/1713/113. In 1676 the Counsel and Solicitor were granted allowances of 40s and 6s 8d respectively for each day's attendance at the Navy Board (Adm. 2/1, 9 Dec. 1676).
[2] Adm. 2/1741 p. 226; Adm. 6/4 p. 25. [3] Adm. 2/1740 pp. 270–3; Adm. 2/1741 p. 143.
[4] Adm. 2/1741 p. 143. The office of Solicitor was held by John Gardiner 1672–9 and William Reyney 1686–96. [5] SPB, i f. 20. [6] Reappointed.

Solicitor 1692–1870

Between 1672 and 1696 the Counsel to the Navy Board was empowered to employ a Solicitor with a salary of £5.[1] In 1692 a distinct office, that of Solicitor for the affairs of the Admiralty and Navy, was appointed by Admiralty warrant with a salary of £100. This office was not filled after 1699.[2]

In 1703 the office of Assistant to the Admiralty Counsel was created with a salary of £400.[3] It was conferred upon an individual who had in the previous year been appointed to the new office of Solicitor of Admiralty Droits.[4] Thereafter these two offices, to which appointments were made by Admiralty warrant, were held concurrently. Their holder was generally referred to as Solicitor rather than Assistant Counsel and this practice has been followed in these lists.

In 1828 the duties of the office were extended and its holder officially designated Solicitor to the Admiralty. At the same time all the fees previously enjoyed by the Solicitor were abolished and he was accorded a salary of £1500 together with an annual allowance of £1000 for Clerks. A further allowance of £100 was made available in 1831.[5]

LIST OF APPOINTMENTS

1692	2 March	Whittaker, E.	1778	30 May	Dyson, J.
			1796	1 March	Bicknell, C.
1703	26 June	Warter, J.	1828	7 Jan.	Jones, C.
1718	3 Dec.	Jobber, T.	1843	8 Dec.	Robson, W. F.
1733	4 April	Winnington, F.	1862	15 Jan.	Skirrow, C. F.
1747	16 June	Ryan, A.	1862	12 May	Bristow, A. R.
1749	24 Jan.	Seddon, S.			

[1] For this office, see Corbett MS, v pp. 144–9. See also p. 78.
[2] SPB, i f. 20; Adm. 2/180 pp. 45–6. [3] SPB, i f. 20.
[4] Admiralty warrant 18 June 1702 (HCA 50/7 f. 154). From 1715 this office was known as that of Comptroller and Solicitor of Admiralty Droits (HCA 50/8 f. 197). The salary attached to it was £200 payable by the Receiver of Droits (*3rd Rept. on Fees*, 122–3).
[5] Adm. 12/245, 27 Dec. 1827; SPB, xiv f. 16.

Judge Advocate of the Fleet 1663–1870

This office, to which appointments were made by Admiralty warrant, was established on a permanent basis in 1663.[1] The salary, which was originally 8s a day (£146 a year), was increased to 10s a day (£182 10s a year) in 1666.[2] From 1824 the office was held concurrently with that of Counsel to the Admiralty.

LIST OF APPOINTMENTS

1663	17 Jan.	Fowler, J.	1744	12 Nov.	Fearne, C.
1672	30 Sept.	Brisbane, J.	1768	19 Feb.	Jackson, G.
1680	29 July	Croone, H.	1824	9 Feb.	Twiss, H.
1689	23 May	Foster, P.	1828	2 June	Shepherd, H. J.
1689	12 Oct.	Bacher, F.	1845	7 Feb.	Godson, R.
1690	23 July	Bathurst, V.	1849	5 Sept.	Crowder, R. B.
1711	13 Sept.	Strahan, W.	1854	17 April	Phinn, T.
1714	22 Dec.	Honywood, E.	1855	6 June	Atherton, W.
1724	1 May	Copeland, J.	1859	16 Dec.	Collier, R. P.
1729	11 Feb.	Hawes, T.	1863	12 Nov.	Phinn, T.[3]
1743	15 June	Kempe, T.	1866	5 Nov.	Huddleston, J. W.

[1] Adm. 2/1733 pp. 54–5. Fowler had acted as Judge Advocate on a temporary basis since 1660 (AO 1/1710/102; AO 1/1711/105; Adm. 2/1725 ff. 48–9).

[2] AO 1/1711/106.   [3] Reappointed.

Deputy Judge Advocate of the Fleet
1668-1870

This office, to which appointments were made by Admiralty warrant, was created in 1668 with a salary of 8s a day (£146 a year).[1] It was discontinued in 1679 as a result of the decision to retrench naval expenditure but was revived in 1684.[2] It was abolished in 1831 but was once again revived, on an unsalaried basis, in 1843.[3]

LIST OF APPOINTMENTS

1668	16 Oct.	Smith, J.		1714	22 Dec.	Copeland, J.
1675	23 Jan.	Southerne, J.		1724	1 May	Bell, W.
1677	12 March	Hewer, W.		1740	20 June	Kempe, T.
				1743	15 June	Fearne, C.
1684	26 Feb.	Walbanke, J.		1744	12 Nov.	Mason, E.
1687	2 Jan.	Atkins, S.		1745	2 March	Atkins, G.
1689	30 May	Tindall, M.		1754	5 Dec.	Clevland, J.
1689	8 Nov.	Jenkins, C.		1762	10 April	Higgens, R.
1692	7 Jan.	Pett, S.		1780	24 July	Binsteed, T.
1693	4 July	Burchett, J.		1804	6 Nov.	Greetham, M.
1694	18 Aug.	Larkin, G.				
1697	21 Oct.	Fawler, J.		1843	16 Jan.	Greetham, G. L.
1703	6 May	Rock, W.		1856	14 Jan.	Hellyer, W. J.
1707	10 Jan.	Ferrabosco, M.		1861	10 May	Eastlake, W.
1707	2 Dec.	Honywood, E.				

[1] Adm. 2/1734 f. 46; AO 1/1712/108.
[2] Adm. 2/1740 pp. 270-3; Sergison MS f. 145.
[3] HC 12 pp. 4, 9 (1843) xxxi, 324, 329.

MARINE DEPARTMENT

Clerks 1755–1809

On the formation of the Marine Department in 1755 provision was made for a clerical staff with salaries payable by the Paymaster of Marines. At first this staff consisted of a First Clerk with a salary of £100 and a Second Clerk with a salary of £70, together with two Extra Clerks.[1] The salary of the First Clerk was increased to £200 in 1756.[2] Fearne, the holder of this office, was then a junior Clerk on the ordinary establishment of the Admiralty. He remained First Clerk after his promotion to the office of Deputy Secretary to the Admiralty in 1764 until his retirement in 1766.[3] His successor as Deputy Secretary, Jackson, was also allowed the salary of £200 attached to the office of First Clerk in the Marine Department.[4]

In 1778 the salary of the Second Clerk was raised to £100 and a Third Clerk was appointed at £70 a year.[5] In 1782 the salary of £200, formerly attached to the first clerkship, was made a permanent part of the remuneration of the Deputy Secretary of the Admiralty who was given the additional title of Deputy Secretary of the Marine Department. At the same time the salaries of the three Clerks were fixed at £130, £80 and £60.[6] In 1784 the third clerkship was abolished and in 1790 the salary attached to the second clerkship was increased to £110.[7]

In 1800 the salaries of the First and Second Clerks were fixed at £300 and £150 respectively and made payable by the Treasurer of the Navy.[8] In 1807 the new salary arrangements for the Senior and Junior Clerks in the Admiralty office were applied to these posts.[9] In 1809 the separate existence of the Marine Department was brought to a close and its clerkships were incorporated into the ordinary establishment of the Admiralty.[10]

LISTS OF APPOINTMENTS

FIRST CLERK

1755	17 July	Fearne, C.	1782	30 June	Madden, J.
1766	11 Nov.	Jackson, G.	1789	7 Oct.	Coombe, G.

[1] Adm. 2/1152 pp. 134–5; *3rd Rept. on Fees*, 116–17. [2] Adm. 2/1153 pp. 271–2.
[3] Adm. 2/1160 p. 187. [4] Adm. 2/1162 p. 202.
[5] Adm. 2/1170 p. 558. [6] Adm. 2/1174 pp. 71, 172.
[7] Adm. 3/99, 12 Feb. 1784; Adm. 2/1175 p. 260; Adm. 2/1180 pp. 263–4.
[8] Order in council 15 Jan. 1800 (HC 138 p. 3 (1816) xiii, 171).
[9] Order in council 28 Oct. 1807 (PC 2/174 pp. 284–6).
[10] SPB, xii ff. 57–8; order in council 14 March 1811 (PC 2/192 pp. 98–100).

Second Clerk

1755	17 July	Clevland, J.	1784	10 Feb.	Coombe, G.
1760	5 May	Madden, J.	1789	7 Oct.	Maxwell, B.
1782	30 June	Bindley, J.	1796	3 Aug.	Moss, S.

Third Clerk

1778	10 June	Bindley, J.	1782	30 June	Coombe, G.

Extra Clerks 1755-82

Provision was made for there to be two Extra Clerks in the Marine Department in 1755, each with a salary of £50, payable by the Paymaster of Marines. The offices were discontinued in 1782.[1]

LIST OF APPOINTMENTS

1755	17 July	Rogers, B.	1770	26 April	Forbes, D.
1755	17 July	Madden, J.	1778	7 July	Coombe, G.
1760	5 May	Parker, H.			

[1] Adm. 2/1152 pp. 134–5; Adm. 2/1174 p. 172; *3rd Rept. on Fees*, 116–17.

MARINE PAY DEPARTMENT

Paymaster of Marines 1755-1831

This office, to which appointments were made by Admiralty warrant, was created in 1755.[1] The salary was fixed at £800, an additional allowance of £200 being provided in time of war.[2] A sum of £100 a year for office rent was made available in 1756.[3] Before 1800 the Paymaster was responsible for paying such Clerks as he required out of his own salary. In that year their salaries were made a charge on the marine contingency fund and the salary of the Paymaster was fixed at £600. At the same time the Paymaster took over the functions of the Agent of Marines.[4] In 1803 the duties of the office were extended and its holder designated Paymaster and Inspector General of Marines with a salary of £1000.[5] The office of Paymaster was abolished in 1831 when its duties were transferred to the Treasurer of the Navy.[6]

LIST OF APPOINTMENTS

1755	5 April	Adair, W.	1812	30 Sept.	Stewart, Hon. E. R.
1756	16 Dec.	Campbell, G.	1813	20 July	Doyle, F. H.
1757	19 April	Tucker, J.	1815	18 Sept.	Chetwynd Stapylton, Hon. G. A.
1778	4 June	Steward, G.			
1792	19 March	Villiers, Hon. G.	1819	8 April	Cockburn, Sir J.
1810	16 Jan.	Phipps, Hon. E.			

[1] Adm. 6/406 pp. 9-11; *3rd Rept. on Fees*, 117-18, 119-20.
[2] Adm. 6/406 pp. 9-11; Adm. 2/1153 pp. 303-4; Adm. 2/1159 pp. 164-5; Adm. 2/1183 pp. 494-5.
[3] Order in council 13 Oct. 1756 (Adm. 2/1153 pp. 286-8).
[4] Order in council 15 Jan. 1800 (HC 138 pp. 7-8 (1816) xiii, 175-6); Adm. 2/1189 pp. 227-9.
[5] Warrant 9 May 1803 (Adm. 6/406).   [6] Order in council 31 Jan. 1831 (PC 2/212 pp. 34-5).

Clerks 1755–1819

On the establishment of the office of Paymaster of Marines in 1755 the Paymaster was provided with a salary out of which he was expected to defray the cost of such clerical assistance as he required. Before 1800 very little information relating to the staff of the office has survived. The Paymaster appears to have appointed two Clerks, known as the First and Second Clerk, from the outset and may have employed Extra Clerks as well.[1] In 1800 the salary of the Paymaster was reduced and provision was made for the salaries of his staff to be charged on public funds and made payable out of the marine contingency fund. The salary of the First Clerk was then fixed at £300 and that of the Second Clerk at £100.[2] In 1807 the salaries were fixed at £450 and £200 respectively.[3] In 1814 a third Clerk was appointed also with a salary of £200.[4] In 1819 these Clerks were absorbed into a classified clerical establishment.[5]

LISTS OF APPOINTMENTS

FIRST CLERK

1755	Madden, J.	1807		Waters, E.
By 1795	Waters, E.[6]	1808	30 Sept.	Hind, T.
1797	Webb, D. C.			

SECOND CLERK

By 1795	Webb, D. C.	1807	31 Dec.	Gardner, G.
1797	Waller, T.			

THIRD CLERK

1814	16 June	Edwards, J.

---

[1] *3rd Rept. on Fees*, 117–18, 120.
[2] Order in council 15 Jan. 1800 (HC 138 pp. 7–8 (1816) xiii, 175–6).
[3] Order in council 11 Nov. 1807 (PC 2/174 pp. 483–5).
[4] SPB, xii ff. 73–4.
[5] Order in council 3 Dec. 1819 (PC 2/201 pp. 595–6).
[6] Deputy Paymaster of Marines 1797–1807.

Extra Clerks 1800-19

In 1800 provision was made for two Extra Clerks in the Marine Pay Department, one with a salary of £80 and the other with a salary of £50.[1] In 1807 the number was fixed at four who were to receive salaries of £80 for under three years' service, £100 for three to five years' service, £120 for five to seven years' service and £140 for more than seven years' service.[2] In 1819 the Extra Clerks were absorbed into a classified clerical establishment.[3]

LIST OF APPOINTMENTS

1800	1 Oct.	Robinson, W.	1803	24 June	Edwards, J.
1801	12 April	Brixey, W.	1807	31 Dec.	Gardner, W.

First Class Clerk 1819-31

In 1819 provision was made for there to be one First Class (or Chief) Clerk in the Marine Pay Department with a salary of £400 rising by annual increments of £10 to £500.[4] The office was discontinued on the abolition of the Department in 1831.[5]

APPOINTMENT

1819   11 Dec.   Hind, T.

[1] Order in council 15 Jan. 1800 (HC 138 pp. 7–8 (1816) xiii, 175–6).
[2] Order in council 11 Nov. 1807 (PC 2/174 pp. 483–5).
[3] Order in council 3 Dec. 1819 (PC 2/201 pp. 595–6).
[4] Order in council 3 Dec. 1819 (PC 2/201 pp. 595–6); SPB, xiii ff. 037–8.
[5] Order in council 31 Jan. 1831 (PC 2/212 pp. 34–5).

Second Class Clerks 1819-31

In 1819 provision was made for there to be two Second Class Clerks in the Marine Pay Department with salaries of £200 rising by annual increments of £10 to £300.[1] A third Second Class Clerk was appointed in 1827.[2] The offices were discontinued in 1831 on the abolition of the Department.[3]

LIST OF APPOINTMENTS

1819	11 Dec.	Gardner, G.	1827	7 April	Edwards, J.
1819	11 Dec.	Robinson, W.			

Third Class Clerks 1819-31

In 1819 provision was made for there to be three Third Class Clerks in the Marine Pay Department.[4] A fourth Third Class Clerk was appointed in 1827.[5] The offices were discontinued in 1831 on the abolition of the Department.[6]

LIST OF APPOINTMENTS

1819	11 Dec.	Brixey, W.	1827	7 April	Bartmore, W.
1819	11 Dec.	Edwards, J.	1827	29 Oct.	Cooper, H.
1819	11 Dec.	Gardner, W.	1827	13 Dec.	Edwards, R.
1824	23 Jan.	Cooper, C.	1830	2 Dec.	Hind, C. W.

[1] Order in council 3 Dec. 1819 (PC 2/201 pp. 595–6); SPB, xiii ff. 037–8.   [2] SPB, xiv f. 19.
[3] Order in council 31 Jan. 1831 (PC 2/212 pp. 34–5).
[4] Order in council 3 Dec. 1819 (PC 2/201 pp. 595–6); SPB, xiii ff. 037–8.   [5] SPB, xiv f. 19.
[6] Order in council 31 Jan. 1831 (PC 2/212 pp. 34–5).

Messenger c. 1807–1831

In 1800 provision was made for a Messenger in the Marine Pay Department with a salary of £50.[1] The salary was raised to £70 in 1807 and to £80 in 1824.[2] The office was discontinued on the abolition of the Department in 1831.[3]

LIST OF APPOINTMENTS

By 1807		Hayward, T.	1813	19 May	Pitts, R.
1809	3 July	Leader, R.	1826	16 Oct.	Elbourn, R.

Office Keeper 1824–31

This office was created in 1824 with a salary of £100 and an annual allowance of £40 for a housemaid. It was discontinued in 1831 on the abolition of the Marine Pay Department.[4]

LIST OF APPOINTMENTS

1824	18 May	Glendenning, R.	1827	11 Dec.	Weaver, W. H.

[1] Order in council 15 Jan. 1800 (HC 138 p. 8 (1816) xiii, 176).
[2] Order in council 11 Nov. 1807 (PC 2/174 pp. 483–5); SPB, xiv f. 21.
[3] Order in council 31 Jan. 1831 (PC 2/212 pp. 34–5).
[4] SPB, xiv f. 21; order in council 31 Jan. 1831 (PC 2/212 pp. 34–5).

Agents of Marines 1756–1800

The offices of Agents of Marines, to which appointments were made by Admiralty warrant, were established in 1756 when it was provided that there should be an Agent for each of the three divisions of Plymouth, Portsmouth and Chatham with a salary of £300 payable by the Paymaster of Marines.[1] In April 1763 the number of Agents was reduced to one who was made responsible for all the divisions.[2] The salary was then fixed at £300 but was raised to £500 in the following month.[3] An additional allowance of £100 was provided in time of war.[4] The office of Agent was abolished in 1800 when its duties were transferred to the Paymaster of Marines.[5]

LIST OF APPOINTMENTS

1756	9 Nov.	Guerin, M. (Plymouth)	1760	5 May	Clevland, J. (Plymouth)
1756	9 Nov.	Winter, J. (Portsmouth)	1763	9 April	Clevland, J.
			1767	16 April	Williams, G.
1756	9 Nov.	Baird, J. (Chatham)	1791	19 July	Cox, C.

[1] Order in council 13 Oct. 1756 (Adm. 2/1153 pp. 287–8).
[2] Order in council 8 April 1763 (Adm. 2/1159 pp. 16–17); *3rd Rept. on Fees*, 120–1.
[3] Adm. 2/1159 pp. 77–8.
[4] Adm. 2/1157 pp. 315–16.
[5] Order in council 15 Jan. 1800 (HC 138 p. 7 (1816) xiii, 175); Adm. 2/1189 pp. 227–9.

NAVAL WORKS DEPARTMENT

Inspector General 1796-1807

This office, to which appointment was made by Admiralty warrant, was created in 1796 with a salary of £750.[1] In 1807 it was transferred from the Admiralty to the Navy Board and given the title of Civil Architect and Engineer of the Navy.[2]

APPOINTMENT

1796   25 March   Bentham, S.

Architect and Engineer 1796-1807

This office, to which appointment was made by Admiralty warrant, was created in 1796 with a salary of £400.[3] In 1807 it was transferred from the Admiralty to the Navy Board and given the title of Assistant Civil Architect and Engineer of the Navy.[4]

LIST OF APPOINTMENTS

1796   25 March   Bunce, S.   1804   3 Jan.   Holl, E.

[1] Order in council 23 March 1796 (*17th Rept. on Finance*, 342–3; warrant 25 March 1796 (Adm. 6/25).
[2] Order in council 28 Oct. 1807 (PC 2/174 pp. 274–6, 284).
[3] Order in council 23 March 1796 (*17th Rept. on Finance*, 342–3); warrant 25 March 1796 (Adm. 6/25).
[4] Order in council 28 Oct. 1807 (PC 2/174 pp. 274–6, 284).

Mechanist 1796-1807

This office, to which appointment was made by Admiralty warrant, was created in 1796 with a salary of £400.[1] In 1807 it was transferred from the Admiralty to the Navy Board and given the title of Mechanist under the Civil Architect and Engineer of the Navy.[2]

LIST OF APPOINTMENTS

1796	25 March	Reke, S.	1799	25 Oct.	Goodrick, S.

Chemist 1796-1807

This office, to which appointment was made by Admiralty warrant, was created in 1796 with a salary of £400.[3] It ceased to exist in 1807 when the Naval Works Department was transferred from the Admiralty to the Navy Board.[4]

APPOINTMENT

1796   25 March   Sadler, J.

Metal Master 1803-7

This office, to which appointment was made by Admiralty warrant, was created in 1803 with a salary of £200.[5] It ceased to exist in 1807 on the transfer of the Naval Works Department from the Admiralty to the Navy Board.[6]

APPOINTMENT

1803   26 April   Sheffield, W. E.

[1] Order in council 23 March 1796 (*17th Rept. on Finance*, 342–3); warrant 25 March 1796 (Adm. 6/25).
[2] Order in council 28 Oct. 1807 (PC 2/174 pp. 274–6, 284).
[3] Order in council 23 March 1796 (*17th Rept. on Finance*, 342–3); warrant 25 March 1796 (Adm. 6/25).
[4] Order in council 28 Oct. 1807 (PC 2/174 pp. 274–6, 284); SPB, iii f. 24.
[5] Order in council 20 April 1803 (PC 2/162 pp. 268–9).
[6] Order in council 28 Oct. 1807 (PC 2/174 pp. 274–6, 284); SPB, iii f. 25.

Secretary 1796-1807

This office was created in 1796 with a salary of £300.[1] In 1807 it was transferred from the Admiralty to the Navy Board and given the title of Extra Assistant to the Civil Architect and Engineer of the Navy.[2]

APPOINTMENT

1796   25 March   Peake, J.

Draftsman 1796-1805

This office was created in 1796 with a salary of £200. It was discontinued in 1805.[3]

APPOINTMENT

1796   13 May   Burr, J.

Clerks 1796-1807

Provision was made for a First and a Second Clerk in the Naval Works Department in 1796 with salaries of £150 and £100 respectively.[4] The second clerkship was discontinued in July 1807.[5] In October 1807 the First Clerk was transferred from the Admiralty to the Navy Board and appointed a Clerk to the Secretary of that Board.[6]

LISTS OF APPOINTMENTS

FIRST CLERK

1796	25 March	Darch, T.	1804	5 July	Rogers, H.
1801	5 Jan.	Upsal, R.			

SECOND CLERK

1796	25 March	Heidekoo, J.	1801	5 Jan.	Heard, W.
1797	22 May	Upsal, R.	1806	30 Jan.	Drummond, D.

[1] Order in council 23 March 1796 (*17th Rept. on Finance*, 342–3); SPB, x f. 40.
[2] Order in council 28 Oct. 1807 (PC 2/174 pp. 274–6, 284).
[3] Order in council 23 March 1796 (*17th Rept. on Finance*, 342–3); SPB, x f. 40; SPB, iii f. 24.
[4] Order in council 23 March 1796 (*17th Rept. on Finance*, 342–3); SPB, x f. 40.
[5] SPB, iii f. 25.   [6] Order in council 28 Oct. 1807 (PC 2/174 pp. 274–6, 284).

Messenger 1796–1807

This office was created in 1796 with a salary of £40.[1] It was transferred to the Navy Board in 1807.[2]

LIST OF APPOINTMENTS

1796	13 May	Fetter, J.	1803	14 July	Howard, W.

[1] Order in council 23 March 1796 (*17th Rept. on Finance*, 342–3); SPB, x f. 40.
[2] Order in council 28 Oct. 1807 (PC 2/174 pp. 274–6, 284); SPB, xii ff. 293–4.

ADMIRALTY COURT
Judge 1660-1870

Until the resignation of the Duke of York in 1673 the Judge was appointed by the Lord High Admiral by letters patent under the seal of the court. From 1673 appointments were made by the crown by letters patent under the great seal with the single exception of Henchman (1714) who was appointed by the Admiralty by letters patent under the seal of the court.[1] Tenure was during pleasure until 1689 and during good behaviour thereafter. In 1689 a salary of £400 was attached to the office payable by the Treasurer of the Navy. Between 1694 and 1714 a further £400 was provided as a reward for attendance on the Privy Council, the Secretaries of State and the Admiralty. This was at first paid out of the Admiralty contingent fund but was transferred to the ordinary establishment in 1698.[2] From 1714 to 1778 the basic salary was £400 with an additional £400 in time of war.[3] In 1725 a further £400 was provided in recognition of the Judge's extra judicial activities and for the making of reports but this was retrenched in the following year.[4] In 1783 an additional allowance of £980 a year was attached to the office and made payable from the time of Marriott's appointment in 1778.[5] In 1798 the salary was fixed at £2500.[6] In addition to his salary the Judge was entitled to certain fees arising from cases in the court.[7] In 1840 these were abolished and a salary of £4000, payable out of the consolidated fund, was provided by statute which also disqualified the Judge from membership of the House of Commons.[8]

LIST OF APPOINTMENTS

1661	4 Feb.	Zouche, R.[9]	1715	23 Aug.	Penrice, H.
1661	12 March	Hyde, T.	1751	19 Dec.	Salusbury, Sir T.
1661	26 Oct.	Exton, J.	1773	4 Nov.	Hay, G.
1668	17 Nov.	Jenkins, L.[10]	1778	12 Oct.	Marriott, Sir J.
1685	1 Oct.	Lloyd, Sir R.	1798	26 Oct.	Scott, Sir W.
1686	6 July	Exton, Sir T.	1828	22 Feb.	Robinson, Sir C.
1686	17 Dec.	Raines, Sir R.	1833	30 May	Nicholl, Sir J.
1689	1 June	Hedges, C.	1838	17 Oct.	Lushington, S.
1714	22 June	Henchman, H.	1867	23 Aug.	Phillimore, Sir R. J.
1714	1 Dec.	Newton, H.			

[1] For this office see Corbett MS, v pp. 35–65; W. Senior, 'Sir Henry Penrice and Sir Thomas Salusbury', *Mariner's Mirror*, xiii (1927), 38–44; 'The Judges of the High Court of Admiralty', ibid., 333–47: 'Judges of the Admiralty—Note', ibid. xiv (1928), 74–5.
[2] SPB, i f. 27.   [3] ibid.; SPB, vi f. 19; SPB, vii f. 21; SPB, v f. 26; SPB, viii f. 42.
[4] SPB, iv f. 19.   [5] SPB, v f. 26.   [6] Order in council 24 Oct. 1798 (PC 2/151 pp. 577–8).
[7] *27th Rept. on Finance*, 334–5.   [8] 3 & 4 Vict., c 66, s 1.
[9] Zouche had originally been appointed in 1641 but had been displaced in 1643.
[10] Jenkins had earlier acted as associate to J. Exton (*CSPD 1664–5*, 427, 490; Corbett MS, v p. 41). By letters patent 12 July 1673 (HCA 50/4 f. 85; C 66/3150) Sir Robert Wiseman was appointed to act as Judge in his absence on diplomatic business.

Registrar 1660-1870

This office was granted by letters patent under seal of the Admiralty Court.[1] Until the resignation of the Duke of York in 1673 the letters patent were issued in the name of the Lord High Admiral; thereafter by the crown. In 1691 Thomas Bedford, who had received a reversionary grant to the office in 1679, had his interest confirmed by letters patent under the great seal.[2] This practice was followed thereafter until the regulation of the office in the nineteenth century. Until 1840 the office was invariably conferred for life with power to appoint deputies; reversionary interests were frequently granted.[3] Following the death of Arden in 1840 the office was regulated by act.[4] This provided that the then deputy should become the principal and that future appointments should be made by the Judge of the Admiralty by letters patent under the seal of the Court and be held during good behaviour. The same act discontinued the previous arrangement whereby the Registrar received his remuneration exclusively in the form of fees which varied according to whether conditions of peace or war prevailed.[5] Thereafter the fees were to be carried to a fund out of which the Registrar and the Marshal were to receive salaries. The salary of the Registrar was fixed at £1400 with provision for it to be increased within a maximum of £2000 in time of war or other exceptional circumstances.

From 1705 it was the practice for the Registrar also to hold the office of Registrar of the Court of Delegates.[6]

LIST OF APPOINTMENTS

1660	6 Sept.	{ Potter, H.[7] { Gee, O.	1758	21 Feb.	Farrant, G. L.
			1790	9 Aug.	Arden, Lord
1705		Crawley, R.	1840	7 Aug.	Swabey, H. B.
1712	21 March	Hill, R.	1853	10 Dec.	Rothery, H. C.
1714	2 Oct.	Hill, S.			

[1] For this office, see Corbett MS, v pp. 81–9; G. H. M. Thompson, *Admiralty Registrars: Some Historical Notes* (London 1958).

[2] Letters patent under seal of Admiralty court 17 April 1679 (HCA 50/4 f. 209) and 15 April 1685 (HCA 50/5 ff. 86–7); letters patent under great seal 8 July 1691 (C 66/3345). Bedford died before succeeding to the office.

[3] Apart from Bedford the following received reversionary grants but did not live to enjoy the office: Charles Hedges (d. c. 1714) by letters patent 13 Dec. 1710 (C 66/3476), Henry Farrant (d. 1727) by letters patent 1 July 1725 (C 66/3559) and Hon. Spencer Perceval (d. 1812) by letters patent 2 July 1764 (C 66/3696).

[4] 3 & 4 Vict., c 66 superseding 50 Geo. III, c 118.   [5] *27th Rept. on Finance*, 336–7.

[6] G. I. O. Duncan, *The High Court of Delegates* (Cambridge 1971), 300.

[7] Potter had originally been appointed in May 1639 but had been suspended in 1644 (Corbett MS, v pp. 81–9).

Marshal 1660-1870

The Marshal was appointed by letters patent under the seal of the Admiralty court.[1] Until 1709 the letters patent were issued in the name of the Lord High Admiral or the Admiralty Board; from then on in that of the crown. Tenure was during pleasure. Originally the remuneration attached to the office was derived exclusively from fees.[2] In 1840 it was enacted that the fees should be carried to a fund out of which the Marshal was to receive a salary of £500 with provision for an increase within a maximum of £800 in time of war or in other exceptional circumstances.[3]

LIST OF APPOINTMENTS

1660	5 July	Joynes, W.	1783	12 Nov.	Crickitt, J.
1689	17 Oct.	Cheeke, J.	1811	30 Oct.	Thornton, R.
1733	9 Aug.	Crespigny, P.	1815	14 March	Lindsay, Hon. H.
1745	7 Feb.	Busby, E.	1844	4 May	Deacon, J.
1751	24 May	Barrington, Hon. D.	1850	1 June	Jones, E.
1753	5 July	Brough, W.			

[1] Corbett MS, v pp. 97-100.
[2] *27th Rept. on Finance*, 336-7.
[3] 3 & 4 Vict., c 66, s 5.

Advocate 1660–1870

Except during the period 1674–89 when he was appointed by royal warrant the Admiralty Advocate was appointed by Admiralty warrant.[1] The salary attached to the office was 20 marks (£13 6s 8d). This appears to have been paid originally out of the perquisites of the Lord High Admiral. From 1674 it was paid by the Treasurer of the Navy.[2] An additional allowance of £200 was provided in time of war.[3] In 1725 a further £200 was provided for making reports but this was retrenched in the following year.[4]

LIST OF APPOINTMENTS

1660	13 June	Hyde, T.	1748	9 Aug.	Salusbury, T.
1661	29 Oct.	Turner, W.	1751	14 Nov.	Pinfold, C.
c. 1670		Walker, Sir W.	1756	17 Feb.	Bettesworth, J.
1674	19 May	Lloyd, R.	1764	14 June	Harris, G.
1685	13 Sept.	Pinfold, T.	1782	21 May	Scott, W.
1686	4 July	Oldys, W.	1788	4 Sept.	Bever, T.
1693	7 Sept.	Littleton, F.	1791	12 Nov.	Battine, W.
1697	16 March	Newton, H.[5]	1811	25 Nov.	Arnold, J. H.
1714	28 Oct.	Penrice, H.	1829	11 March	Dodson, J.
1715	15 Aug.	Fuller, R.	1834	25 Oct.	Phillimore, J.
1727	30 March	Sayer, E.	1855	3 Feb.	Phillimore, R. J.
1731	1 Oct.	Isham, E.	1862	3 Sept.	Twiss, T.
1742	20 March	Strahan, W.	1868	31 Jan.	Deane, J. P.

[1] For this office, see Corbett MS, v pp. 133–4.

[2] *A Descriptive Catalogue of the Naval Manuscripts in the Pepysian Library*, ed. J. R. Tanner, ii (Navy Records Soc., xxvii, 1904), 306–7; AO 1/1716/123.

[3] SPB, ii f. 20; SPB, i f. 27; SPB, vi f. 19; SPB, vii f. 22; SPB, v f. 26; SPB, viii f. 43; SPB, iii f. 125; SPB, xii f. 325.   [4] Corbett MS, v p. 134; SPB, iv f. 19.

[5] In 1708 Nathaniel Lloyd was appointed Deputy Advocate during Newton's absence abroad (HCA 50/8 ff. 24, 82–3).

Proctor 1660–1870

The Admiralty Proctor was appointed by Admiralty warrant. He received no salary but was paid fees for the work which he undertook.[1]

LIST OF APPOINTMENTS

1660	16 July	Budd, R.	1745	7 Feb.	Crespigny, P.
1673	28 July	Franklyn, S.	1763	24 Dec.	Crespigny, P. C.
1700	16 May	Glasier, J.	1766	4 Oct.	Gostling, G.
1709	20 June	Exton, E.	1777	2 May	Gostling, G.
1718	14 May	Sayer, G.	1820	29 May	Townsend, W.
1727	5 Aug.	Sayer, E.	1866	11 Oct.	Stokes, H. G.

Receiver of Droits 1691–1857

The office of Receiver of Droits, the full title of which was Receiver of the Rights and Perquisites of the Admiralty, was established on a permanent basis in 1691.[2] Appointments were usually made by Admiralty warrant although both Byng (1727) and Goldsworthy (1733) received warrants of appointment from the crown.[3] The salary, which was paid out of the receipts from the perquisites, was originally £300. It was raised to £400 in 1800.[4] In 1854 provision was made for the office to be abolished on the next vacancy when its duties were to be transferred to the Board of Trade.[5] The office accordingly ceased to exist in 1857.

LIST OF APPOINTMENTS

1691	31 July	Rainsford, F.	1782	30 Aug.	Crespigny, C. C.
1695	13 Sept.	Corbett, A.	1818	31 Jan.	Hampson, G. F.
1702	27 June	Dod, J.	1833	27 June	Callander, A. J.
1720	14 Nov.	Byng, R.	1844	1 Jan.	Baillie Hamilton, G.
1733	13 June	Goldsworthy, B.			
1774	24 Jan.	Jackson, J.			

[1] Corbett MS, v p. 137.
[2] For this office, see Corbett MS, v pp. 105–23. For earlier arrangements for the collection of the droits, see Adm. 6/404 pp. 1–2; *CSPD 1673*, 415.
[3] *3rd Rept. on Fees*, 106, 122; HCA 50/7 p. 156; HCA 50/8 p. 159.
[4] Order in council 15 Jan. 1800 (HC 138 pp. 8–10 (1816) xiii, 176–8).
[5] 17 & 18 Vict., c 120, s 10.

Periodic Lists of Officials

LIST OF OFFICIALS AT ACCESSION OF ANNE
8 MARCH 1702

Lord High Admiral
 Pembroke, Earl of
Secretary
 Burchett, J.
Chief Clerk
 Fawler, J.
Clerks
 Poole, T. P.
 Pett, P.
 Halford, E.
 Gordon, G.
 Gibbs, T.
 Drake, J.
 Dod, J.
 Crosfield, R.
Head Messenger
 Baker, J.

Messenger
 Golding, E.
Porter
 Thompson, W.
Watchman
 Lindsey, J.
Housekeeper
 Baker, M.
Necessary Woman
 Buck, E.
Gardener
 Cooke, F.
Counsel
 Lechmere, T.
Judge Advocate of the Fleet
 Bathurst, V.

Deputy Judge Advocate of the Fleet
 Fawler, J.

ADMIRALTY COURT

Judge
 Hedges, Sir C.
Registrar
 Gee, Sir O.
Marshal
 Cheeke, J.
Advocate
 Newton, Sir H.
Proctor
 Glasier, J.
Receiver of Droits
 Corbett, A.

LIST OF OFFICIALS AT ACCESSION OF GEORGE I
1 AUGUST 1714

Commissioners
 Strafford, Earl of
 Leake, Sir J.
 Drake, Sir W.
 Wishart, Sir J.
 Clarke, G.
 Beaumont, Sir G.
Secretary
 Burchett, J.
Deputy Secretary
 Fawler, J.
Chief Clerk
 Burt, E.

Clerks
 Crosfield, R.
 Barnett, P.
 Pembroke, W.
 Crickett, P.
 Allen, C.
 Newsom, J.
Head Messenger
 Bennet, L.
Messengers
 Owen, P.
 Elliston, R.
Porter
 Thompson, W.

Watchmen
 Lindsey, J.
 Pratt, B.
 Waldron, R.
Housekeeper
 Bennet, A.
Necessary Woman
 Lindsey, A.
Gardener
 Cooke, F.
Counsel
 Ettrick, W.
Solicitor
 Warter, J.

Judge Advocate of the Fleet
Strahan, W.
Deputy Judge Advocate of the Fleet
Honywood, E.

ADMIRALTY COURT
Judge
Henchman, H.
Registrar
Hill, R.
Marshal
Cheeke, J.

Advocate
Newton, Sir H.
Proctor
Exton, E.
Receiver of Droits
Dod, J.

LIST OF OFFICIALS AT ACCESSION OF GEORGE II
11 JUNE 1727

Commissioners
Berkeley, Earl of
Cockburn, J.
Chetwynd, W. R.
Norris, Sir J.
Wager, Sir C.
Oxenden, Sir G.
Lyttelton, Sir T.
Secretary
Burchett, J.
Chief Clerk
Corbett, T.
Clerks
Hawes, T.
Young, W.
Westcomb, G.
Osborn, R.
Ram, A.
Milnes, J.
Borrodale, J. A.
Extra Clerks
(?) Troughton, J.
(Possibly others)

Head Messenger
Bennet, L.
Messengers
Gould, J.
Rogers J.
Porter
Elliston, R.
Watchmen
Blasedale, A.
Kettlewell, J.
Mears, H.
Housekeeper
Head, E.
Necessary Woman
Roberts, M.
Gardener
Cooke, J.
Counsel
Baynes, J.
Solicitor
Jobber, T.

Judge Advocate of the Fleet
Copeland, J.
Deputy Judge Advocate of the Fleet
Bell, W.

ADMIRALTY COURT
Judge
Penrice, Sir H.
Registrar
Hill, S.
Marshal
Cheeke, J.
Advocate
Sayer, E.
Proctor
Sayer, G.
Receiver of Droits
Byng, Hon. R.

LIST OF OFFICIALS AT ACCESSION OF GEORGE III
25 OCTOBER 1760

Commissioners
Anson, Lord
Boscawen, Hon. E.
Hay, G.
Hunter, T. O.
Elliot, G.
Forbes, Hon. J.
Stanley, H.

First Secretary
Clevland, J.
Second Secretary
Stephens, P.
Clerks
Fearne, C.
Borrodale, J. A.
Burchett, G. A.

Phillips, E.
Clevland, J.
Alcock, J.
Ibbetson, J.
Extra Clerks
Parker, H.
Bullock, D.
Hastings, H.

Bryer, W.
Fouace, C.
Cooke, G. A.
Wright, C.
Ward, E.
Pollock, W.
Davie, C.
Jeafryson, S.
Irish, T.
Head Messenger
Doody, H.
Messengers
Cooke, W.
Hutchinson, R.
Porter
Collett, J.
Watchmen
Spike, A.
White, W.
Hutchinson, R.
Housekeeper
Bell, E.
Necessary Woman
Johnston, C.
Gardener
Tucker, J.

Inspector of Repairs
Glanville, B.
Counsel
Hussey, R.
Solicitor
Seddon, S.
Judge Advocate of the Fleet
Fearne, C.
Deputy Judge Advocate of the Fleet
Clevland, J.

MARINE
DEPARTMENT
Secretary
Clevland, J.
First Clerk
Fearne, C.
Second Clerk
Madden, J.
Extra Clerks
Rogers, B.
Parker, H.

MARINE PAY
DEPARTMENT
Paymaster of Marines
Tucker, J.
First Clerk
Madden, J.
Second Clerk
(Name unknown)
Agents of Marines
Winter, J. (Portsmouth)
Baird, J. (Chatham)
Clevland, J. (Plymouth)

ADMIRALTY
COURT
Judge
Salusbury, Sir T.
Registrar
Farrant, G. L.
Marshal
Brough, W.
Advocate
Bettesworth, J.
Proctor
Crespigny, P.
Receiver of Droits
Goldsworthy, B.

LIST OF OFFICIALS FOLLOWING REORGANISATION
15 JANUARY 1800

Commissioners
Spencer, Earl
Arden, Lord
Stephens, Sir P.
Gambier, J.
Young, W.
Wallace, T.
Man, R.
First Secretary
Nepean, E.
Second Secretary
Marsden, W.
Chief Clerk
Wright, C.
Senior Clerks
Robinson, R.

Gimber, W.
Kite, T.
Gascoigne, W.
Pearce, W.
Hollinworth, M.
Junior Clerks[1]
Banes, E.
Raymond, A. M.
Wright, H.
Reynolds, W.
Dyer, J.
Hollinworth, T.
Riley, R.
Sayer, C.
Thurtle, S.
Barker, J. D.

Extra Clerks[2]
Amedroz, H. F.
Martin, R.
Fisher, J.
Cowcher, W. P.
Darch, T.
Evans, J.
Greaves, R.
Translator
Maxwell, R.
Private Secretary to First Lord
Harrison, J.
Head Messenger
Millman, W.

[1] Appointments not complete until 19 Dec. 1800. [2] Appointments not complete until 16 Feb. 1801.

Messengers
Powell, J.
Eastwood, J.
Extra Messengers
Winchester, J.
Evans, E.
Porter
Housen, G.
Watchmen
Crockford, J.
Sandford, T.
Munday, J.
Necessary Woman
Hill, E.
Gardener
Combe, D.
Hydrographer
Dalrymple, A.
Inspector of Telegraphs
Roebuck, G.

MARINE
DEPARTMENT
First Secretary
Nepean, E.

Second Secretary
Marsden, W.
First Clerk
Coombe, G.
Second Clerk
Moss, S.

MARINE PAY
DEPARTMENT
Paymaster of Marines
Villiers, Hon. G.
First Clerk
Webb, D. C.
Second Clerk
Waller, T.

NAVAL WORKS
DEPARTMENT
Inspector General
Bentham, S.
Architect and Engineer
Bunce, S.
Mechanist
Goodrick, S.
Chemist
Sadler, J.

Secretary
Peake, J.
Draftsman
Burr, J.
First Clerk
Darch, T.
Second Clerk
Upsal, R.
Messenger
Fetter, J.

ADMIRALTY
COURT
Judge
Scott, Sir W.
Registrar
Arden, Lord
Marshal
Crickitt, J.
Advocate
Battine, W.
Proctor
Gostling, G.
Receiver of Droits
Crespigny, C. C.

LIST OF OFFICIALS FOLLOWING REORGANISATION
30 JANUARY 1816

Commissioners
Melville, Viscount
Yorke, Sir J. S.
Johnstone Hope, G.
Warrender, Sir G.
Osborn, J.
Paulet, Lord H.
Blachford, B. P.
First Secretary
Croker, J. W.
Second Secretary
Barrow, J.
Chief Clerk
Pearce, W.
First Class Clerks
Dyer, J.
Riley, R.
Sayer, C.

Thurtle, S.
Amedroz, H. F.
Evans, J.
Finlaison, J.
Darch, T.
Second Class Clerks
Shepherd, G.
Bedford, H.
Innes, J. W.
Barker, F. E.
Clifton, M. W.
Mends, M. B.
Hay, J. H.
Third Class Clerks
Creswell, W.
Gibson, J.
Mountain, W. J.
Croasdaile, R.

Barker, G. R.
Rouse, J.
Biggs, L. J.
Holworthy, C. D.
Templeman, G.
Houghton, G. R.
Ryland, F.
Miller, J.
Hardman, J.
Translator
Amedroz, H. F.
Private Secretaries
To First Lord
Hay, R. W.
To First Secretary
Biggs, L. J.
To Second Secretary
Gibson, J.

Head Messenger
Millman, W.
Board Room Messengers
Nye, J. J.
Lilburn, G.
Heald, W.
Porter
Newbegin, J.
Watchmen
Smith, J.
Legatt, J.
Barlow, J.
Necessary Woman
Hill, E.
Gardener
Kitchen, W.
Hydrographer
Hurd, T.
Inspector of Telegraphs
Roebuck, G.

Counsel
Jervis, T.
Solicitor
Bicknell, C.
Judge Advocate of the Fleet
Duckett, Sir G.

MARINE PAY
DEPARTMENT
Paymaster of Marines
Chetwynd Stapylton,
Hon. G. A.
First Clerk
Hind, T.
Second Clerk
Gardner, G.
Third Clerk
Edwards, J.
Extra Clerks
Robinson, W.

Brixey, W.
Gardner, W.
Messenger
Pitts, R.

ADMIRALTY
COURT
Judge
Scott, Sir W.
Registrar
Arden, Lord
Marshal
Lindsay, Hon. H.
Advocate
Arnold, J. H.
Proctor
Gostling, G.
Receiver of Droits
Crespigny, Sir C. C.

LIST OF OFFICIALS AT 31 DECEMBER 1870

Commissioners
Childers, H. C. E.
Dacres, Sir S. C.
Robinson, Sir R. S.
Hay, Lord J.
Camperdown, Earl of
First Secretary
Baxter, W. E.
Second Secretary
Lushington, V.
Chief Clerk
Wolley, T.
First Class Clerks
James, T.
Hay, J. H.
Innes, A. W.
Bell, R.
Kennedy, C. S.
Kempe, C. N.
Second Class Clerks
Swainson, E. N.
Noel, J. G.
Scott, J.
Senior, J.
Spalding, A. F. M.

Gordon, F. F.
Domvile, H. W.
Miller, J. V.
Dormer, Hon. H. F.
Macgregor, E.
de Vismes, A. M.
Awdry, R. D.
*Third Class (First
Section) Clerks*
Knox, A. E. E.
Wilson, H. J. C.
Carmichael, J. M.
Jeffreys, M. D.
Gambier, J. W. M.
Vansittart Neale, H. J.
Primrose, E. M.
Caulfield, M. P. F.
Thomas, C. I.
Yorke, H. F. R.
Hodgson, T. H.
Birch, C. C.
*Third Class (Second
Section) Clerks*
Lambert, G. T.
Macgregor, A.

Daly, J. F.
Giffard, J. H.
Maude, C. J.
Dacres, S. L.
Dalrymple Hay, W. A.
Stuart, H. N.
Digest Writers
Baker, J.
Abbot, T. C.
Index Writers
Smith, W.
Pickard, J. J.
Librarian
Thorburn, R.
Private Secretaries
To First Lord
Scudamore Stanhope,
C. S.
To First Secretary
Awdry, R. D.
To Second Secretary
Vansittart Neale, H. J.
Head Messenger
Winter, N.

Board Room Messengers
Styan, W.
Wild, A.
Ansell, J.
Weaver, J. F.
Roberts, J.
Porter
Carter, T.
Hydrographer
Richards, G. H.
Counsel
Huddleston, J. W.

Solicitor
Bristow, A. R.
Judge Advocate of the Fleet
Huddleston, J. W.
Deputy Judge Advocate of the Fleet
Eastlake, W.

ADMIRALTY COURT

Judge
Phillimore, Sir R. J.
Registrar
Rothery, H. C.
Marshal
Jones, E.
Advocate
Deane, J. P.
Proctor
Stokes, H. G.

Alphabetical List of Officials

Abbot, T. C. *Digest Writer* 9 Jan. 1863 (Adm. 12/730).

Adair, William *Paymaster of Marines* 5 April 1755–16 Dec. 1756 (Adm. 6/406 pp. 9–11). Res. 16 Dec. 1756 (ibid. pp. 34–5).

Adam, Charles (ktd. 10 Aug. 1835) *First Naval Lord* 1 Nov.–23 Dec. 1834; 25 April 1835–8 Sept. 1841; 24 July 1846–20 July 1847.

Adams, James *Commissioner* 19 Feb. 1801–15 May 1804.

Affleck, Philip *Commissioner* 26 April 1793–7 March 1795.

Aislabie, John *Commissioner* 4 Oct. 1710–9 April 1714.

Alcock, James *Extra Clerk* in office by 15 Nov. 1740 (SPB, vi f. 7; Adm. 3/44, 13 Nov. 1740). *Clerk* 6 June 1753–24 Aug. 1773 (Adm. 3/63). Res. 25 Aug. 1773 (Adm. 3/80).

Alderson, Francis J. *Third Class Clerk* 30 Dec. 1853–31 March 1855 (Adm. 12/570). *Third Class (Second Section) Clerk* 31 March 1855–17 March 1857 (Adm. 12/602; *Navy Lists*). Res. 17 March 1857 (Adm. 12/634).

Allen, Charles *Clerk* pd. from 30 May 1708 by order 11 June 1708 (SPB, i f. 43). Left office 17 Jan. 1715 on app. as Clerk of Cheque and Storekeeper, Harwich (ibid.).

Allen, Timothy Curtis *Extra Clerk* 26 Aug. 1807–30 Jan. 1808 (SPB, iii f. 14). Dis. 30 Jan. 1808 (SPB, xii ff. 37–8).

Allpuss, Robert *Watchman* 10 April 1773–10 Feb. 1784 (SPB, v f. 27). D. 10 Feb. 1784 (ibid.).

Alves, William *Supernumerary Clerk* pd. from 7 July 1812 to 25 Dec. 1815 (SPB, xii ff. 45–6). *Third Class Clerk* 6 May 1818–1 Sept. 1819 (SPB, xiii ff. 021–2). Res. 1 Sept. 1819 on app. as Agent to Naval Hospital, Malta (Adm 12/193, 23 Aug. 1819).

Amedroz, Henry Frederick *Extra Clerk* 10 Jan. 1799–11 June 1802 (SPB, ix f. 11). *Junior Clerk* 11 June 1802–15 March 1811 (SPB, iii f. 11). *Senior Clerk* 15 March 1811–5 Feb. 1816 (SPB, xii ff. 15–16). *First Class Clerk* 5 Feb. 1816–14 May 1832 (SPB, xiii ff. 017–18). *Chief Clerk* 14 May 1832–5 Jan. 1849 (SPB, xiv f. 4). Res. 5 Jan. 1849 (Adm. 12/506).

   Translator 11 April 1800–22 April 1845 (SPB, ix f. 11). Res. 22 April 1845 (Adm. 12/442).

Amedroz, Henry Frederick *Third Class Clerk* 15 Dec. 1834–25 July 1846 (Adm. 12/298). *Second Class Clerk* 25 July 1846–20 Dec. 1856/20 March 1857 (Adm. 12/458). *First Class Clerk* app. between 20 Dec. 1856 and 20 March 1857 (*Navy Lists*). Ret. c. 18 May 1869 (ibid.; PMG 24/10).

   Translator 22 April 1845–c. 18 May 1869 (Adm. 12/442).

Anderson, Noel Robert *Third Class (Second Section) Clerk* 7 July 1858–20 Dec. 1861/20 March 1862 (Adm. 12/650). *Acting Third Class (First Section) Clerk* app. between 20 Dec. 1861 and 20 March 1862 (*Navy Lists*). *Third Class (First Section) Clerk* app. between 20 Sept. and 20 Dec. 1862 (ibid.). *Acting Second Class Clerk* 9

Oct.–6 Nov. 1866 (Adm. 12/778). *Second Class Clerk* 6 Nov. 1866–15 Oct. 1868 (ibid.). D. 15 Oct. 1868 (Adm. 12/810; death certificate).

Anglesey, Arthur (Annesley) 1st Earl of *Commissioner* 9 July 1673–14 May 1679.

Ansell, J. *Board Room Messenger* 28 Oct. 1867 (Adm. 2/794).

Anson, George (cr. Lord **Anson** 15 July 1747) *Commissioner* 27 Dec. 1744–22 June 1751. *First Lord* 22 June 1751–17 Nov. 1756; 2 July 1757–6 June 1762. D. 6 June 1762.

Apsley, Henry (Bathurst) *styled* Lord *Commissioner* 31 Dec. 1783–12 Aug. 1789.

Arden, Lord *see* **Perceval,** Hon. Charles George

Arlington, Henry (Bennet) 1st Earl of *Commissioner* 9 July 1673–14 May 1679.

Arnold, James Henry *Advocate* 25 Nov. 1811–11 March 1829 (HCA 50/13 p. 231). Res. 11 March 1829 (HCA 50/16 ff. 50–1).

Arrow, James *Inspector of Repairs* 8 Aug. 1774–29 Sept. 1785 (SPB, v f. 27). Left office 29 Sept. 1785 (SPB, viii f. 45).

Ashley, Anthony (Ashley Cooper) *styled* Lord *Civil Lord* 23 Dec. 1834–25 April 1835.

Atherton, William *Counsel and Judge Advocate of the Fleet* 6 June 1855–16 Dec. 1859 (Adm. 12/602, under Admiralty Courts). Left office 16 Dec. 1859 on app. as Solicitor General (app. of Collier; *London Gazette* no. 22337).

Atkins, George *Deputy Judge Advocate of the Fleet* 2 March 1745–3 Dec. 1754 (Adm. 6/16 p. 451). D. 3 Dec. 1754 (SPB, vii f. 22).

Atkins, Samuel *Clerk* app. Clerk to Hewer, Chief Clerk to Pepys as Secretary 1674 (MS Rawlinson A 181 f. 4); app. Clerk by Pepys 1677 (ibid.). Left office with Pepys May 1679 (ibid. f. 250); probably reapp. by Pepys May 1684; occ. first on list of his Clerks 1 Jan. 1687 (Pepys Library no. 2867 p. 13); probably succ. J. Walbanke as Chief Clerk Dec. 1686; last occ. 23 Aug. 1688 (A. Bryant, *Samuel Pepys: the Saviour of the Navy*, 2nd ed. (London 1949), 398–9). Probably left office with Pepys March 1689.
Deputy Judge Advocate of the Fleet 2 Jan. 1687–30 May 1689 (Sergison MS f. 157). Left office 30 May 1689 (app. of Tindall; AO 1/1718/128).

Atkins, William *Clerk* 11 Aug.–c. 4 Nov. 1727 (Adm. 3/36). D. by 4 Nov. 1727 (SPB, iv f. 7).

Aubrey, John *Commissioner* 18 July 1782–10 April 1783.

Auckland, George (Eden) 2nd Lord (cr. Earl of **Auckland** 21 Dec. 1839) *First Lord* 11 June–23 Dec. 1834; 25 April–19 Sept. 1835; 13 July 1846–1 Jan. 1849. D. 1 Jan. 1849.

Austen, Robert *Commissioner* 23 Jan. 1691–c. 23 Aug. 1696. Buried 23 Aug. 1696 at Bexley, Kent (parish register).

Awdry, Richard Davis *Temporary Clerk* 23 March 1861–27 Feb. 1862 (Adm. 12/698). *Third Class (Second Section) Clerk* 27 Feb. 1862–8 Feb. 1866 (Adm. 12/714). *Acting Third Class (First Section) Clerk* 8 Feb.–28 Sept. 1866 (Adm. 12/778). *Third Class (First Section) Clerk* 28 Sept. 1866–31 March 1870 (ibid.). *Second Class Clerk* 31 March 1870 (Adm. 12/846).
Private Secretary: to Second Secretary (Romaine) 17 Aug. 1865–15 Oct. 1866 (Adm. 12/762); *to First Secretary* (Baxter) 14 Jan. 1869 (Adm. 12/828).

Aylmer, Matthew *Commissioner* 16 April 1717–19 March 1718.

Bacher, Frederick *Judge Advocate of the Fleet* 12 Oct. 1689–4 July 1690 (Sergison MS f. 171). D. 4 July 1690 (AO 1/1719/132).

Baillie, George *Commissioner* 14 Oct. 1714–16 April 1717.

Baillie Hamilton, George *Private Secretary to First Lord* (Melville) 3 April 1823–Sept. 1827 (SPB, xiv f. 4).

Baillie Hamilton, Gerard *Receiver of Droits* 1 Jan. 1844– c. 20 March 1857 (HCA 50/20 p. 1). Last occ. 20 March 1857 (*Navy List*).

Baillie Hamilton, William Alexander *Private Secretary to First Lord* (Haddington) 10 Sept. 1841–28 Jan. 1845 (Adm. 12/383). *Second Secretary* 28 Jan. 1845–22 May 1855 (Adm. 12/426). Res. 22 May 1855 (Adm. 12/602).

Baird, James *Agent of Marines* (*Chatham*) 9 Nov. 1756–9 April 1763 (Adm. 6/406 p. 33). Discharged 9 April 1763 (ibid.; app. of J. Clevland, jun.).

Baker, James *Temporary Clerk* app. 17 May 1855 (Adm. 12/602). No further occ.

Baker, James *Digest Writer* 9 Jan. 1863 (Adm. 12/730).

Baker, John *Porter* pd. from 30 Sept. 1694 by order 18 Jan. 1695 (SPB, i f. 20). Discharged 24 June 1698 by order 20 Sept. 1698 (ibid.). *Head Messenger* 20 Sept. 1698–20 April 1708 (ibid.). Discharged 20 April 1708 by order 14 June 1708 (ibid.).

Baker, Margaret *Housekeeper* pd. from 20 May 1695 by order 17 Dec. 1697 (SPB, i f. 20). Discharged 20 April 1708 by order 14 June 1708 (ibid.).

Balfour, Archibald *Acting Third Class* (*Second Section*) *Clerk* 19 April–1 June 1859 (Adm. 12/666). *Third Class* (*Second Section*) *Clerk* 1 June 1859–30 Oct. 1861 (ibid.). Res. 30 Oct. 1861 (Adm. 12/698).

Baltimore, Charles (Calvert) 5th Lord *Commissioner* 19 March 1742–25 April 1745.

Banes, Edward *Extra Clerk* 28 Aug. 1780–11 April 1800 (Adm. 3/91). *Junior Clerk* 11 April 1800–12 Feb. 1801 (SPB, ix f. 82). *Senior Clerk* 12 Feb. 1801–16 Dec. 1815 (ibid.). Ret. 16 Dec. 1815 (SPB, xii ff. 13–14).

Barham, Lord *see* **Middleton**, Sir Charles

Baring, Sir Francis Thornhill, 3rd Bart. *First Lord* 18 Jan. 1849–2 March 1852.

Baring, Thomas George (*styled* Hon. 4 Jan. 1866) *Private Secretary to First Lord* (Wood) 8 March 1855–21 March 1857 (Adm. 12/602). Res. 21 March 1857 (Adm. 12/634). *Civil Lord* 30 May 1857–8 March 1858. *First Secretary* 30 April–16 July 1866 (Adm. 12/778).

Barker, Francis Eccles *Extra Clerk* 8 June 1805–6 Sept. 1809 (SPB, iii f. 14). *Junior Clerk* 6 Sept. 1809–5 Feb. 1816 (SPB, xii ff. 23–4). *Second Class Clerk* 5 Feb. 1816–5 June 1824 (SPB, xiii ff. 019–20). Res. 5 June 1824 (SPB, xiv f. 6).

Barker, George Rickards *Extra Clerk* 4 Sept. 1809–5 Feb. 1816 (SPB, xii ff. 39–40). *Third Class Clerk* 5 Feb. 1816–2 June 1829 (SPB, xiii ff. 021–2). *Second Class Clerk* 2 June 1829–21 July 1832 (SPB, xiv f. 6). Ret. 21 July 1832 (ibid.).

Barker, James Douglas *Extra Clerk* 19 June 1795–19 Dec. 1800 (SPB, viii f. 15). *Junior Clerk* 19 Dec. 1800–26 April 1802 (SPB, ix f. 84). Dis. 26 April 1802 (SPB, iii f. 11).

Barkham, Simon Devert *Extra Clerk* 16 March 1769–22 Dec. 1777 (Adm. 3/76). *Clerk* 22 Dec. 1777–13 March 1790 (Adm. 3/82). Dis. 13 March 1790 (Adm. 3/107).

Barlow, John *Watchman* 14 Jan. 1812–26 March 1821 (SPB, xii ff. 67–8). Left office 26 March 1821 (SPB, xiii ff. 029–30).

Barnes, Moses *Extra Clerk* 3 May 1804–26 Aug. 1807 (SPB, iii f. 14). *Junior Clerk* 26 Aug. 1807–5 Feb. 1816 (ibid. f. 11). Ret. 5 Feb. 1816 (SPB, xii ff. 23–4).

Barnett, Philip *Clerk* pd. from 13 Oct. 1705 by order 13 Dec. 1705 (SPB, i f. 43). Discharged 16 Jan. 1715 by order 17 Jan. 1715 (ibid.).

Barrington, Hon. Daines *Marshal* 24 May 1751–5 July 1753 (HCA 50/11 f. 76). Left office 5 July 1753 (ibid. f. 91).

Barrington, Hon. George *Fourth Naval Lord* 25 Nov. 1830–13 April 1833.

Barrington, William Wildman (Barrington) 2nd Viscount *Commissioner* 25 Feb. 1746–9 April 1754.

Barrow, George *Third Class Clerk* 23 Feb. 1824–16 Sept. 1825 (SPB, xiv f. 7). Res. 16 Sept. 1825 on app. as Clerk, Colonial Office (ibid.; D. M. Young, *The Colonial Office in the Early 19th Century* (London 1961), 271).

Barrow, John (cr. Bart. 30 March 1835) *Second Secretary* 22 May 1804–9 Feb. 1806 (SPB, iii f. 4). Left office 9 Feb. 1806 (ibid.). Reapp. 9 April 1807 (ibid.). Ret. 28 Jan. 1845 (Adm. 12/442).

Barrow, John *Third Class Clerk* 17 Nov. 1824–20 July 1832 (SPB, xiv f. 8). *Second Class Clerk* 20 July 1832–4 May 1844 (Adm. 12/284). *First Class Clerk* 4 May 1844–21 March 1857 (Adm. 12/426). Ret. 21 March 1857 (Adm. 12/634).

Barrow, Peter *Third Class Clerk* 21 Jan. 1833–17 Oct. 1834 (Adm. 12/290). Res. 17 Oct. 1834 (Adm. 12/298).

Barsley, Edward *Porter* pd. from 25 March 1686 to 25 March 1688 (AO 1/1717/127).

Bartmore, William *Third Class Clerk* (*Marine Pay Department*) 7 April 1827–11 Jan. 1831 (SPB, xiv f. 18). *Second Class Clerk* (*Marine Pay Department*) 11 Jan.–31 March 1831 (ibid.). Discharged 31 March 1831 by order 1 July 1831 (ibid.).

Baston, Thomas *Clerk* pd. from 24 June 1694 by order 26 Sept. 1694 (SPB, ii ff. 50–1). Pd. to 25 March 1699 (Adm. 20/71 no. 1410).

Bateman, John (Bateman) 2nd Viscount *Commissioner* 29 Dec. 1755–17 Nov. 1756.

Bathurst, Villiers *Judge Advocate of the Fleet* 23 July 1690–8 Sept. 1711 (Sergison MS f. 185). D. 8 Sept. 1711 (*Collins's Peerage of England*, ed. Sir E. Brydges (London 1812), v, 86).

Battine, William *Advocate* 12 Nov. 1791–25 Nov. 1811 (HCA 50/13 ff. 204–5). Left office 25 Nov. 1811 (app. of Arnold).

Baxter, William Edward *First Secretary* 22 Dec. 1868 (Adm. 12/810).

Bayham, Viscount *see* **Pratt, Hon. John Jeffreys**

Baylee, Henry William *Third Class Clerk* 19 April 1837–8 Oct. 1847 (Adm. 12/332). *Second Class Clerk* 8 Oct. 1847–30 Sept. 1849 (Adm. 12/474). D. 30 Sept. 1849 (Adm. 46/186 no. 1918).

Baynes, John *Counsel* 4 Oct. 1726–26 Feb. 1737 (SPB, iv f. 19; SPB, vi f. 19). D. 26 Feb. 1737 (SPB, vi f. 19).

Beauclerk, Lord Vere *Commissioner* 13 March 1738–19 March 1742; 27 Nov. 1744–18 Nov. 1749.

Beaufort, Francis (ktd. 29 April 1848) *Hydrographer* 19 May 1829–25 Jan. 1855 (SPB, xiv f. 9). Res. 25 Jan. 1855 (Adm. 12/602, app. of Washington).

Beaumont, Sir George, 4th Bart. *Commissioner* 9 April–14 Oct. 1714.

Bedford, Henry *Extra Clerk* 3 May 1804–30 April 1807 (SPB, iii f. 13). *Junior Clerk* 30 April 1807–5 Feb. 1816 (ibid. f. 11). *Second Class Clerk* 5 Feb. 1816–2 June 1826 (SPB, xiii ff. 019–20). *First Class Clerk* 2 June 1826–4 May 1844 (SPB, xiv f. 5). Ret. 4 May 1844 (Adm. 12/426).

Bedford, Henry Charles Grosvenor *Extra Clerk* 12 Nov. 1842–27 Feb. 1847 (Adm. 12/395). *Third Class Clerk* 27 Feb. 1847–31 March 1855 (Adm. 12/474). *Third Class*

(First Section) Clerk 31 March 1855–1 Aug. 1857 (Adm. 12/602; *Navy Lists*). Left office 1 Aug. 1857 on app. as Storekeeper, Sheerness (*Navy List*).

Bedford, John (Russell) 4th Duke of *First Lord* 27 Dec. 1744–26 Feb. 1748.

Belgrave, Robert (Grosvenor) *styled* Viscount *Commissioner* 12 Aug. 1789–27 June 1791.

Bell, Elizabeth *Housekeeper* 13 May 1752–15 Jan. 1800 (SPB, vii f. 22). Office abolished 15 Jan. 1800 (HC 138 p. 4 (1816) xiii, 172).

Bell, John Craigie *Third Class Clerk* 20 April 1837–2 Feb. 1841 (Adm. 12/332). Res. 2 Feb. 1841 (Adm. 12/383).

Bell, Robert *Third Class Clerk* 2 Feb. 1841–16 Aug. 1854 (Adm. 12/383). *Second Class Clerk* 16 Aug. 1854–21 Oct. 1867 (Adm. 12/586). *First Class Clerk* 21 Oct. 1867 (Adm. 12/794).

Bell, Thomas *Extra Clerk* 5 May 1753–5 Nov. 1756 (SPB, vii f. 7). Left office 5 Nov. 1756 (ibid.).

Bell, William *Deputy Judge Advocate of the Fleet* 1 May 1724–20 June 1740 (Adm. 6/13 ff. 70, 155). Res. 20 June 1740 on app. as Commissioner of Sick and Wounded (Adm. 6/15 ff. 301, 308–9).

Bell, William Hamilton *Third Class Clerk* 13 May 1836–5 Nov. 1842 (Adm. 12/320). Res. 5 Nov. 1842 (Adm. 12/395).

Belson, Joseph *Extra Clerk* 1 March 1759–5 May 1760 (SPB, vii f. 7). Discharged 5 May 1760 (ibid.). Reapp. 4 May 1764 (Adm. 3/72). *Clerk* 28 March 1777–14 Jan. 1799 (SPB, v f. 6). D. 14 Jan. 1799 (SPB, ix f. 9).

Bennet, Anne *Housekeeper* pd. from 26 May 1713 by order 20 June 1713 (SPB, i f. 20). D. 29 April 1726 (SPB, iv f. 20).

Bennet, Luke *Messenger* pd. from 4 July 1705 by order 28 Sept. 1705 (SPB, i f. 20). *Head Messenger* pd. from 21 April 1708 by order 14 June 1708 (ibid.). D. 5 Oct. 1733 (SPB, vi f. 20).

Bennet, Thomas *Clerk* pd. from 6 March 1708 by order 24 March 1708 (SPB, i f. 43). Discharged 29 May 1708 by order 11 June 1708 (ibid.).

Bentham, Samuel *Inspector General of Naval Works* 25 March 1796–28 Oct. 1807 (Adm. 6/25). Transferred to Navy Board 28 Oct. 1807 as Civil Architect and Engineer of the Navy (PC 2/174 pp. 274–6, 284).

Bere, Julian *Extra Clerk* 31 Aug. 1744–26 Feb. 1745 (Adm. 3/48). Left office 26 Feb. 1745 on app. as Purser of the *Dreadnought* (SPB, vi f. 7).

Beresford, Sir John Poo, 1st Bart. *Second Naval Lord* 23 Dec. 1834–25 April 1835.

Berkeley, Charles Paget Fitzhardinge *Extra Clerk* 5 May 1847–4 June 1850 (Adm. 12/522). *Third Class Clerk* 4 June 1850–31 March 1855 (Adm. 46/184 no. 544; Adm. 46/186 no. 1918). *Third Class (First Section) Clerk* 31 March 1855–2 Sept. 1858 (Adm. 12/602; *Navy Lists*). Res. 2 Sept. 1858 (Adm. 12/650).

Berkeley, James (Berkeley) 3rd Earl of *First Lord* 16 April 1717–2 Aug. 1727.

Berkeley, Lionel Spencer *Extra Clerk* 7 Nov. 1738–15 April 1741 (Adm. 3/43; SPB, vi f. 7). Left office 15 April 1741 on app. as Purser of the *Bedford* (SPB, vi f. 7).

Berkeley, Hon. Maurice Frederick Fitzhardinge (ktd. 5 July 1855) *Fourth Naval Lord* 13 April 1833–23 Dec. 1834; 22 July 1837–5 March 1839. *Third Naval Lord* 13 July 1846–23 Dec. 1847. *Second Naval Lord* 23 Dec. 1847–13 Feb. 1852. *First Naval Lord* 13 Feb.–2 March 1852. *Second Naval Lord* 5 Jan. 1853–3 June 1854. *First Naval Lord* 3 June 1854–24 Nov. 1857.

Bettesworth, John *Advocate* 17 Feb. 1756–14 June 1764 (HCA 50/11 f. 107). Left office 14 June 1764 (app. of G. Harris).

Bever, Thomas *Advocate* 4 Sept. 1788–8 Nov. 1791 (HCA 50/13 ff. 169–70). D. 8 Nov. 1791 (*Gent. Mag.* (1791), lx(2), 1068).

Bickerton, Sir Richard, 2nd Bart. *Commissioner* 6 April 1807–25 March 1812.

Bicknell, Charles *Solicitor* 1 March 1796–10 Dec. 1827 (SPB, ix f. 55; HCA 50/17 f. 212). Ret. 10 Dec. 1827 (SPB, xiv f. 16).

Biggs, Lewis James *Extra Clerk* 15 March 1811–5 Feb. 1816 (SPB, xii ff. 41–2). *Third Class Clerk* 5 Feb. 1816–17 July 1821 (SPB, xiii ff. 021–2). *Second Class Clerk* 17 July–24 Dec. 1821 (ibid. ff. 019–20). *Third Class Clerk* 24 Dec. 1821–1822 Jan. 1822 (ibid.). *Second Class Clerk* 22 Jan. 1822–14 May 1832 (ibid.). *First Class Clerk* 14 May 1832–22 May 1833 (SPB, xiv f. 5). Ret. 22 May 1833 (Adm. 12/290).
  Private Secretary to First Secretary (Croker) 5 Feb. 1812–17 July 1821 (SPB, xii ff. 41–2; SPB, xiii ff. 019–20).

Bindley, John *Extra Clerk* 9 March 1771–10 June 1778 (Adm. 3/78). *Third Clerk* (*Marine Department*) 10 June 1778–30 June 1782 (Adm. 2/1170 p. 558). *Second Clerk* (*Marine Department*) 30 June 1782–9 Feb. 1784 (Adm. 2/1174 p. 172). Dis. 9 Feb. 1784 (Adm. 2/1175 p. 262).
  Translator 5 March 1776–8 Feb. 1784 (SPB, v f. 7). Discharged 8 Feb. 1784 (ibid.).

Binsteed, Thomas *Deputy Judge Advocate of the Fleet* 24 July 1780–3 Nov. 1804 (Adm. 6/22 p. 154). D. 3 Nov. 1804 (SPB, iii f. 125).

Birch, Claude Churchill *Temporary Clerk* 12 Feb.–22 Oct. 1866 (Adm. 12/778). *Third Class* (*Second Section*) *Clerk* 22 Oct. 1866–31 March 1870 (ibid.). *Third Class* (*First Section*) *Clerk* 31 March 1870 (Adm. 12/846).

Bird, William *Clerk* 22 March 1723–28 July 1725 (Adm. 2/195 p. 578). D. 28 July 1725 (SPB, iv f. 7).

Blachford, Barrington Pope *Commissioner* 23 Aug. 1814–14 May 1816. D. 14 May 1816 (SPB, xii f. 4).

Blackie, Helen *Necessary Woman* 26 March 1823–3 March 1832 (SPB, xiv f. 12). D. 3 March 1832 (ibid.).

Blanckley, Thomas Riley *Extra Clerk* in office by 15 Nov. 1740 (SPB, v f. 7; Adm. 3/44, 13 Nov. 1740). *Clerk* 18 June 1743–4 May 1753 (Adm. 3/47). D. 4 May 1753 (SPB, vii f. 7).

Blasedale, Alexander *Watchman* 27 Oct. 1719–22 Oct. 1742 (SPB, i f. 20). D. 22 Oct. 1742 (SPB, vi f. 20).

Blount, Leonora Ann *Housekeeper* 28 May 1851–c. 26 Jan. 1865 (Adm. 12/538). Left office by 26 Jan. 1865 (Adm. 12/762).

Borrodale, Jasper Aris *Clerk* 30 Sept. 1725–5 Oct. 1768 (Adm. 3/35). Res. 5 Oct. 1768 (Adm. 3/76).

Boscawen, Hon. Edward *Commissioner* 22 June 1751–10 Jan. 1761. D. 10 Jan. 1761 (SPB, vi f. 2).

Bowers, Richard *Extra Clerk* 23 Feb. 1748–30 April 1749 (SPB, vi f. 7). Discharged 30 April 1749 (ibid.).

Bowles, Benjamin *Clerk* pd. from 26 Dec. 1703 by order 27 March 1704 (SPB, i f. 42). Left office 9 June 1707 on app. as Victualling Agent, Gibraltar (ibid.; Adm. 2/186 p. 318).

Bowles, Phineas *Secretary* occ. from 6 March 1689 to 15 Jan. 1690 (Adm. 2/377, 378).

Bowles, William *Third Naval Lord* 22 May 1844–13 July 1846.

Braddyll, Clarence *Extra Clerk* 22 June 1846–15 March 1848 (Adm. 12/458). *Acting Third Class Clerk* 15 March 1848–9 Jan. 1849 (Adm. 12/490). *Third Class Clerk* 9 Jan. 1849–31 March 1855 (Adm. 12/506). *Third Class (First Section) Clerk* 31 March 1855–14 Nov. 1857 (Adm. 12/602; *Navy Lists*). Ret. 14 Nov. 1857 (Adm. 12/634).

Bradley, Samuel *Clerk* pd. from 26 Dec. 1694 to 25 March 1697 (Adm. 20/63 no. 1370; Adm. 20/67 no. 2313) and from 26 March to 24 June 1700 (Adm. 20/74 no. 912).

Bradshaw, Thomas *Commissioner* 6 May 1772–6 Nov. 1774. D. 6 Nov. 1774 (SPB, v f. 2).

Braithwaite, Thomas *Extra Clerk and Translator* 8 May 1787–18 June 1788 (Adm. 3/103). Discharged 18 June 1788 (Adm. 3/104).

Brandreth, Thomas *Private Secretary to First Lord* (Lowry Corry) 9 March 1867–Dec. 1868 (Adm. 12/794).

Breaks,— *Temporary Clerk* app. 23 June 1858 (Adm. 12/650). No further occ.

Brecknock, George Charles (Pratt) *styled* Earl of *Member of Council* 4 Feb.–19 Sept. 1828. *Commissioner* 19 Sept. 1828–15 July 1829.

Brett, Charles *Commissioner* 1 April 1782–10 April 1783; 31 Dec. 1783–16 July 1788.

Brett, Sir Piercy, kt. *Commissioner* 11 Dec. 1766–28 Feb. 1770.

Bridgeman, William *Secretary* first occ. 6 Aug. 1694 (Adm. 2/385). Discharged 24 June 1698 by order 15 July 1698 (SPB, i f. 1).

Bridgwater, John (Egerton) 3rd Earl of *First Lord* 31 May 1699–19 March 1701. D. 19 March 1701.

Briggs, John Henry *Third Class Clerk* 19 April 1827–15 Dec. 1834 (SPB, xiv f. 8). *Second Class Clerk* 15 Dec. 1834–9 Jan. 1849 (Adm. 12/298). *First Class Clerk* 9 Jan. 1849–13 July 1865 (Adm. 12/506). *Chief Clerk* 13 July 1865–28 March 1870 (Adm. 12/846). Ret. 28 March 1870 (Adm. 12/762).
  Reader 18 June 1841–13 July 1865 (Adm. 12/383).

Briggs, John Thomas *Private Secretary to First Lord* (Graham) 29 Nov.–11 Dec. 1830 (SPB, xiv f. 4).

Brisbane, John *Judge Advocate of the Fleet* 30 Sept. 1672–29 July 1680 (AO 1/1713/113). Left office 29 July 1680 (app. of Croone).
  Secretary occ. from 3 Feb. 1680 to 20 May 1684 (Adm. 2/1753, 1754).

Brisbane, Thomas *Extra Clerk* 8 July 1778–12 Oct. 1780 (Adm. 3/85). Dis. 12 Oct. 1780 (SPB, v f. 7).

Bristol, Earl of *see* **Hervey**, Hon. Augustus John

Bristow, Alfred Rhodes *Solicitor* 12 May 1862 (*Navy List*).

Brixey, William *Extra Clerk (Marine Pay Department)* 12 April 1801–11 Dec. 1819 (SPB, xii ff. 75–6). *Third Class Clerk (Marine Pay Department)* 11 Dec. 1819–23 Sept. 1830 (SPB, xiii ff. 037–8). Ret. 23 Sept. 1830 (SPB, xiv f. 19).

Brodie, Alexander *Extra Clerk* 28 Aug. 1805–11 Feb. 1807 (SPB, iii f. 14). Res. 11 Feb. 1807 (ibid.).

Brodrick, Henry (*styled* Hon. 2 Dec. 1863) *Temporary Clerk* 20 Jan. 1862–5 June 1863 (Adm. 12/714). *Third Class (Second Section) Clerk* 5 June 1863–6 Nov. 1866

(Adm. 12/730). *Third Class (First Section) Clerk* 6 Nov. 1866–c. 18 May 1869 (*Navy Lists*). Ret. c. 18 May 1869 (PMG 24/10).

Brodrick, Hon. Thomas   *Counsel* 12 Dec. 1791–16 Jan. 1795 (SPB, viii f. 42). Left office 16 Jan. 1795 (app. of S. Perceval).

Brooke Pechell, Sir Samuel John, 3rd Bart.   *Third Naval Lord* 25 Nov. 1830–23 Dec. 1834. *Fourth Naval Lord* 5 March 1839–25 June 1841. *Third Naval Lord* 25 June–8 Sept. 1841.

Brough, William   *Marshal* 5 July 1753–c. 12 Nov. 1783 (HCA 50/11 ff. 90–1). D. by 12 Nov. 1783 (HCA 50/13 f. 99).

Brouncker, William (Brouncker) 2nd Viscount   *Commissioner* 19 Feb. 1681–5 April 1684. D. 5 April 1684.

Brydges, Hon. James   *Member of Council* 29 March 1703–5 April 1705. Res. 5 April 1705 (Adm. 3/19).

Bryer, William   *Extra Clerk* 6 May 1755–5 Oct. 1768 (Adm. 3/63). *Clerk* 5 Oct. 1768–17 Jan. 1790 (Adm. 3/76). D. 17 Jan. 1790 (SPB, viii f. 13).

Buck, Elizabeth   *Necessary Woman* pd. from 24 June 1694 by order 26 Sept. 1694 (SPB, i f. 21; SPB, ii ff. 50–1). D. 1 Sept. 1706 (AO 1/1726/148).

Buck, Thomas   *Watchman* pd. from 25 June 1698 by order 1 Oct. 1698 (SPB, i f. 20). Discharged 29 Sept. 1699 (ibid.).

Buckingham, George (Villiers) 2nd Duke of   *Commissioner* 9 July 1673–31 Oct. 1674.

Buckley, Alfred   *Third Class Clerk* 12 May 1854–31 March 1855 (Adm. 12/586). *Third Class (Second Section) Clerk* 31 March 1855–15 June 1859 (Adm. 12/602; *Navy Lists*). *Third Class (First Section) Clerk* 15 June 1859–24 April 1865 (Adm. 12/666). Res. 24 April 1865 (Adm. 12/762).

Budd, Richard   *Proctor* app. 16 June 1660 (Adm. 2/1732 f. 5). No further occ.

Budge, William   *Private Secretary to First Lord* (Melville) 12 July 1804–May 1805 (SPB, iii f. 5).

Budgett, John   *Clerk* pd. from 21 Oct. 1706 by order 10 April 1707 (SPB, i f. 43). Discharged 5 March 1708 by order 24 March 1708 (ibid.).

Buller, James   *Commissioner* 6 April 1807–25 March 1812.

Buller, John   *Commissioner* 31 July 1765–22 Sept. 1780.

Bullock, Daniel   *Extra Clerk* 11 June 1753–10 May 1770 (SPB, vii f. 7). D. 10 May 1770 (SPB, v f. 7).

Bunce, Samuel   *Architect and Engineer of Naval Works* 25 March 1796–18 Oct. 1802 (Adm. 6/25). D. 18 Oct. 1802 (SPB, iii f. 23).

Bunter, Edward J.   *Third Class Clerk* 27 Oct. 1836–18 July 1840 (Adm. 12/320). Res. 18 July 1840 (Adm. 12/368).

Burchett, George Anne   *Clerk* 4 Nov. 1727–31 July 1761 (Adm. 3/36). Res. 31 July 1761 (Adm. 3/69).

Burchett, Josiah   *Clerk* entered service of Pepys c. 1680 (*Letters and Diary of Samuel Pepys*, ed. R. G. Howarth (London 1932), 181). Probably app. Clerk by Pepys May 1684; occ. 1 Jan. 1687 (Pepys Library no. 2867 p. 13). Dis. Aug. 1687 (Howarth, *Letters*, 181). Probably reapp. by P. Bowles March 1689; occ. 4 May 1689 (Adm. 2/377). Probably left office 19 Jan. 1691 on app. as Secretary to Admiral Edward Russell (*Bull. Inst. Hist. Research*, xiv (1936–7), 53). Reapp. by 18 July 1693; signed Secretary's letters, probably as Chief Clerk, from 18 July to 26 Aug. 1693 (Adm. 2/384). Probably left office 24 April 1694 on app. as Secretary to Admiral Edward

Russell (*Bull. Inst. Hist. Research*, xiv (1936–7), 53). *Secretary* 26 Sept. 1694–14 Oct. 1742 (Adm. 2/16 p. 414). Ret. 14 Oct. 1742 (SPB, iv f. 6; Adm. 3/46, 12 and 14 Oct. 1742).

Deputy Judge Advocate of the Fleet 4 July 1693–18 Aug. 1694 (Sergison MS f. 200). Left office 18 Aug. 1694 (app. of Larkin).

Burr, James *Draftsman* (*Naval Works Department*) 13 May 1796–28 April 1805 (SPB, x f. 40). Left office 28 April 1805 (SPB, iii f. 24).

Burrard Neale, Sir Harry, 2nd Bart. *Commissioner* 17 Jan.–13 Sept. 1804; 10 Feb. 1806–6 April 1807.

Burrows, James *Messenger* pd. from 24 June 1694 by order 26 Sept. 1694 (SPB, ii ff. 50–1). Pd. to 25 Dec. 1696 (AO 1/1721/138). Left office on app. as Doorkeeper, Registry Office (ibid.).

Burt, Edward *Chief Clerk* transferred to Admiralty 1694 from office of Chief Clerk to Surveyor of Navy (SPB, ii f. 3); pd. from 24 June 1694 by order 26 Sept. 1694 (ibid. ff. 50–1). Pd. to 24 June 1696 when app. Secretary, Registry Office (SPB, i f. 17; SPB, ii f. 35). Reapp. 19 Nov. 1705 (Adm. 2/185 p. 205). D. 15 Sept. 1722 (Adm. 2/195 p. 576).

Busby, Edward *Marshal* 7 Feb. 1745–17 May 1751 (HCA 50/11 ff. 8–9). D. 17 May 1751 (*Gent. Mag.* (1751), xx, 236).

Butler, Elizabeth *Necessary Woman* 3 Aug. 1775–9 Dec. 1793 (SPB, v f. 27). D. 9 Dec. 1793 (SPB, viii f. 45).

Butler, Thomas *Messenger* 30 Sept. 1763–4 July 1778 (SPB, v f. 27). Left office 4 July 1778 on app. as Porter, Woolwich Dockyard (ibid.).

Byng, Sir George, kt. (cr. Bart. 15 Nov. 1715; Viscount **Torrington** 21 Sept. 1721) *Commissioner* 8 Nov. 1709–19 Jan. 1714; 14 Oct. 1714–30 Sept. 1721. *First Lord* 2 Aug. 1727–17 Jan. 1733. D. 17 Jan. 1733.

Byng, Robert (*styled* Hon. 21 Sept. 1721) *Receiver of Droits* 14 Nov. 1720–13 June 1733 (HCA 50/9 ff. 43, 155–6). Left office 13 June 1733 (app. of Goldsworthy).

Caley, Robert *Supernumerary Clerk* pd. from 2 Feb. to 24 June 1813 (SPB, xii ff. 45–6).

Callander, Alexander James *Receiver of Droits* 27 June 1833–1 Jan. 1844 (HCA 50/20 ff. 14–15). Res. 1 Jan. 1844 (HCA 50/22 ff. 1–2).

Callander, Robert John *Third Class Clerk* 13 April 1854–31 March 1855 (Adm. 12/586). *Third Class* (*Second Section*) *Clerk* 31 March 1855–21 Feb. 1859 (Adm. 12/602; *Navy Lists*). *Acting Third Class* (*First Section*) *Clerk* 21 Feb.–1 June 1859 (Adm. 12/666). *Third Class* (*First Section*) *Clerk* 1 June 1859–21 Nov. 1865 (ibid.). *Acting Second Class Clerk* 21 Nov. 1865–22 Jan. 1866 (Adm. 12/762). *Second Class Clerk* 22 Jan.–8 Feb. 1866 (Adm. 12/778). Res. 8 Feb. 1866 (ibid.).

Private Secretary to First Secretary (Lowry Corry) 9 March 1858–June 1859 (Adm. 12/650).

Campbell, Frederick Archibald *Private Secretary to First Lord* (Somerset) 20 March–July 1866 (Adm. 12/778).

Campbell, George *Paymaster of Marines* 16 Dec. 1756–19 April 1757 (Adm. 6/406 pp. 34–5). Left office 19 April 1757 (ibid. pp. 45–6).

Campbell, John *Commissioner* 22 May 1736–19 March 1742.

Camperdown, Robert Adam Philips Haldane (Haldane Duncan) 3rd Earl of *Civil Lord* 12 July 1870.

Cane *see* **Du Cane**

Capel, Hon. Sir Henry, kt. *First Lord* 14 May 1679–19 Feb. 1681.

Carbery, Earl of *see* **Vaughan,** Lord

Carmichael, James Morse *Temporary Clerk* 10 April 1862–12 May 1865 (Adm. 12/714). *Third Class (Second Section) Clerk* 12 May 1865–6 Nov. 1866 (Adm. 12/762). *Acting Third Class (First Section) Clerk* 6 Nov. 1866–20 March/20 June 1867 (Adm. 12/778). *Third Class (First Section) Clerk* app. between 20 March and 20 June 1867 (*Navy Lists*).

Carnegie, Hon. Swynfen Thomas *Fourth Naval Lord* 28 Jan.– 23 April 1859.

Carroll, Herbert Alexander *Temporary Clerk* 18 Dec. 1855–17 June 1856 (Adm. 12/602). *Third Class (Second Section) Clerk* 17 June 1856–20 Dec. 1861/20 March 1862 (Adm. 12/618). *Third Class (First Section) Clerk* app. between 20 Dec. 1861 and 20 March 1862 (*Navy Lists*). *Acting Second Class Clerk* 8 Feb.–27 Aug. 1866 (Adm. 12/778). D. 27 Aug. 1866 (*Gent. Mag.* (1866), clix, 557).

Carter, Thomas *Porter* 2 April 1862 (Adm. 12/714).

Carteret, Sir George, 1st Bart. *Commissioner* 9 July 1673–14 May 1679.

Carysfort, John (Proby) 1st Lord *Commissioner* 6 April–2 July 1757; 1 Jan. 1763–31 July 1765.

Castlereagh, Frederick William Robert (Stewart) *styled* Viscount *Commissioner* 15 July 1829–25 Nov. 1830.

Cator, Frederick Henry *Temporary Clerk* 30 Oct.–18 Dec. 1855 (Adm. 12/602). *Acting Third Class (Second Section) Clerk* 18 Dec. 1855–12 May 1856 (ibid.). Res. 12 May 1856 (Adm. 12/618).

Caulfield, Marcus Piers Francis *Temporary Clerk* 25 June 1863–17 Feb. 1866 (Adm. 12/730). *Third Class (Second Section) Clerk* 17 Feb. 1866–2 Dec. 1869 (Adm. 12/778). *Third Class (First Section) Clerk* 2 Dec. 1869 (Adm. 12/828).

Cavendish, Philip *Commissioner* 19 March 1742–14 July 1743. D. 14 July 1743 (SPB, vi f. 2).

Chatham, John (Pitt) 2nd Earl of *First Lord* 16 July 1788–19 Dec. 1794.

Cheeke, John *Marshal* 17 Oct. 1689–28 July 1733 (HCA 50/6 f. 21; HCA 50/7 ff. 51–2, 105–6; HCA 50/8 ff. 7–9, 49–50; HCA 50/9 f. 115). D. 28 July 1733 (*Gent. Mag.* (1733), iii, 381).

Chetwynd, William Richard *Commissioner* 16 April 1717–2 Aug. 1727.

Chetwynd Stapylton, Hon. Granville Anson *Paymaster of Marines* 18 Sept. 1815–8 April 1819 (SPB, xii ff. 73–4). Left office 8 April 1819 (SPB, xiii ff. 033–4).

Chetwynd Stapylton, Henry Edward *Extra Clerk* 17 Dec. 1844–24 May 1847 (Adm. 12/426). *Third Class Clerk* 24 May 1847–31 March 1855 (Adm. 12/474). *Third Class (First Section) Clerk* 31 March 1855–16 April 1857 (Adm. 12/602; *Navy Lists*). Res. 16 April 1857 (Adm. 12/634).

    Private Secretary to First Secretary (Osborne) 6 Jan. 1853–13 March 1857 (Adm. 12/570). Res. 13 March 1857 (Adm. 12/634).

Chicheley, Sir John, kt. *Commissioner* 20 Jan. 1682–19 May 1684; 8 March 1689–5 June 1690.

Chicheley, Sir Thomas, kt. *Commissioner* 26 Sept. 1677–14 May 1679.

Childers, Hugh Culling Eardley *Civil Lord* 22 April 1864–23 Jan. 1866. *First Lord* 18 Dec. 1868.

Chirm, Thomas *Watchman* 21 March 1751–25 Dec. 1754 (SPB, vi f. 20). Res. 25 Dec. 1754 (SPB, vii f. 23).

Chown, William *Board Room Messenger* 24 Aug. 1841–19 June 1850 (Adm. 12/383).

Left office 19 June 1850 on app. as Head Messenger, Naval Departments, Somerset House (Adm. 12/522).

Christie, John *Board Room Messenger* 27 May 1820–c. 28 Aug. 1846 (SPB, xiii ff. 027–8). D. by 28 Aug. 1846 (Adm. 12/458).

Christie, William Dougal *Private Secretary to First Lord* (Minto) 27 April–Sept. 1841 (Adm. 12/383).

Churchill, George *Commissioner* 28 Oct. 1699–26 Jan. 1702. *Member of Council* 22 May 1702–28 Oct. 1708.

Clack (*later* **Johnston**), Christian *Necessary Woman* 19 Dec. 1729–14 April 1762 (SPB, iv f. 20). D. 14 April 1762 (SPB, vii f. 23).

Clack, Jane *Necessary Woman* 15 April 1762–25 May 1767 (SPB, vii f. 23). D. 25 May 1767 (SPB, v f. 27).

Clarence, William Henry 1st Duke of *Lord High Admiral* 2 May 1827–19 Sept. 1828.

Claridge, Thomas *Messenger* pd. from 24 June 1694 by order 26 Sept. 1694 (SPB, ii ff. 50–1). Discharged 24 June 1698 by order 20 Sept. 1698 (ibid.).

Clarke, Charles *Counsel* 1 March 1742–9 Feb. 1743 (SPB, vi f. 9). Left office 9 Feb. 1743 on app. as Baron of Exchequer (ibid.; C 66/3612).

Clarke, George *Secretary* 20 May 1702–25 Oct. 1705 (SPB, i f. 1; James and Shaw, Admiralty Administration, 183). *Commissioner* 20 Dec. 1710–14 Oct. 1714.

Clerk, Sir George, 6th Bart. *Commissioner* 15 March 1819–2 May 1827. *Member of Council* 4 Feb.–19 Sept. 1828. *Commissioner* 19 Sept. 1828–31 July 1830.

Clevland, John *Second Secretary* 1 Aug. 1746–30 April 1751 (Adm. 3/55). *Secretary* 30 April 1751–16 Oct. 1759 (d. of Corbett; Adm. 3/62, 2 May 1751). *First Secretary* 16 Oct. 1759–18 June 1763 (Adm. 3/67). D. 18 June 1763 (SPB, vi f. 6).

Clevland, John *Extra Clerk* 10 Dec. 1751–5 May 1753 (Adm. 3/62). *Clerk* 5 May 1753–12 Nov. 1766 (Adm. 3/63). Res. 12 Nov. 1766 (Adm. 3/73).
Deputy Judge Advocate of the Fleet 5 Dec. 1754–10 April 1762 (Adm. 6/18 p. 117; Adm. 6/19 p. 322). Left office 10 April 1762 on app. as Accountant, Sixpenny Office (Adm. 6/19 pp. 398–9).
Second Clerk (Marine Department) 17 July 1755–5 May 1760 (Adm. 2/1152 pp. 134–5). *Agent of Marines (Plymouth)* 5 May 1760–9 April 1763 (Adm. 6/406 pp. 67–8). *Agent of Marines* 9 April 1763–16 April 1767 (Adm. 6/406). Res. 16 April 1767 (ibid.; app. of G. Williams).

Clifton, Francis *Third Class Clerk* 1 Jan. 1827–25 May 1833 (SPB, xiv f. 8). *Second Class Clerk* 25 May 1833–13 March 1841 (Adm. 12/290). Left office 13 March 1841 on app. as Naval Storekeeper, Malta (Adm. 12/383; *Navy List*).

Clifton, Joseph B. *Supernumerary Clerk* pd. from 26 Dec. 1812 to 25 Dec. 1814 (SPB, xii ff. 45–6).

Clifton, Marshall Waller *Extra Clerk* 9 Sept. 1805–15 March 1811 (SPB, iii f. 14). *Junior Clerk* 15 March 1811–5 Feb. 1816 (SPB, xii ff. 25–6). *Second Class Clerk* 5 Feb. 1816–21 Aug. 1819 (SPB, xiii ff. 019–20). *First Class Clerk* 21 Aug. 1819–22 Jan. 1822 (ibid. ff. 017–18). Left office 22 Jan. 1822 on app. as Secretary, Victualling Board (ibid.).

Clifton, W. C. *Temporary Clerk* app. 24 Sept. 1858 (Adm. 12/650). No further occ.

Clifton, Waller *Third Class Clerk* 11 June 1832–17 Feb. 1841 (SPB, xiv f. 8). *Second Class Clerk* 17 Feb. 1841–30 Dec. 1853 (Adm. 12/383). *First Class Clerk* 30 Dec. 1853–31 July 1869 (Adm. 12/570). Ret. 31 July 1869 (Adm. 12/828).

Private Secretary to First Secretary (Wood, More O'Ferrall) 11 April 1837–17 Feb. 1841 (Adm. 12/332; Adm. 12/383, 17 Feb. 1841).

Clutterbuck, Thomas *Commissioner* 15 June 1732–5 May 1741.

Cockayne Cust *see* **Cust**

Cockburn, Sir George, kt. *Commissioner* 2 April 1818–2 May 1827. *Member of Council* 2 May 1827–19 Sept. 1828. *Commissioner* 19 Sept. 1828–25 Nov. 1830. *First Naval Lord* 23 Dec. 1834–25 April 1835; 8 Sept. 1841–13 July 1846.

Cockburn, Sir James, 9th Bart. *Paymaster of Marines* 8 April 1819–31 Jan. 1831 (SPB, xiii ff. 033–4). Office abolished 31 Jan. 1831 (PC 2/212 pp. 34–5). App. Inspector General of Marines 7 March 1831 (SPB, xiii f. 16).

Cockburn, John *Commissioner* 16 April 1717–15 June 1732; 19 March 1742–27 Dec. 1744.

Cockerell, Samuel Pepys *Inspector of Repairs* 30 Sept. 1785–15 Jan. 1800 (SPB, viii f. 45). Office abolished 15 Jan. 1800 (HC 138 p. 4 (1816) xiii, 172).

Cole, Edward *Clerk* pd. from 15 Nov. 1702 (SPB, i f. 6). Left office 14 May 1711 on app. as Storekeeper, Plymouth (ibid. f. 42; Adm. 2/190 p. 115).

Cole, John George *Private Secretary to First Lord* (de Grey) 31 Dec. 1834–April 1835 (Adm. 12/298).

Coling, Richard *Clerk* pd. from 16 Nov. 1699 by order 29 Nov. 1699 (SPB, i f. 6). Discharged 23 April 1700 by order 8 June 1700 (ibid.; Adm. 20/74 no. 906).

Collett, James *Messenger* 5 Aug. 1748–5 June 1756 (SPB, iv f. 20). *Porter* 5 June 1756–30 Sept. 1763 (SPB, vii f. 22). *Head Messenger* 30 Sept. 1763–31 March 1768 (SPB, v f. 26). D. 31 March 1768 (ibid.).

Collier, Robert Porrett *Counsel and Judge Advocate of the Fleet* 16 Dec. 1859–2 Oct. 1863 (*Navy List*). Left office 2 Oct. 1863 on app. as Solicitor General (*London Gazette* no. 22776).

Colpoys, Sir John, kt. *Commissioner* 15 May 1804–2 May 1805.

Combe, Davis *Gardener* 27 Feb. 1786–11 Aug. 1812 (SPB, viii f. 44). Ret. 11 Aug. 1812 (SPB, xii ff. 69–70).

Cooke, Charles Edward Stephen *Third Class Clerk* 22–31 March 1855 (Adm. 12/602). *Third Class (Second Section) Clerk* 31 March 1855–18 July 1861 (ibid.; *Navy Lists*). *Acting Third Class (First Section) Clerk* 18 July 1861–20 Dec. 1861/20 March 1862 (Adm. 12/698). *Third Class (First Section) Clerk* app. between 20 Dec. 1861 and 20 March 1862 (*Navy Lists*). Res. 8 July 1862 (Adm. 12/714).

Cooke, Francis *Gardener* originally pd. from contingent fund; pd. by Treasurer of Navy from 25 Dec. 1699 by order 1 Feb. 1700 (SPB, i f. 20); pd. jointly with J. Cooke from 10 April 1716 to 24 June 1717 (ibid.; Adm. 2/194 p. 256).

Cooke, George Anne *Extra Clerk* 22 March 1756–8 Dec. 1764 (SPB, vii f. 7). Left office 8 Dec. 1764 on app. as Purser of the *Albion* (SPB, v f. 7).

Cooke, James *Gardener* pd. jointly with F. Cooke from 10 April 1716 to 24 June 1717 and singly thereafter (SPB, i f. 20; SPB, iv f. 20). D. 12 March 1741 (SPB, vi f. 20).

Cooke, William *Messenger* 5 June 1756–30 Sept. 1763 (SPB, vii f. 22). *Porter* 30 Sept. 1763–21 April 1768 (SPB, v f. 26). *Head Messenger* 21 April 1768–c. 9 Feb. 1781 (ibid.). D. by 9 Feb. 1781 (ibid.).

Coombe, George *Extra Clerk (Marine Department)* 7 July 1778–30 June 1782 (Adm. 2/1170 p. 558). *Third Clerk (Marine Department)* 30 June 1782–10 Feb. 1784 (Adm. 2/1174 p. 172). *Second Clerk (Marine Department)* 10 Feb. 1784–7

Oct. 1789 (Adm. 2/1175 p. 260). *First Clerk* (*Marine Department*) 7 Oct. 1789–4 Sept. 1809 (Adm. 2/1180 pp. 65–6). Ret. 4 Sept. 1809 (SPB, xii ff. 57–8).

Cooper, Astley Paston   *Extra Clerk* 22 July 1846–9 Jan. 1849 (Adm. 12/458). *Acting Third Class Clerk* 9 Jan.–30 Nov. 1849 (Adm. 12/506). Res. 30 Nov. 1849 (ibid.). *Third Class Clerk* 30 Dec. 1853–31 March 1855 (Adm. 12/570). *Third Class* (*Second Section*) *Clerk* 31 March 1855–3 Oct. 1856 (Adm. 12/602; *Navy Lists*). Left office 3 Oct. 1856 on app. as Storekeeper, Trincomalee (*Navy List*).

Cooper, Charles   *Third Class Clerk* (*Marine Pay Department*) 23 Jan. 1824–18 Oct. 1827 (SPB, xiv f. 19). D. 18 Oct. 1827 (ibid.).

Cooper, George   *Clerk* pd. from 19 Jan. 1706 by order 21 Jan. 1706 (SPB, i f. 43). Discharged 25 March 1708 by order 11 June 1708 (ibid.).

Cooper, Henry   *Third Class Clerk* (*Marine Pay Department*) 29 Oct. 1827–1831 (SPB, xiv f. 19). Office abolished 1831 (ibid.; PC 2/212 pp. 34–5).

Copeland, John   *Deputy Judge Advocate of the Fleet* 22 Dec. 1714–1 May 1724 (Adm. 6/12 f. 12). *Judge Advocate of the Fleet* 1 May 1724–10 Feb. 1729 (Adm. 6/13 ff. 69, 155). D. 10 Feb. 1729 (SPB, iv f. 19).

Corbett, Andrew   *Receiver of Droits* 13 Sept. 1695–27 June 1702 (HCA 50/6 f. 129). Left office 27 June 1702 (app. of Dod).

Corbett, John   *Extra Clerk* 10 Nov. 1746–30 April 1749 (SPB, vi f. 7). Discharged 30 April 1749 (ibid.). Reapp. 6 June 1749 (Adm. 3/61). *Clerk* 2 May 1751–5 May 1753 (Adm. 3/62). D. 5 May 1753 (SPB, vii f. 7).

Corbett, Thomas   *Clerk* 17 Jan. 1715–15 March 1723 (Adm. 2/193 pp. 127–8). *Chief Clerk* 15 March 1723–27 July 1728 (Adm. 3/34). *Deputy Secretary* 27 July 1728–29 April 1741 (Adm. 6/13 p. 213). *Secretary* 29 April 1741–30 April 1751 (PC 2/96 pp. 442, 447–8, 455; SPB, vi f. 6). D. 30 April 1751 (SPB, vi f. 6).

Cornwallis, Charles (Cornwallis) 3rd Lord   *First Lord* 10 March 1692–15 April 1693.

Corry *see* **Lowry Corry**

Coventry, Hon. Henry   *Commissioner* 9 July 1673–14 May 1679.

Coventry, Hon. William (ktd. 26 June 1665)   *Secretary* occ. from 2 July 1660 to 4 Sept. 1667 (James and Shaw, Admiralty Administration, 182).

Cowcher, William Pollock   *Extra Clerk* 12 March 1799–28 March 1803 (SPB, ix f. 11). *Junior Clerk* 28 March–14 May 1803 (SPB, iii f. 11). Res. 14 May 1803 (ibid.).

Cowper, Hon. William Francis   *Civil Lord* 13 July 1846–2 March 1852; 5 Jan. 1853–8 March 1855.

Cox, Charles   *Agent of Marines* 19 July 1791–15 Jan. 1800 (Adm. 6/406). Office abolished 15 Jan. 1800 (HC 138 p. 7 (1816) xiii, 175; Adm. 2/1189 pp. 227–9).

Cox, Henry   *Porter* 3 Feb. 1837–c. 11 June 1846 (Adm. 12/332). D. by 11 June 1846 (Adm. 12/458).

Cox, William   *Extra Clerk* 30 Nov. 1741–4 April 1746 (SPB, vi f. 7). D. 4 April 1746 (ibid.).

Craven, William (Craven) 1st Earl of   *Commissioner* 26 Sept. 1677–14 May 1679.

Crawley, Richard   *Registrar* grant in reversion by letters patent under seal of Admiralty court 1 Sept. 1698 (HCA 50/6 ff. 200–1); confirmed by letters patent under great seal 12 Oct. 1698 (ibid. ff. 202–3; C 66/3406); succ. 1705 (d. of Gee). D. 21 March 1712 (G. I. O. Duncan, *The High Court of Delegates* (Cambridge 1971), 300).

Crespigny, Claude Champion (cr. Bart. 31 Aug. 1805)   *Receiver of Droits* 30 Aug. 1782–29 Jan. 1818 (HCA 50/13 ff. 78–9). D. 29 Jan. 1818 (*Gent. Mag.* (1818), lxxxvii(1), 187).

Crespigny, Philip *Marshal* 9 Aug. 1733–7 Feb. 1745 (HCA 50/10 f. 80). *Proctor* 7 Feb. 1745–24 Dec. 1763 (HCA 50/11 ff. 9–10). Res. 24 Dec. 1763 (HCA 50/12 f. 3).

Crespigny, Philip Champion *Proctor* 24 Dec. 1763–26 Sept. 1766 (HCA 50/12 f. 3). Left office 26 Sept. 1766 on app. as King's Proctor (ibid. f. 70).

Creswell, William *Extra Clerk* 26 Aug. 1807–5 Feb. 1816 (SPB, iii f. 14). *Third Class Clerk* 5 Feb. 1816–21 Aug. 1819 (SPB, xiii ff. 021–2). *Second Class Clerk* 21 Aug. 1819–17 April 1821 (ibid. ff. 019–20). Res. 17 April 1821 (ibid.).

Crickett, Peter *Clerk* pd. from 26 Jan. 1708 by order 24 March 1708 (SPB, i f. 43). D. 26 May 1717 (Adm. 2/194 p. 282).

Crickitt, John *Marshal* 12 Nov. 1783–30 Oct. 1811 (HCA 50/13 f. 99). D. 30 Oct. 1811 (*Gent. Mag.* (1811), lxxxi(2), 288).

Croasdaile, Richard *Extra Clerk* 30 Jan. 1808–5 Feb. 1816 (SPB, xii ff. 39–40). *Third Class Clerk* 5 Feb. 1816–6 May 1818 (SPB, xiii ff. 021–2). Left office 6 May 1818 on app. as Naval Storekeeper, Jamaica (ibid.).

Crockford, John *Watchman* 24 June 1788–8 Dec. 1811 (SPB, viii f. 44). D. 8 Dec. 1811 (SPB, xii ff. 67–8).

Croker, John William *First Secretary* 12 Oct. 1809–29 Nov. 1830 (SPB, xii ff. 7–8; SPB, xiv f. 3).

Croker, Thomas Crofton *Third Class Clerk* 21 Aug. 1819–14 May 1832 (SPB, xiii ff. 021–2). *Second Class Clerk* 14 May 1832–5 April 1837 (SPB, xiv f. 6). *First Class Clerk* 5 April 1837–9 Feb. 1850 (Adm. 12/332). Ret. 9 Feb. 1850 (Adm. 12/522).

Croone, Henry *Judge Advocate of the Fleet* 29 July 1680–23 May 1689 (Sergison MS ff. 129, 147). Left office 23 May 1689 (app. of Bacher).

Crosfield, Robert *Clerk* pd. from 26 Dec. 1700 by order c. 25 March 1701 (SPB, i f. 6). Left office 4 Jan. 1715 on app. as Clerk of Survey, Plymouth (ibid. f. 42; Adm. 6/12 f. 14).

Crowder, Richard Budden *Counsel and Judge Advocate of the Fleet* 5 Sept. 1849–24 March 1854 (Adm. 12/506). Left office 24 March 1854 on app. as Justice, Common Pleas (app. of Phinn; C 66/4985).

Currie, Charles *Extra Clerk* 28 May 1846–9 Oct. 1847 (Adm. 12/458). *Acting Third Class Clerk* 9 Oct. 1847–7 March 1848 (Adm. 12/474). Res. 7 March 1848 (Adm. 12/490).

Cust (from 27 Jan. 1772 **Cockayne Cust**), Francis *Counsel* 28 March 1770–1 Dec. 1791 (SPB, v f. 28). D. 1 Dec. 1791 (SPB, viii f. 42).

Cutforth, James *Extra Clerk* 20 Sept. 1794–29 Sept. 1800 (Adm. 3/114). Res. 29 Sept. 1800 (SPB, ix f. 10).

Dacres, Sir Sydney Colpoys, kt. *Second Naval Lord* 13 July 1866–18 Dec. 1868. *First Naval Lord* 18 Dec. 1868.

Dacres, Sydney Lambert *Third Class (Second Section) Clerk* 10 Dec. 1867 (Adm. 12/794).

Dale, Robert *Extra Clerk* 12 April 1776–16 Aug. 1778 (SPB, v f. 7). Res. 16 Aug. 1778 (ibid.).

Dalmeny, Archibald (Primrose) *styled* Lord *Civil Lord* 25 April 1835–8 Sept. 1841.

Dalrymple, Alexander *Hydrographer* 13 Aug. 1795–28 May 1808 (Adm. 6/25 ff. 211–12). Ret. 28 May 1808 (Adm. 6/30 f. 114).

Dalrymple Hay, Sir John Charles, 3rd Bart. *Fourth Naval Lord* 13 July 1866–18 Dec. 1868.

Dalrymple Hay, William Archibald *Third Class (Second Section) Clerk* 4 Nov. 1868 (Adm. 12/810).

Daly, James Frederick *Third Class (Second Section) Clerk* 22 Dec. 1866 (Adm. 12/778).

Danby, Earl of *see* **Osborne**, Viscount

Dancer, Francis *Extra Clerk* 21 March 1757–15 April 1759 (SPB, vii f. 7). Left office 15 April 1759 (ibid.).

Daniell, Stanley W. *Temporary Clerk* 26 June 1860–26 Aug. 1861 (Adm. 12/682). *Third Class (Second Section) Clerk* 26 Aug. 1861–21 Nov. 1865 (Adm. 12/698). *Acting Third Class (First Section) Clerk* 21 Nov. 1865–22 Jan. 1866 (Adm. 12/762). *Third Class (First Section) Clerk* 22 Jan.–4 Oct. 1866 (Adm. 12/778). Res. 4 Oct. 1866 (ibid.).

Darby, George *Commissioner* 22 Sept. 1780–1 April 1782.

Darch, Thomas *First Clerk (Naval Works Department)* 25 March 1796–19 Dec. 1800 (SPB, x f. 20). *Extra Clerk* 19 Dec. 1800–3 May 1804 (SPB, ix f. 11). *Junior Clerk* 3 May 1804–5 Feb. 1816 (SPB, iii f. 11). *First Class Clerk* 5 Feb. 1816–14 May 1832 (SPB, xiii ff. 017–18). Ret. 14 May 1832 (SPB, xiv f. 5).

Daunt, T. C. *Temporary Clerk* app. 17 March 1858 (Adm. 12/650). No further occ.

Davie, Charles *Extra Clerk* 16 April 1759–18 Aug. 1762 (SPB, vii f. 7). Left office 18 Aug. 1762 (ibid.).

Davies, William *Extra Clerk* 14 Oct. 1742–30 Sept. 1744 (Adm. 3/46). Left office 30 Sept. 1744 (SPB, vi f. 7).

Dawson, George Robert *First Secretary* 24 Dec. 1834–27 April 1835 (Adm. 12/298).

Deacon, John *Marshal* 4 May 1844–21 May 1850 (HCA 50/22 pp. 19–20). D. 21 May 1850 (*Gent. Mag.* (1850), cxxvii, 223).

Deane, James Parker *Advocate* 31 Jan. 1868 (HCA 50/24 pp. 414–16).

Deans Dundas, James Whitley *Fourth Naval Lord* 25 June–8 Sept. 1841. *Second Naval Lord* 13 July 1846–20 July 1847. *First Naval Lord* 20 July 1847–13 Feb. 1852.

de Grey, Thomas Philip (de Grey) 2nd Earl *First Lord* 23 Dec. 1834–25 April 1835.

Delaval, Sir Ralph, kt. *Commissioner* 15 April 1693–2 May 1694.

Denison, John Evelyn *Member of Council* 2 May 1827–4 Feb. 1828.

de Vismes, Alexander Montgomery *Temporary Clerk* 4 April 1859–27 Feb. 1862 (Adm. 12/666). *Third Class (Second Section) Clerk* 27 Feb. 1862–22 Jan. 1866 (Adm. 12/714). *Acting Third Class (First Section) Clerk* 22 Jan.–20 March/20 June 1866 (Adm. 12/778). *Third Class (First Section) Clerk* app. between 20 March and 20 June 1866 (*Navy Lists*). *Second Class Clerk* 31 March 1870 (Adm. 12/846).

Dickenson, William *Commissioner* 15 May 1804–10 Feb. 1806.

Digby, Henry (Digby) 7th Lord *Commissioner* 20 April 1763–31 July 1765.

Dod, John *Receiver of Droits* 27 June 1702–c. 14 Nov. 1720 (HCA 50/7 ff. 117, 158; HCA 50/8 f. 108; HCA 50/9 f. 4). D. by 14 Nov. 1720 (HCA 50/9 f. 43).

Dodd, Joseph *Clerk* pd. from 23 April 1700 by order 28 June 1700 (SPB, i f. 6). Discharged 16 Sept. 1709 by order 26 Sept. 1709 (ibid. f. 42).

Dodington, George *Commissioner* 8 Nov. 1709–20 Dec. 1710; 14 Oct. 1714–16 April 1717.

Dodson, John *Advocate* 11 March 1829–25 Oct. 1834 (HCA 50/16 ff. 50–1). Left office 25 Oct. 1834 on app. as King's Advocate (app. of J. Phillimore; C 66/4444).

Domett, William *Commissioner* 9 May 1808–23 Oct. 1813.

Domvile, Herbert Winnington   *Third Class (Second Section) Clerk* 29 Oct. 1858–20 Sept./20 Dec. 1862 (Adm. 12/650). *Acting Third Class (First Section) Clerk* app. between 20 Sept. and 20 Dec. 1862 (*Navy Lists*). *Third Class (First Section) Clerk* 13 July 1865–7 Oct. 1867 (Adm. 12/762). *Second Class Clerk* 7 Oct. 1867 (Adm. 12/794).

Doody, Henry   *Head Messenger* 8 Oct. 1733–29 Sept. 1763 (SPB, vi f. 20). D. 29 Sept. 1763 (SPB, v f. 26).

Dormer, Hon. Hubert Francis   *Third Class (Second Section) Clerk* 17 Aug. 1859–13 July 1865 (Adm. 12/666). *Acting Third Class (First Section) Clerk* app. 13 July 1865 (Adm. 12/762). *Third Class (First Section) Clerk* app. between 20 Sept. and 20 Dec. 1865 (*Navy Lists*). *Second Class Clerk* 27 Oct. 1868 (Adm. 12/810).

Douglas, William Robert Keith   *Commissioner* 8 Feb.–23 March 1822; 16 Feb. 1824–2 May 1827. *Member of Council* 2 May 1827–4 Feb. 1828.

Downing, William   *Watchman* 14 Jan. 1773–27 March 1777 (SPB, v f. 27). *Messenger* 27 March 1777–6 Nov. 1781 (ibid.). D. 6 Nov. 1781 (ibid.).

Doyle, Francis Hastings   *Paymaster of Marines* 20 July 1813–12 Sept. 1815 (Adm. 6/406). Left office 12 Sept. 1815 (SPB, xii ff. 73–4).

Drake, Sir Francis Samuel, 1st Bart.   *Commissioner* 12 Aug.–18 Nov. 1789. D. 18 Nov. 1789 (SPB, viii f. 1).

Drake, Joseph   *Clerk* pd. from 16 Nov. 1699 by order 29 Nov. 1699 (SPB, i f. 6). Discharged 24 June 1708 (ibid. f. 42).

Drake, Sir William, 4th Bart.   *Commissioner* 4 Oct. 1710–14 Oct. 1714.

Drinkwater, Edward   *Third Class Clerk* 14 May 1832–10 Oct. 1836 (SPB, xiv f. 8). Res. 10 Oct. 1836 (Adm. 12/320).
   Private Secretary to First Secretary (Elliot) 18 Aug. 1832–Dec. 1834 (Adm. 12/284).

Drummond, David   *Second Clerk (Naval Works Department)* 30 Jan. 1806–13 July 1807 (SPB, x f. 40). Left office 13 July 1807 (SPB, iii f. 25).

Drummond, Hon. James Robert   *Private Secretary to First Lord* (Wood) 1 May 1857–March 1858 (Adm. 12/634). *Fourth Naval Lord* 8 March 1858–28 Jan. 1859; 15 June 1861–9 May 1866.

Drummond, Walter   *Extra Clerk* Oct. 1847–30 Dec. 1853 (Adm. 1/5660 p. 177). *Third Class Clerk* 30 Dec. 1853–31 March 1855 (Adm. 12/570). *Third Class (Second Section) Clerk* 31 March–15 Dec. 1855 (Adm. 12/602; *Navy Lists*). *Acting Third Class (First Section) Clerk* 15 Dec. 1855–15 March 1856 (Adm. 12/602). *Third Class (First Section) Clerk* 15 March 1856–27 Aug. 1859 (Adm. 12/618). *Acting Second Class Clerk* 27 Aug. 1859–18 July 1861 (Adm. 12/666). *Second Class Clerk* 18 July 1861–5 Oct. 1866 (Adm. 12/698). Ret. 5 Oct. 1866 (Adm. 12/778).

Du Cane, Charles   *Civil Lord* 13 July 1866–3 Sept. 1868.

Duckett see **Jackson,** George

Duncannon, Frederick (Ponsonby) *styled* Viscount   *Commissioner* 1 April–18 July 1782; 10 April–31 Dec. 1783.

Duncannon, William (Ponsonby) *styled* Viscount   *Commissioner* 27 June 1746–17 Nov. 1756.

Duncombe, Hon. Arthur   *Fourth Naval Lord* 2 March 1852–5 Jan. 1853.

Dundas, Hon. George Heneage Lawrence   *Second Naval Lord* 25 Nov. 1830–1 Aug. 1834. *First Naval Lord* 1 Aug.–7 Oct. 1834. D. 7 Oct. 1834 (Burke, *Peerage*, under Zetland, Marquess of).

Dundas, Henry *Third Class (Second Section) Clerk* 6 Feb. 1858–20 Dec. 1861/20 March 1862 (Adm. 12/650). *Acting Third Class (First Section) Clerk* app. between 20 Dec. 1861 and 20 March 1862 (*Navy Lists*). *Third Class (First Section) Clerk* app. between 20 Sept. and 20 Dec. 1862 (ibid.). *Acting Second Class Clerk* 28 Sept.–9 Oct. 1866 (Adm. 12/778). *Second Class Clerk* 9 Oct. 1866–23 March 1870 (ibid.). Ret. 23 March 1870 (Adm. 12/846).

Dundas, William *Commissioner* 25 March 1812–23 Aug. 1814.

Dundas *see also* **Deans Dundas** *and* **Saunders Dundas**

Dyer, John *Extra Clerk* 12 March 1793–11 April 1800 (Adm. 3/110). *Junior Clerk* 11 April 1800–26 Aug. 1807 (SPB, ix f. 83). *Senior Clerk* 26 Aug. 1807–5 Feb. 1816 (SPB, iii f. 9). *First Class Clerk* 5 Feb. 1816–21 Aug. 1819 (SPB, xiii ff. 017–18). *Chief Clerk* 21 Aug. 1819–14 May 1832 (ibid. ff. 015–16). Ret. 14 May 1832 (SPB, xiv f. 4; Adm. 12/284).

Dyer, John Jones *Third Class Clerk* 22 Jan. 1822–14 May 1832 (SPB, xiii ff. 023–4). *Second Class Clerk* 14 May 1832–20 April 1838 (SPB, xiv f. 6). *First Class Clerk* 20 April 1838–18 Nov. 1853 (Adm. 12/344). *Chief Clerk* 18 Nov. 1853–21 March 1857 (Adm. 12/570). Ret. 21 March 1857 (Adm. 12/634).
    Private Secretary to First Secretary (Elliot) 10 Feb. 1831–31 May 1832 (SPB, xiv f. 7).

Dyson, James *Solicitor* 30 May 1778–1 March 1796 (SPB, v f. 28). Left office 1 March 1796 (app. of Bicknell).

Eastlake, William *Deputy Judge Advocate of the Fleet* 10 May 1861 (Adm. 12/699, under Courts Martial).

Eastwood, John *Messenger* 20 Feb. 1798–19 April 1806 (SPB, ix f. 58). D. 19 April 1806 (SPB, iii f. 17).

Eden, Charles *Private Secretary to First Lord* (Auckland, Baring) 13 Nov. 1848–Feb. 1852 (Adm. 12/490; Adm. 12/506, 16 Jan. 1849). *Third Naval Lord* 28 June 1859–15 June 1861. *Second Naval Lord* 15 June 1861–13 July 1866.

Eden, Henry *Private Secretary to First Lord* (Auckland) 13 July 1846–13 Nov. 1848 (Adm. 12/458). Left office 13 Nov. 1848 (Adm. 12/490). *Second Naval Lord* 8 March 1855–2 April 1857. *Third Naval Lord* 2 April–24 Nov. 1857. *Second Naval Lord* 24 Nov. 1857–8 March 1858.

Edgcumbe, Frederick *Private Secretary to First Lord* (Yorke) 7 May 1810–March 1812 (SPB, xii f. 10).

Edgcumbe, Hon. Richard *Commissioner* 29 Dec. 1755–17 Nov. 1756.

Edwards, James *Extra Clerk* 22 April–23 Aug. 1780 (Adm. 3/90, 2 Sept. 1780). Res. 23 Aug. 1780 (SPB, v f. 7).

Edwards, John *Clerk* 17 Jan. 1715–27 Aug. 1716 (Adm. 2/193 pp. 127–8). Res. 27 Aug. 1716 (Adm. 2/194 p. 89).

Edwards, John *Extra Clerk (Marine Pay Department)* 24 June 1803–16 June 1814 (SPB, xii ff. 75–6). *Third Clerk (Marine Pay Department)* 16 June 1814–11 Dec. 1819 (ibid. ff. 73–4). *Third Class Clerk (Marine Pay Department)* 11 Dec.1819–7 April 1827 (SPB, xiii ff. 037–8). *Second Class Clerk (Marine Pay Department)* 7 April 1827–10 Jan. 1831 (SPB, xiv f. 18). D. 10 Jan. 1831 (ibid.).

Edwards, Robert *Third Class Clerk (Marine Pay Department)* 13 Dec. 1827–19 April 1831 (SPB, xiv f. 19). Discharged 19 April 1831 (ibid.).

Egmont, John (Perceval) 2nd Earl of *First Lord* 16 Sept. 1763–15 Sept. 1766.

Elbourn, Robert *Messenger (Marine Pay Department)* 16 Oct. 1826–7 March 1831

(SPB, xiv f. 21). Transferred to office of Inspector General of Marines 7 March 1831 (ibid.).

Eliot, Hon. Henry Cornwallis *Third Class Clerk* 22–24 Feb. 1855 (Adm. 12/602). Left office 24 Feb. 1855 (ibid.).

Eliot, Hon. William *Commissioner* 10 July 1800–17 Jan. 1804.

Ellenborough, Edward (Law) 1st Earl of *First Lord* 13 Jan.–13 July 1846.

Elliot, Amyand Powney Charles *Extra Clerk* 5 April–22 May 1841 (Adm. 12/383). Res. 22 May 1841 (ibid.).

Elliot, Hon. George *First Secretary* 29 Nov. 1830–24 Dec. 1834 (SPB, xiv f. 3). *Third Naval Lord* 25 April 1835–22 July 1837.

Elliot, Gilbert *Commissioner* 17 Nov. 1756–19 March 1761.

Elliot, Gilbert John *Third Class Clerk* 21 March 1836–2 Oct. 1837 (Adm. 12/320). Res. 2 Oct. 1837 (Adm. 12/332).

Ellis, Nathaniel *Supernumerary Clerk* pd. from 26 March 1812 to 24 June 1813 (SPB, xii ff. 45–6).

Ellis, Welbore *Commissioner* 23 June 1747–29 Dec. 1755.

Elliston, George *Porter* 30 April 1731–2 April 1732 (SPB, iv f. 20). D. 2 April 1732 (ibid.).

Elliston, Richard *Messenger* pd. from 22 Feb. 1711 by order 28 Feb. 1711 (SPB, i f. 20). *Porter* 17 Sept. 1714–30 April 1731 (SPB, iv f. 20). Left office 30 April 1731 (ibid.). Reapp. 3 April 1732 (Adm. 3/40). Left office by 5 July 1732 (app. of Mears).

Ernle, Sir John, kt. *Commissioner* 26 Sept. 1677–14 May 1679.

Ettrick, William *Counsel* 18 Feb. 1703–8 Dec. 1708 (SPB, i f. 20). Left office 8 Dec. 1708 (app. of Phipps). Reapp. 11 June 1711 (SPB, i f. 20). Discharged 18 Jan. 1715 (ibid.; app. of G. Townsend).

Evans, Evan *Extra Messenger* 13 Aug. 1795–11 April 1800 (SPB, viii f. 43). Left office 11 April 1800 (SPB, ix f. 57).

Evans, James *Extra Clerk* 16 Feb. 1801–3 May 1804 (SPB, ix f. 85). *Junior Clerk* 3 May 1803–30 July 1814 (SPB, iii f. 11). *Senior Clerk* 30 July 1814–5 Feb. 1816 (SPB, xii ff. 15–16). *First Class Clerk* 5 Feb. 1816–2 June 1826 (SPB, xiii ff. 017–18). D. 2 June 1826 (*Gent. Mag.* (1826), xcvi(1), 571).

Evans, Robert Spike *Third Class Clerk* 1 Jan. 1827–2 May 1833 (SPB, xiv f. 8). *Second Class Clerk* 2 May 1833–8 Oct. 1847 (Adm. 12/290). *First Class Clerk* 8 Oct. 1847–16 July 1861 (Adm. 12/474). Ret. 16 July 1861 (Adm. 12/698).

Evans, William Frederick *Third Class Clerk* 19 June–3 July 1832 (SPB, xiv f. 8; Adm. 12/284). Left office 3 July 1832 on app. as Third Class Clerk, Accountant General of Navy (Adm. 12/284). Reapp. 28 March 1835 (Adm. 12/308). *Second Class Clerk* 24 May 1847–18 July 1861 (Adm. 12/474). *First Class Clerk* 18 July 1861–17 Oct. 1867 (Adm. 12/698). D. 17 Oct. 1867 (death certificate; Adm. 12/794, 18 Oct. 1867).

Exton, Everard *Proctor* 20 June 1709–13 May 1718 (HCA 50/8 ff. 43–4, 83–4, 195). D. 13 May 1718 (*Hist. Reg. Chron.* (1718), iii, 22).

Exton, John *Judge* 26 Oct. 1661–c. 22 Oct. 1668 (HCA 50/3 ff. 210–13). Buried 22 Oct. 1668 (*The Registers of St. Bene't and St. Peter, Paul's Wharf, London*, ed. W. A. Littledale (Harleian Soc. 1909–12), iv, 62).

Exton, Sir Thomas, kt. *Judge* 6 July–17 Dec. 1686 (HCA 50/5 ff. 136–8; C 66/3287). Left office 17 Dec. 1686 (app. of Raines).

Fairborne, Sir Stafford, kt. *Member of Council* 8 Feb. 1706–20 June 1708.

Fairfax, Robert *Member of Council* 20 June–28 Oct. 1708.

Falkland, Anthony (Carey) 5th Viscount *Commissioner* 23 Jan. 1691–15 April 1693. *First Lord* 15 April 1693–2 May 1694.

Fanshawe, Edward Gennys *Third Naval Lord* 25 March 1865–13 July 1866.

Farrant, Godfrey Lee *Registrar* grant in reversion by letters patent under seal of Admiralty court 30 June 1725 (HCA 50/9 ff. 81–3); confirmed by letters patent under great seal 1 July 1725 (C 66/3559); succ. 21 Feb. 1758 (d. of S. Hill). D. 9 Aug. 1790 (*Gent. Mag.* (1790), lx(2), 768).

Fawcett, William *Extra Clerk* 18 June 1743–17 Nov. 1744 (Adm. 3/47). Left office 17 Nov. 1744 on app. as Purser of the *Portland* (Adm. 3/49; Adm. 6/16 p. 387).

Fawler, John *Chief Clerk* pd. from 24 June 1694 by order 26 Sept. 1694 (SPB, ii ff. 50–1). *Deputy Secretary* 15 Nov. 1705–11 Nov. 1714 (Adm. 6/8 f. 201; Adm. 6/9 f. 77). Left office 11 Nov. 1714 on app. as Commissioner of Navy (SPB, i f. 42; C 66/3502).

    Deputy Judge Advocate of the Fleet 21 Oct. 1697–6 May 1703 (Adm. 6/4 f. 120). Discharged 6 May 1703 (SPB, ii f. 6).

Fearne, Charles *Extra Clerk* in office by 30 May 1738 (Adm. 3/43). *Clerk* 7 Nov. 1738–4 July 1763 (ibid.). *Chief Clerk* 4 July 1763–28 June 1764 (Adm. 3/71). *Deputy Secretary* 28 June 1764–10 Nov. 1766 (Adm. 6/20 p. 35). Res. 10 Nov. 1766 (Adm. 3/73).

    Deputy Judge Advocate of the Fleet 15 June 1743–12 Nov. 1744 (Adm. 6/16 pp. 192–3). *Judge Advocate of the Fleet* 12 Nov. 1744–28 Jan. 1768 (ibid. pp. 382–3). D. 28 Jan. 1768 (SPB, v f. 103).

    First Clerk (Marine Department) 17 July 1755–11 Nov. 1766 (Adm. 2/1152 pp. 134–5). Left office 11 Nov. 1766 (Adm. 2/1162 p. 202).

Fearne, Thomas William *Extra Clerk* 21 Jan. 1761–12 Nov. 1766 (Adm. 3/68). *Clerk* 12 Nov. 1766–25 March 1795 (Adm. 3/73). Res. 25 March 1795 (SPB, viii f. 13).

Fenwick, Henry *Civil Lord* 23 Jan.–10 April 1866.

Ferrabosco, Mossom *Deputy Judge Advocate of the Fleet* 10 Jan.–22 Oct. 1707 (Adm. 6/9 f. 46). D. 22 Oct. 1707 (SPB, i f. 18).

Fetter (*later* **Laplume**), George Philip *Porter* 4 Nov. 1817–1 April 1820 (SPB, xii ff. 65–6). *Board Room Messenger* 1 April 1820–26 July 1841 (SPB, xiii ff. 027–8). Left office 26 July 1841 on app. as Head Messenger, Naval Departments, Somerset House (Adm. 12/383). *Head Messenger* 10 Aug. 1841–7 July 1854 (ibid.). Ret. 7 July 1854 (Adm. 12/586).

Fetter, John *Messenger (Naval Works Department)* 26 Dec. 1796–13 July 1803 (SPB, x f. 40). D. 13 July 1803 (SPB, iii f. 26).

Finch, Hon. Daniel (*styled* Lord **Finch** 12 May 1681; succ. as 2nd Earl of **Notting-ham** 18 Dec. 1682) *Commissioner* 14 May 1679–19 Feb. 1681. *First Lord* 19 Feb. 1681–19 May 1684.

Finch, Heneage (Finch) 1st Lord *Commissioner* 31 Oct. 1674–14 May 1679.

Finlaison, John *Keeper of Records* 21 Aug. 1809–5 Feb. 1816 (SPB, xii ff. 55–6). *First Class Clerk* 5 Feb. 1816–24 Dec. 1821 (SPB, xiii ff. 017–18). Res. 24 Dec. 1821 on app. as Actuary and Accountant, Check Department, National Debt office (ibid.; *Summary of Minutes of Commissioners for Reduction of National Debt* (London 1961), 181).

Fisher, John *Extra Clerk* 25 Jan. 1799–30 June 1803 (SPB, ix f. 11). *Junior Clerk*

30 June 1803–1 July 1813 (SPB, iii f. 11). *Senior Clerk* 1 July 1813–5 Feb. 1816 (SPB, xii ff. 15–16). Ret. 5 Feb. 1816 (ibid.).

Fisher, Susannah   *Housekeeper* 24 Oct. 1739–c. 15 March 1740 (SPB, vi f. 20). D. by 15 March 1740 (ibid.).

Fisher, William   *Clerk* pd. from 28 Feb. 1709 by order 24 March 1709 (SPB, i f. 43). Discharged 24 June 1713 by order 27 June 1713 (ibid.).

Fitzgerald, Maurice   *Civil Lord* 23 Dec. 1834–25 April 1835.

Fitzroy, Hon. Henry   *Civil Lord* 12 Feb. 1845–13 July 1846.

Fonblanque, Bentham Albany   *Third Class Clerk* 30 Dec. 1853–31 March 1855 (Adm. 12/570). *Third Class (Second Section) Clerk* 31 March 1855–29 Jan. 1858 (Adm. 12/602; *Navy Lists*). *Third Class (First Section) Clerk* 29 Jan. 1858–20 Dec. 1861/20 March 1862 (Adm. 12/650). *Acting Second Class Clerk* app. between 20 Dec. 1861 and 20 March 1862 (*Navy Lists*). *Second Class Clerk* 13 July–1 Nov. 1865 (Adm. 12/762). Ret. 1 Nov. 1865 (ibid.).

Forbes, David   *Extra Clerk (Marine Department)* 26 April 1770–7 July 1778 (Adm. 2/1165 p. 1). Left office 7 July 1778 (Adm. 12/1170 p. 558).

Forbes, Hon. John   *Commissioner* 13 Dec. 1756–6 April 1757; 2 July 1757–20 April 1763.

Forrest, William   *Third Class Clerk* 31 Oct.–3 Nov. 1840 (Adm. 12/368). App. cancelled 3 Nov. 1840 (ibid.).

Forster, Thomas R.   *Extra Clerk* 28 Sept. 1807–18 Jan. 1815 (SPB, iii f. 14). Left office 18 Jan. 1815 on app. as Naval Storekeeper, Jamaica (SPB, xii f. 40).

Foster, Philip   *Judge Advocate of the Fleet* 23 May–12 Oct. 1689 (Sergison MS f. 162). Removed from office 12 Oct. 1689 (ibid. f. 171).

Fouace, Charles   *Extra Clerk and Translator* 22 Dec. 1755–25 Dec. 1775 (SPB, vii f. 7). Res. 25 Dec. 1775 (SPB, v f. 7).

Fowler, John   *Judge Advocate of the Fleet* 17 Jan. 1663–c. 30 Sept. 1672 (Adm. 2/1733 pp. 54–5). Left office c. 30 Sept. 1672 (app. of J. Brisbane).

Fox, Hon. Charles James   *Commissioner* 28 Feb. 1770–6 May 1772.

Frankland, Sir Thomas, 3rd Bart.   *Commissioner* 13 May 1730–19 March 1742.

Frankland, William   *Commissioner* 23 Oct. 1806–6 April 1807.

Franklyn, Samuel   *Proctor* 28 July 1673–c. 13 May 1700 (Adm. 2/1736 pp. 46–8). D. by 13 May 1700 (*CSPD 1700–2*, 37; HCA 50/7 f. 28).

Frederick, Charles   *Fourth Naval Lord* 28 June 1859–15 June 1861. *Third Naval Lord* 15 June 1861–25 March 1865.

Fremantle, Thomas Francis   *Commissioner* 23 Oct. 1806–6 April 1807.

French, George   *Extra Clerk* 17 Nov. 1744–21 May 1749 (Adm. 3/49). Left office 21 May 1749 on app. as Clerk, Navy Office (SPB, vi f. 7).

Freshfield, James   *Extra Clerk* 18 May 1778–25 March 1795 (Adm. 3/84). Res. 25 March 1795 (SPB, viii f. 14).

Fuller, Richard   *Advocate* 15 Aug. 1715–5 Oct. 1726 (HCA 50/8 ff. 185–6). D. 5 Oct. 1726 (*Hist. Reg. Chron.* (1726), xi, 38).

Gage, Sir William Hall, kt.   *Second Naval Lord* 8 Sept. 1841–13 July 1846.

Gambier, James (cr. Lord **Gambier** 9 Nov. 1807)   *Commissioner* 7 March 1795–19 Feb. 1801; 15 May 1804–10 Feb. 1806; 6 April 1807–9 May 1808.

Gambier, James William Morley   *Temporary Clerk* 11 April 1862–13 Dec. 1865 (Adm. 12/714). *Third Class (Second Section) Clerk* 13 Dec. 1865–21 Oct. 1867 (Adm. 12/762). *Third Class (First Section) Clerk* 21 Oct. 1867 (Adm. 12/794).

Gardner, Alan (cr. Bart. 9 Sept. 1794) *Commissioner* 19 Jan. 1790–7 March 1795.

Gardner, Francis Charles *Third Class Clerk* 11 June 1832–c. 13 May 1836 (SPB, xiv f. 8). D. by 13 May 1836 (app. of W. H. Bell; Adm. 47/5).

Gardner, George *Second Clerk* (*Marine Pay Department*) 31 Dec. 1807–11 Dec. 1819 (SPB, xii ff. 73–4). *Second Class Clerk* (*Marine Pay Department*) 11 Dec. 1819–30 June 1831 (SPB, xiii ff. 037–8). Ret. 30 June 1831 (SPB, xiv f. 18).

Gardner, William *Extra Clerk* (*Marine Pay Department*) 31 Dec. 1807–11 Dec. 1819 (SPB, xii ff. 75–6). *Third Class Clerk* (*Marine Pay Department*) 11 Dec. 1819–21 Jan. 1824 (SPB, xiii ff. 037–8). D. 21 Jan. 1824 (SPB, xiv f. 19).

Garlies, George (Stewart) *styled* Lord *Commissioner* 2 May 1805–10 Feb. 1806.

Garner, John *Supernumerary Clerk* pd. from 26 March 1812 to 25 March 1813 (SPB, xii ff. 45–6).

Garthshore, William *Commissioner* 19 Feb. 1801–17 Jan. 1804.

Gascoigne, William *Extra Clerk* 8 April 1777–16 June 1795 (SPB, v f. 7). *Clerk* 16 June 1795–7 Feb. 1800 (SPB, viii f. 13). *Senior Clerk* 7 Feb. 1800–25 Jan. 1801 (SPB, ix f. 81). D. 25 Jan. 1801 (ibid.).

Gascoyne, Bamber *Commissioner* 16 July 1779–1 April 1782.

Gashry, Francis *Clerk of Journals* 8 Dec. 1738–7 March 1741 (Adm. 3/43). Office discontinued 7 March 1741 (Adm. 3/45).

Gaspy, John *Porter* pd. from 25 March 1688 to 20 Feb. 1689 (AO 1/1717/127; AO 1/1719/132).

Gee, Orlando (ktd. 18 Aug. 1682) *Registrar* 6 Sept. 1660–1705 (HCA 50/3 ff. 35–6). D. 1705 (*Notes and Queries*, xl, 22).

George, Prince *Lord High Admiral* 20 May 1702–28 Oct. 1708. D. 28 Oct. 1708.

Gibbs, Thomas *Clerk* pd. from 24 June 1694 by order 26 Sept. 1694 (SPB, ii ff. 50–1). Left office 18 Nov. 1695 on app. as Muster Master of Fleet at Deal (Adm. 20/65 no. 396); again pd. from 13 Sept. 1701 by order 18 Oct. 1701 (SPB, i f. 6; Adm. 20/76 no. 211); payment ceased 24 June 1702 (AO 1/1724/144).

Gibson, John *Extra Clerk* 26 Aug. 1807–5 Feb. 1816 (SPB, iii f. 24). *Third Class Clerk* 5 Feb. 1816–11 April 1822 (SPB, xiii ff. 021–2). D. 11 April 1822 (SPB, xiv f. 7).
    Private Secretary to Second Secretary (Barrow) 5 Feb. 1812–26 June 1821 (SPB, xii ff. 39–40). Office discontinued 26 June 1821 (SPB, xiii ff. 021–2).

Giffard, Edward *Third Class Clerk* 12 July 1833–26 Aug. 1841 (Adm. 12/290). *Second Class Clerk* 26 Aug. 1841–16 Aug. 1854 (Adm. 12/383). *First Class Clerk* 16 Aug. 1854–22 Feb. 1855 (Adm. 12/586). Left office 22 Feb. 1855 on app. as Secretary, Transport Board (Adm. 12/602); reapp. 21 March 1857 (Adm. 12/634). D. 1 Oct. 1867 (death certificate; Adm. 12/794, 18 Oct. 1867).
    Private Secretary to First Secretary (Dawson) 15 Jan.–April 1835 (Adm. 12/308).

Giffard, John Hardinge *Third Class* (*Second Section*) *Clerk* 22 Dec. 1866 (Adm. 12/778).

Giffard, John William *Third Class Clerk* 1 Sept. 1827–12 July 1833 (SPB, xiv f. 8). Res. 12 July 1833 (Adm. 12/290).

Giles, John *Board Room Messenger* 28 Aug. 1846–28 Oct. 1867 (Adm. 12/458). Ret. 28 Oct. 1867 (Adm. 12/794).

Gilly, William Octavius Shakespeare *Extra Clerk* 2 Nov. 1841–17 Dec. 1844 (Adm. 12/383). *Third Class Clerk* 17 Dec. 1844–31 March 1855 (Adm. 12/426). *Third Class* (*First Section*) *Clerk* 31 March 1855–27 Aug. 1859 (Adm. 12/602; *Navy Lists*). Ret. 27 Aug. 1859 (Adm. 12/666).

Gimber, William *Extra Clerk* 22 Feb. 1771–18 Jan. 1790 (Adm. 3/78). *Clerk* 18 Jan. 1790–7 Feb. 1800 (Adm. 3/107). *Senior Clerk* 7 Feb. 1800–2 May 1804 (SPB, ix f. 81). Ret. 2 May 1804 (SPB, iii f. 7).

Gipps, George *Private Secretary to First Lord* (Auckland) 16 June–Dec. 1834 (Adm. 12/298); 27 April–22 June 1835 (Adm. 12/308). Res. 22 June 1835 (ibid.).

Glanville, Benjamin *Inspector of Repairs* 1 April 1731–c. 8 Aug. 1774 (Adm. 3/39; SPB, iv f. 20). D. by 8 Aug. 1774 (SPB, v f. 27).

Glasier, Jeffrey *Proctor* 16 May 1700–c. 20 June 1709 (HCA 50/7 ff. 28, 83, 110). D. by 20 June 1709 (app. of E. Exton; *CTB*, xxiv, 213).

Glendenning, Robert *Office Keeper* (*Marine Pay Department*) 18 May 1824–11 Dec. 1827 (SPB, xiv f. 21). Res. 11 Dec. 1827 (ibid.).

Glenorchy, John (Campbell) *styled* Lord *Commissioner* 5 May 1741–19 March 1742.

Godson, Richard *Counsel and Judge Advocate of the Fleet* 7 Feb. 1845–1 Aug. 1849 (Adm. 12/442). D. 1 Aug. 1849 (death certificate; Adm. 12/506).

Golding, Edward *Messenger* pd. from 26 Dec. 1696 to 3 July 1705 (SPB, i f. 20; AO 1/1725/147).

Golding, Edward *Private Secretary to First Lord* (Grenville) 3 Oct. 1806–April 1807 (SPB, iii f. 5).

Golding, Reuben *Clerk* pd. from 24 June 1702 to 25 Dec. 1703 (Adm. 20/77 no. 3982; AO 1/1725/146). Left office 10 Dec. 1703 on app. as Clerk of Survey, Plymouth (Adm. 3/19; Adm. 6/8 f. 33; SPB, i f. 6).

Goldsworthy, Burrington *Receiver of Droits* 13 June 1733–c. 24 Jan. 1774 (HCA 50/10 f. 159; HCA 50/12 ff. 53–4). D. by 24 Jan. 1774 (HCA 50/12 f. 204).

Goodrick, Simon *Mechanist of Naval Works* 25 Oct. 1799–28 Oct. 1807 (Adm. 6/27 f. 88). Transferred to Navy Board 28 Oct. 1807 as Mechanist under Civil Architect and Engineer of the Navy (PC 2/174 pp. 274–6, 284).

Gordon, Francis Frederick *Third Class* (*Second Section*) *Clerk* 20 July 1858–20 Sept./20 Dec. 1862 (Adm. 12/650). *Acting Third Class* (*First Section*) *Clerk* app. between 20 Sept. and 20 Dec. 1862 (*Navy Lists*). *Third Class* (*First Section*) *Clerk* 26 April 1865–8 May 1867 (Adm. 12/762). *Second Class Clerk* 8 May 1867 (Adm. 12/794).

Gordon, George *Clerk* pd. from 1 Aug. 1695 by order 18 Oct. 1695 (Adm. 20/65 no. 730). Discharged 24 June 1698 by order 15 July 1698 (SPB, i f. 6); again pd. from 26 March 1699 by order 27 June 1699 (ibid.; Adm. 20/71 no. 2570). D. 22 Oct. 1712 (Adm. 2/191 p. 98).

Gordon, Hon. William *Fourth Naval Lord* 8 Sept. 1841–17 Feb. 1846.

Gordon Lennox, Lord Henry *First Secretary* 16 July 1866–22 Dec. 1868 (Adm. 12/778).

Gostling, George *Proctor* 4 Oct. 1766–2 May 1777 (HCA 50/12 ff. 70–1). Res. 2 May 1777 (ibid. ff. 209–10).

Gostling, George *Proctor* 2 May 1777–27 May 1820 (HCA 50/12 ff. 209–10). D. 27 May 1820 (*Gent. Mag.* (1820), xc(1), 570).

Gough, Benjamin *Messenger* 8 Dec. 1738–18 July 1748 (SPB, iv f. 20). Left office 18 July 1748 (ibid.).

Gough, Joseph *Messenger* 25 Feb. 1734–7 Dec. 1738 (SPB, iv f. 20). Left office 7 Dec. 1738 (ibid.).

Gould, John *Messenger* 9 Nov. 1715–2 Oct. 1729 (SPB, i f. 20). Left office 2 Oct. 1729 on app. as Gunner of the *Weymouth* (SPB, iv f. 20).

Gower *see* **Leveson Gower**

Graham, George *Private Secretary to First Lord* (Graham) 26 May 1831–June 1834 (SPB, xiv f. 4).

Graham, Sir James Robert George, 2nd Bart. *First Lord* 25 Nov. 1830–11 June 1834; 5 Jan. 1853–8 March 1855.

Graham, William Charles *Third Class Clerk* 14 June 1832–19 March 1836 (SPB, xiv f. 8). D. 19 March 1836 (Adm. 12/320; *Gent. Mag.* (1836), cvi(1), 564).

Grant, Henry *Private Secretary to First Lord* (Grey/Howick) 14 March–Sept. 1806 (SPB, iii f. 5).

Grant, Thomas George *Third Class Clerk* 13 March 1841–22 Feb. 1855 (Adm. 12/383). *Second Class Clerk* 22 Feb. 1855–3 Feb. 1859 (Adm. 12/602). Left office 3 Feb. 1859 on app. as Acting Storekeeper, Deptford (Adm. 12/666). App. Storekeeper, Gosport 18 May 1859 (ibid).

    Private Secretary to First Secretary (O'Brien Stafford) 3 March 1852–Jan. 1853 (Adm. 12/554).

Graves, Francis *Extra Clerk* 1 April–26 Aug. 1841 (Adm. 12/383). *Third Class Clerk* 26 Aug. 1841–31 March 1855 (ibid.). *Third Class (First Section) Clerk* 31 March–15 Dec. 1855 (Adm. 12/602; *Navy Lists*). *Acting Second Class Clerk* 15 Dec. 1855–20 Dec. 1856/2 March 1857 (Adm. 12/602). *Second Class Clerk* app. between 20 Dec. 1856 and 20 March 1857 (*Navy Lists*). Ret. 10 June 1869 (Adm. 12/828).

    Private Secretary to Second Secretary (Baillie Hamilton, Phinn) 29 Jan. 1845–16 March 1857 (Adm. 12/442; Adm. 12/602, 18 June 1855).

Graydon, Robert *Extra Clerk* 31 Aug. 1744–3 Sept. 1747 (Adm. 3/48). D. 3 Sept. 1747 (SPB, vi f. 7).

Greaves, Richard *Extra Clerk* 16 Feb. 1801–11 June 1802 (SPB, ix f. 85). Res. 11 June 1802 (SPB, iii f. 13).

Greetham, George Lamburn *Deputy Judge Advocate of the Fleet* 16 Jan. 1843–14 Jan. 1856 (Adm. 12/411, under Courts Martial). Res. 14 Jan. 1856 (Adm. 12/619, under Courts Martial).

Greetham, Moses *Deputy Judge Advocate of the Fleet* 6 Nov. 1804–23 July 1831 (Adm. 6/29 f. 2) D. 23 July 1831 (SPB, xiv f. 15).

Grenville, George (*styled* Hon. 13 Sept. 1749) *Commissioner* 27 Dec. 1744–23 June 1747. *First Lord* 18 Oct. 1762–20 April 1763.

Grenville, Thomas *First Lord* 29 Sept. 1806–6 April 1807.

Greville, Hon. Charles Francis *Commissioner* 22 Sept. 1780–1 April 1782.

Grey, Hon. Charles (*styled* Viscount **Howick** 11 April 1806) *First Lord* 10 Feb.–29 Sept. 1806.

Grey, Hon. Frederick William (ktd. 2 Jan. 1857) *Private Secretary to First Lord* (Auckland) 22 June–Sept. 1835 (Adm. 12/308). *Frist Naval Lord* 15 June 1861–13 July 1866.

Grey *see also* **de Grey**

Groves, James *Board Room Messenger* 7 April 1845–20 April 1864 (Adm. 12/442). Ret. 20 April 1864 (Adm. 12/746).

Guerin, Maynard *Agent of Marines* (*Plymouth*) 9 Nov. 1756–4 May 1760 (Adm. 6/406 p. 33). D. 4 May 1760 (*Gent. Mag.* (1760), xxx, 249).

Guion, Daniel *Extra Clerk* 12 Feb. 1742–10 Oct. 1752 (SPB, vi f. 7). Left office 10 Oct. 1752 (ibid.).

Guy, James *Porter* 11 June 1846–14 March 1862 (Adm. 12/458). Ret. 14 March 1862 (Adm. 12/714).

Haddington, Thomas (Hamilton) 9th Earl of *First Lord* 8 Sept. 1841–13 Jan. 1846.

Hales, Edward (succ. as 3rd Bart. between 22 Aug. 1683 and 17 April 1684) *Commissioner* 14 May 1679–19 May 1684.

Halford, Edward *Clerk* pd. from 24 June 1694 by order 26 Sept. 1694 (SPB, ii ff. 50–1); pd. to 24 June 1697 (SPB, i f. 6; Adm. 20/67 no. 2418); again pd. from 26 March 1700 by order 28 June 1700 (SPB, i f. 6; Adm. 20/74 no. 909). D. 9 Nov. 1702 (SPB, i f. 6).

Halifax, George (Montagu Dunk) 2nd Earl of *First Lord* 17 June–18 Oct. 1762.

Halifax, H. F. *Temporary Clerk* 29 July 1858–c. 24 July 1860 (Adm. 12/650). D. by 24 July 1860 (Adm. 12/682).

Hall, Robert *Private Secretary to First Lord* (Somerset) 27 April 1863–20 March 1866 (Adm. 12/730).

Halsey, Sarah *Housekeeper* pd. from 21 April 1708 by order 14 June 1708 (SPB, i f. 20). D. 25 May 1713 (ibid.).

Halsted, William Anthony *Third Class Clerk* 10 May–10 Sept. 1824 (SPB, xiv f. 7). Res. 10 Sept. 1824 (ibid.).

Hamilton, Lord Archibald *Commissioner* 19 May 1729–13 March 1738; 19 March 1742–25 Feb. 1746.

Hamilton, Richard Wynne *Third Class Clerk* 1 May 1837–9 Oct. 1847 (Adm. 12/332). *Acting Second Class Clerk* 9 Oct. 1847–9 Jan. 1849 (Adm. 12/474). *Second Class Clerk* 9 Jan. 1849–10 Oct. 1858 (Adm. 12/506). D. 10 Oct. 1858 (Adm. 12/650).

Hamilton *see also* **Baillie Hamilton**

Hampson, George Francis (succ. as 8th Bart. 12 Feb. 1820) *Receiver of Droits* 31 Jan. 1818–8 May 1833 (HCA 50/16 ff. 168–9). D. 8 May 1833.

Hardman, James *Supernumerary Clerk* pd. from 26 Dec. 1811 to 25 Dec. 1814 (SPB, xii ff. 45–6). *Extra Clerk* 18 Jan. 1815–5 Feb. 1816 (ibid. ff. 41–2). *Third Class Clerk* 5 Feb. 1816–15 April 1825 (SPB, xiii ff. 021–2). D. 15 April 1825 (SPB, xiv f. 7).

Hardy, Sir Charles, kt. *Commissioner* 13 Dec. 1743–27 Nov. 1744. D. 27 Nov. 1744 (SPB, vi f. 2).

Hardy, Sir Thomas Masterman, 1st Bart. *First Naval Lord* 25 Nov. 1830–1 Aug. 1834.

Harland, Sir Robert, 1st Bart. *Commissioner* 1 April 1782–30 Jan. 1783.

Harris, Alexander *Head Messenger* pd. from c. Feb. 1666 to 24 June 1682 (AO 1/1711/106; AO 1/1716/122). Discharged 24 June 1682 (Adm. 2/1754 p. 87).

Harris, George *Advocate* 14 June 1764–21 May 1782 (HCA 50/12 f. 45). Left office 21 May 1782 (app. of W. Scott).

Harris, James *Commissioner* 1 Jan.–20 April 1763.

Harris, John *Porter* pd. from 1 Jan. 1676 to 25 March 1678 (AO 1/1715/120).

Harris, John *Extra Clerk* 5 April 1746–24 June 1747 (SPB, vi f. 7). Discharged 24 June 1747 (ibid.).

Harrison, John *Private Secretary to First Lord* (Spencer) 7 Feb. 1800–Feb. 1801 (SPB, ix ff. 8, 80).

Hartington, Spencer Compton (Cavendish) *styled* Marquess of *Civil Lord* 27

March–30 April 1863. Left office 30 April 1863 on app. as Under Secretary of State, War Office (Adm. 12/730).

Hartwell, Marmaduke *Porter* his widow pd. for quarter from 24 June to 29 Sept. 1694 (SPB, ii ff. 50–1).

Hastings, Henry *Extra Clerk* 26 Feb. 1745–30 April 1749 (Adm. 3/50). Discharged 30 April 1749 (ibid.); reapp. 8 Feb. 1755 (SPB, vii f. 7). *Clerk* 31 July 1761–21 Dec. 1777 (Adm. 3/69). D. 21 Dec. 1777 (SPB, v f. 6).

Haversham, John (Thomson) 1st Lord *Commissioner* 31 May 1699–26 Jan. 1702.

Hawdon, George *Extra Clerk* 13 Aug. 1796–31 Dec. 1798 (SPB, ix f. 11). Removed from office 31 Dec. 1798 (ibid.).

Hawes, Thomas *Clerk* 17 Jan. 1715–14 Oct. 1742 (Adm. 2/193 pp. 127–8). *Chief Clerk* 14 Oct. 1742–14 June 1743 (Adm. 3/46). D. 14 June 1743 (SPB, vi f. 6). *Judge Advocate of the Fleet* 11 Feb. 1729–14 June 1743 (Adm. 6/14 f. 12).

Hawke, Sir Edward, kt. *First Lord* 11 Dec. 1766–12 Jan. 1771.

Hay, Edward *Supernumerary Clerk* pd. from 26 Dec. 1811 to 24 June 1814 (SPB, xii ff. 45–6).

Hay, George (ktd. 11 Nov. 1773) *Commissioner* 17 Nov. 1756–6 April 1757; 2 July 1757–31 July 1765. *Judge* 4 Nov. 1773–6 Oct. 1778 (HCA 50/12 ff. 147–52). D. 6 Oct. 1778 (*Gent. Mag.* (1778), xlviii, 495).

Hay, Lord John (d. 1851) *Fourth Naval Lord* 13 July 1846–23 Dec. 1847. *Third Naval Lord* 23 Dec. 1847–9 Feb. 1850.

Hay, Lord John (d. 1916) *Fifth Naval Lord* 10 April–9 May 1866. *Fourth Naval Lord* 9 May–13 July 1866. *Third Naval Lord* 18 Dec. 1868.

Hay, John Holman *Extra Clerk* 5 May 1807–1 July 1813 (SPB, iii f. 14). *Junior Clerk* 1 July 1813–5 Feb. 1816 (SPB, xii ff. 25–6). *Second Class Clerk* 5 Feb. 1816–2 June 1829 (SPB, xiii ff. 019–20). *First Class Clerk* 2 June 1829–5 Jan. 1849 (SPB, xiv f. 5). *Chief Clerk* 5 Jan. 1849–17 Nov. 1853 (Adm. 12/506). D. 17 Nov. 1853 (*Gent. Mag.* (1854), cxxxiv(1), 439).

Hay, John Holman *Third Class Clerk* 5 May 1837–4 June 1850 (Adm. 12/332). *Second Class Clerk* 4 June 1850–13 July 1865 (Adm. 46/184 no. 544; Adm. 46/186 no. 1918). *First Class Clerk* 13 July 1865 (Adm. 12/762).

Hay, Robert William *Private Secretary to First Lord* (Melville) 22 June 1812–3 April 1823 (SPB, xii f. 10).

Hay *see also* **Dalrymple Hay**

Haynes, John *Board Room Messenger* 27 April 1827–7 April 1845 (SPB, xiv f. 10). Ret. 7 April 1845 (Adm. 12/442).

Haysom, James *Messenger* 26 April 1768–28 March 1777 (SPB, v f. 27). Left office 28 March 1777 on app. as Messenger, Navy Office (ibid.).

Hayter, Thomas *Secretary* occ. from 22 May 1679 to 3 Feb. 1680 (James and Shaw, Admiralty Administration, 182; Adm. 2/1752).

Hayward, Thomas *Messenger* (*Marine Pay Department*) pd. from 31 Dec. 1807 to 25 March 1809 (SPB, xii ff. 77–8). Left office 25 March 1809 (ibid.).

Head, Elizabeth *Housekeeper* 3 Jan.–13 Sept. 1727 (SPB, iv f. 20). Discharged 13 Sept. 1727 (ibid.).

Heald, William *Board Room Messenger* 19 May 1813–6 April 1820 (SPB, xii ff. 63–4). D. 6 April 1820 (SPB, xiii ff. 027–8).

Heard, William *Second Clerk* (*Naval Works Department*) 5 Jan. 1801–5 May 1805 (SPB, x f. 40). Left office 5 May 1805 (SPB, iii f. 25).

Hedges, Sir Charles, kt. *Judge* 1 June 1689–10 June 1714 (HCA 50/6 ff. 5–8; HCA 50/7 ff. 121–5, 188–96; C 66/3327, 3428, 3454). D. 10 June 1714 (SPB, i f. 27).

Heidekoo, John *Second Clerk (Naval Works Department)* 25 March–25 Dec. 1796 (SPB, x f. 40). Res. 25 Dec. 1796 (ibid.).

Hellyer, William John *Deputy Judge Advocate of the Fleet* 14 Jan. 1856–23 April 1861 (Adm. 12/619, under Courts Martial). D. 23 April 1861 (Adm. 12/699, under Courts Martial; death certificate).

Henchman, Humphrey *Judge* 22 June–1 Dec. 1714 (HCA 50/8 ff. 121–6). Removed from office 1 Dec. 1714 (app. of Newton).

Herbert, Arthur (cr. Earl of **Torrington** 29 May 1689) *Supernumerary Commissioner* 22 Aug. 1683–17 April 1684. *Commissioner* 17 April–19 May 1684. *First Lord* 8 March 1689–20 Jan. 1690.

Herbert, Hon. Sidney *First Secretary* 10 Sept. 1841–4 Feb. 1845 (Adm. 46/92 no. 3596). Left office 4 Feb. 1845 on app. as Secretary at War (Adm. 12/442).

Herbert, Sir Thomas, kt. *Third Naval Lord* 2 March 1852–5 Jan. 1853.

Hervey, Hon. Augustus John (succ. as 3rd Earl of **Bristol** 18 March 1775) *Commissioner* 2 Feb. 1771–12 April 1775.

Hewer, William *Clerk* probably app. by Pepys June 1673; occ. 22 Dec. 1673 (Pepys Library no. 2849 p. 435); probably app. Chief Clerk in succession to Southerne; occ. as such 1674 (MS Rawlinson A 181 f. 4); signed Secretary's letters 26 Aug. 1674 and 18 Feb. 1679 (Pepys Library no. 2850 p. 287; ibid. no. 2856 p. 82). Probably left office with Pepys May 1679.
   Deputy Judge Advocate of the Fleet 12 March 1677–29 Dec. 1679 (Adm. 2/1738 f. 92). Discharged 29 Dec. 1679 (Adm. 2/1740 pp. 270–3; AO 1/1716/124).

Heywood, John Modyford *Commissioner* 31 Dec. 1783–2 April 1784.

Hickes, William *Extra Clerk* 24 June 1747–30 April 1749 (Adm. 3/57). Discharged 30 April 1749 (SPB, vi f. 7).

Higgens, Richard *Deputy Judge Advocate of the Fleet* 10 April 1762–c. 24 July 1780 (Adm. 6/19 p. 399). D. by 24 July 1780 (SPB, v f. 26).

Hill, Elizabeth *Necessary Woman* 27 March 1794–15 May 1816 (SPB, viii f. 45). Ret. 15 May 1816 (SPB, xii ff. 67–8).

Hill, John *Messenger* 7 Nov. 1781–21 May 1792 (SPB, v f. 27). Left office 21 May 1792 on app. as Porter, Sheerness Dockyard (SPB, viii f. 44).

Hill, Richard *Member of Council* 22 May 1702–28 Oct. 1708. *Registrar* grant in reversion by letters patent under seal of Admiralty court 27 Nov. 1710 (HCA 50/8 ff. 96–8); confirmed by letters patent under great seal 13 Dec. 1710 (C 66/3476); succ. 21 March 1712 (d. of Crawley). Surrendered office by 2 Oct. 1714 (HCA 50/8 ff. 131–2).

Hill, Samuel *Registrar* 2 Oct. 1714–21 Feb. 1758 (HCA 50/8 ff. 131–2; C 66/3499). D. 21 Feb. 1758 (*Gent. Mag.* (1758), xxviii, 146).

Hind, Charles Whiston *Third Class Clerk (Marine Pay Department)* 2 Dec. 1830–30 June 1831 (SPB, xiv f. 19). Discharged 30 June 1831 (ibid.).

Hind, Thomas *First Clerk (Marine Pay Department)* 30 Sept. 1808–11 Dec. 1819 (SPB, xii ff. 73–4). *First Class Clerk (Marine Pay Department)* 11 Dec. 1819–30 June 1831 (SPB, xiii ff. 037–8). Discharged 30 June 1831 (SPB, xiv f. 17).

Hinsom, Thomas *Clerk* pd. from 28 Feb. 1711 by order 28 Sept. 1711 (SPB, i f. 43). Discharged 24 June 1713 by order 27 June 1713 (ibid.); reapp. 17 Jan. 1715 (Adm. 2/193 pp. 127–8). Dis. 5 May 1716 (Adm. 2/194 p. 8).

Hodgson, Thomas Hesketh *Temporary Clerk* 26 Jan.–24 Oct. 1866 (Adm. 12/778). *Third Class (Second Section) Clerk* 24 Oct. 1866–31 March 1870 (ibid.). *Third Class (First Section) Clerk* 31 March 1870 (Adm. 12/846).

Holburne, Francis *Commissioner* 28 Feb. 1770–2 Feb. 1771.

Holl, Edward *Architect and Engineer of Naval Works* 3 Jan. 1804–28 Oct. 1807 (Adm. 6/28 f. 197). Transferred to Navy Board 28 Oct. 1807 as Assistant Architect and Engineer of the Navy (PC 2/174 pp. 274–6, 284).

Holland, Elizabeth *Housekeeper* 14 Sept. 1727–c. 24 Oct. 1739 (SPB, iv f. 20). D. by 24 Oct. 1739 (SPB, vi f. 20).

Hollinworth, Mitchell *Extra Clerk* 6 April 1779–11 March 1799 (Adm. 3/88). *Clerk* 11 March 1799–7 Feb. 1800 (SPB, ix f. 9). *Senior Clerk* 7 Feb. 1800–25 Aug. 1807 (ibid. f. 82). Ret. 25 Aug. 1807 (SPB, iii f. 8).

Hollinworth, Thomas *Extra Clerk* 19 June 1795–19 Dec. 1800 (SPB, viii f. 15). *Junior Clerk* 19 Dec. 1800–20 Jan. 1803 (SPB, ix f. 83). Left office 20 Jan. 1803 on app. as Clerk of Ropeyard, Woolwich (SPB, iii f. 10).

Holworthy, Charles Desborough *Extra Clerk* 15 March 1811–5 Feb. 1816 (SPB, xii ff. 41–2). *Third Class Clerk* 5 Feb. 1816–1 Nov. 1827 (SPB, xiii ff. 021–2). Left office 1 Nov. 1827 on app. as Agent to Naval Hospital, Malta (SPB, xiv f. 7).

Honywood, Edward *Clerk* pd. from 25 Dec. 1704 (AO 1/1725/147; SPB, i f. 43). Discharged 25 Jan. 1708 by order 24 March 1708 (SPB, i f. 43).
    Deputy Judge Advocate of the Fleet 2 Dec. 1707–22 Dec. 1714 (Adm. 6/9 f. 107). *Judge Advocate of the Fleet* 22 Dec. 1714–16 April 1724 (Adm. 6/12 f. 12). D. 16 April 1724 (SPB, iv f. 19).

Hood, Samuel (Hood) 1st Lord *Commissioner* 16 July 1788–7 March 1795.

Hope *see* **Johnstone Hope**

Hopkins, Richard *Commissioner* 1 April 1782–10 April 1783; 2 April 1784–27 June 1791.

Hopwood, Thomas *Extra Clerk* 12 Oct. 1744–11 Dec. 1748 (Adm. 3/49). D. 11 Dec. 1748 (SPB, vi f. 7).

Hore, Herbert Francis *Third Class Clerk* 27 July 1832–11 March 1841 (Adm. 12/284). Res. 11 March 1841 (Adm. 12/383).

Hornby, Phipps (ktd. 7 April 1852) *Second Naval Lord* 2 March 1852–5 Jan. 1853.

Hotham, Hon. Sir Henry, kt. *Commissioner* 2 April 1818–23 March 1822; 19 Sept. 1828–25 Nov. 1830.

Houblon, Sir John, kt. *Commissioner* 2 May 1694–31 May 1699.

Houghton, George Robert *Extra Clerk* 5 Feb. 1812–5 Feb. 1816 (SPB, xii ff. 41–2). *Third Class Clerk* 5 Feb. 1816–17 June 1824 (SPB, xiii ff. 021–2). *Second Class Clerk* 17 June 1824–15 Dec. 1834 (SPB, xiv f. 6). *First Class Clerk* 15 Dec. 1834–16 April 1838 (Adm. 12/298). Ret. 16 April 1838 (Adm. 12/344).

Houghton, John Horatio Nelson *Third Class Clerk* 14 May 1832–5 April 1837 (SPB, xiv f. 8). *Second Class Clerk* 5 April 1837–18 Nov. 1853 (Adm. 12/332). *First Class Clerk* 18 Nov. 1853–31 Dec. 1869 (Adm. 12/570). Ret. 31 Dec. 1869 (Adm. 12/828).
    Private Secretary to First Secretary (Wood) 28 April 1835–11 April 1837 (Adm. 12/308).

Housen, George *Porter* 23 Dec. 1786–1 May 1804 (SPB, viii f. 44). Ret. 1 May 1804 (SPB, iii f. 18).

Howard, Charles *Extra Clerk* 19 Aug. 1762–7 Oct. 1765 (SPB, vii f. 7). Left office 7 Oct. 1765 on app. as Clerk of Cheque and Storekeeper, Harwich (SPB, v f. 30).

Howard, William *Messenger (Naval Works Department)* 14 July 1803–28 Oct. 1807 (SPB, iii f. 26). Transferred to Navy Board 28 Oct. 1807 (PC 2/174 pp. 274–6, 284; SPB, xii ff. 293–4).

Howe, Philip *Extra Clerk* 24 June 1766–21 Feb. 1771 (Adm. 3/74). Res. 21 Feb. 1771 (SPB, v f. 7).

Howe, Richard (Howe) 4th Viscount *Commissioner* 20 April 1763–31 July 1765. *First Lord* 30 Jan.–10 April 1783; 31 Dec. 1783–16 July 1788.

Howick, Viscount *see* **Grey,** Hon. Charles

Howison, Thomas *Extra Clerk* 4 Sept. 1747–30 April 1749 (SPB, vi f. 7). Discharged 30 April 1749 (ibid.); reapp. 2 May 1751 (Adm. 3/62). D. 6 Dec. 1751 (SPB, vii f. 7).

Huddleston, John Walter *Counsel and Judge Advocate of the Fleet* 5 Nov. 1866 (Adm. 12/778).

Hunter, James *Counsel* 1 March 1737–25 Feb. 1742 (SPB, vi f. 19). D. 25 Feb. 1742 (ibid.).

Hunter, Thomas Orby *Commissioner* 17 Nov. 1756–6 April 1757; 2 July 1757–20 April 1763.

Hurd, Thomas *Hydrographer* 28 May 1808–29 April 1823 (Adm. 6/30 f. 114). D. 29 April 1823 (SPB, xiv f. 9).

Hussey, Richard *Counsel* 15 Feb. 1757–7 Feb. 1770 (SPB, vii f. 21). Res. 7 Feb. 1770 (Adm. 3/77).

Hutchinson, Charles *Clerk* pd. from 25 June 1698 by order 3 Aug. 1698 (SPB, i f. 6). Left office 20 May 1701 on app. as Muster Master and Storekeeper, West Indies Fleet (Adm. 20/75 nos. 1747, 1748).

Hutchinson, Richard *Watchman* 25 Dec. 1754–9 April 1773 (SPB, vii f. 23). Dis. 9 April 1773 (SPB, v f. 27).

Hutchinson, Richard *Messenger* 5 June 1756–21 April 1768 (SPB, vii f. 22). *Porter* 21 April 1768–22 Dec. 1786 (SPB, v f. 26). D. 22 Dec. 1786 (SPB, viii f. 44).

Hyde, Thomas *Advocate* 13 June 1660–12 March 1661 (Adm. 2/1725 f. 2). *Judge* 12 March–c. 26 Oct. 1661 (HCA 50/3 ff. 137–42). D. by 26 Oct. 1661 (app. of J. Exton).

Hyde, Lord *see* **Villiers,** Hon. Thomas

Ibbetson, John *Extra Clerk* 8 Feb. 1755–16 Oct. 1759 (Adm. 3/63). *Clerk* 16 Oct. 1759–12 June 1782 (Adm. 3/67). *Deputy Secretary* 12 June 1782–13 Jan. 1783 (Adm. 6/22 p. 479). *Second Secretary* 31 Jan. 1783–2 March 1795 (Adm. 3/96). Res. 2 March 1795 (SPB, viii f. 12).

Innes, Alexander William *Third Class Clerk* 5 Nov. 1840–12 April 1854 (Adm. 12/368). *Second Class Clerk* 12 April 1854–7 Oct. 1867 (Adm. 47/23). *First Class Clerk* 7 Oct. 1867 (Adm. 12/784).

Innes, John William *Extra Clerk* 3 May 1804–28 Sept. 1807 (SPB, iii f. 14). *Junior Clerk* 28 Sept. 1807–5 Feb. 1816 (ibid. f. 11). *Second Class Clerk* 5 Feb. 1816–22 Jan. 1822 (SPB, xiii ff. 017–18). *First Class Clerk* 22 Jan. 1822–24 May 1847 (ibid). D. 24 May 1847 (Adm. 12/474).

Irish, Thomas *Extra Clerk* 6 May 1760–1 March 1764 (SPB, vii f. 7). Left office 1 March 1764 on app. as Purser of the *Tyger* (SPB, v f. 7).

Isham, Edmund (succ. as 6th Bart. 5 March 1737) *Advocate* 1 Oct. 1731–19 March 1742 (HCA 50/10 ff. 48–9). Res. 19 March 1742 (SPB, vi f. 19).

Ives, George *Board Room Messenger* 23 Sept. 1860–c. 29 July 1868 (Adm. 12/682). D. by 29 July 1868 (Adm. 12/810).

Jackson (*from* 3 Feb. 1797 **Duckett**), George (cr. Bart. 28 July 1791) *Deputy Secretary* 11 Nov. 1766–12 June 1782 (Adm. 6/20 p. 143). Res. 12 June 1782 (Adm. 3/95).

  First Clerk (*Marine Department*) 11 Nov. 1766–12 June 1782 (Adm. 2/1162 p. 202). Res. 12 June 1782 (Adm. 2/1174 p. 71).

  Judge Advocate of the Fleet 19 Feb. 1768–15 Dec. 1822 (Adm. 6/20 p. 195). D. 15 Dec. 1822 (SPB, xiv f. 15).

Jackson, John *Receiver of Droits* 24 Jan. 1774–30 Aug. 1782 (HCA 50/12 ff. 204–5). Dis. 30 Aug. 1782 (HCA 50/13 f. 78).

Jackson, John *Third Class Clerk* 17 Oct. 1834–4 May 1844 (Adm. 12/298). *Second Class Clerk* 4 May 1844–1 April 1857 (Adm. 12/426). *Acting First Class Clerk* 1 April 1857–7 April 1858 (Adm. 12/634). *First Class Clerk* 7 April 1858–2 March 1870 (Adm. 12/650). Ret. 2 March 1870 (Adm. 12/846).

Jackson, R. H. S. *Extra Clerk* 14 Jan. 1845–28 May 1846 (Adm. 12/442). Res. 28 May 1846 (Adm. 12/458).

James, Thomas *Third Class Clerk* 4 May 1837–5 Jan. 1849 (Adm. 12/332). *Acting Second Class Clerk* 5 Jan. 1849–4 June 1850 (Adm. 46/173 no. 143). *Second Class Clerk* 4 June 1850–10 March 1862 (Adm. 46/184 no. 544; Adm. 46/186 no. 1918). *First Class Clerk* 10 March 1862 (Adm. 12/714).

  Private Secretary to First Secretary (Ward) 14 June 1848–May 1849 (Adm. 12/490).

Jeafryson, Shuckburgh *Extra Clerk* 18 Oct. 1759–30 June 1764 (Adm. 3/67). Left office 30 June 1764 on app. as Purser of the *Soverano* (SPB, v f. 7).

Jefferson, Thomas *Watchman* 5 July 1732–20 March 1751 (SPB, iv f. 20). D. 20 March 1751 (SPB, vi f. 20).

Jeffreys, Marmaduke Darell *Temporary Clerk* 10 April 1862–24 July 1865 (Adm. 12/714). *Third Class* (*Second Section*) *Clerk* 24 July 1865–7 Oct. 1867 (Adm. 12/762). *Third Class* (*First Section*) *Clerk* 7 Oct. 1867 (Adm. 12/794).

Jenkins, Cloudesley *Deputy Judge Advocate of the Fleet* 8 Nov. 1689–7 Jan. 1692 (Sergison MS f. 174). Left office 7 Jan. 1692 (app. of S. Pett; AO 1/1719/133).

Jenkins, Leoline (ktd. 7 Jan. 1670) *Judge* 17 Nov. 1668–1 Sept. 1685 (HCA 50/4 ff. 11–15, 85–93; C 66/3150). D. 1 Sept. 1685 (HCA 50/4 f. 111).

Jenkinson, Charles *Commissioner* 11 Dec. 1766–8 March 1768.

Jennings, Sir John, kt. *Commissioner* 14 Oct. 1714–16 April 1717; 19 March 1718–1 June 1727.

Jervis, Swynfen *Counsel* 5 June 1747–14 Feb. 1757 (SPB, vi f. 19). Left office 14 Feb. 1757 (SPB, vii f. 21).

Jervis, Thomas *Counsel* 20 Feb. 1801–8 Feb. 1824 (SPB, ix f. 55). Left office 8 Feb. 1824 on app. as Second Justice, Chester (SPB, xiv f. 16; C 66/4268).

Jesse, John Heneage *Third Class Clerk* 26 Oct. 1829–28 March 1835 (SPB, xiv f. 8). *Second Class Clerk* 28 March 1835–4 June 1850 (Adm. 12/308). *First Class Clerk* 4 June 1850–3 April 1867 (Adm. 46/184 no. 544; Adm. 46/186 no. 1918). Ret. 3 April 1867 (Adm. 12/794).

Jobber, Thomas *Solicitor* 3 Dec. 1718–29 March 1733 (SPB, iv f. 19; SPB, vi f. 19; HCA 50/8 f. 220: HCA 50/9 f. 118). D. 29 March 1733 (SPB, vi f. 19).

Johnston *see* **Clack**, Christian

Johnstone Hope, George *Commissioner* 25 March 1812–18 May 1813; 23 Oct. 1813–2 April 1818.

Johnstone Hope, William (ktd. 1815) *Commissioner* 6 April 1807–30 March 1809; 13 March 1820–2 May 1827. *Member of Council* 2 May 1827–12 March 1828.

Jolliffe, William *Commissioner* 10 April–31 Dec. 1783.

Jones, Charles *Solicitor* 7 Jan. 1828–27 Sept. 1843 (SPB, xiv f. 16). D. 27 Sept. 1843 (*Gent. Mag.* (1843), cxiii(2), 556).

Jones, Evan *Marshal* 1 June 1850 (HCA 50/22 ff. 238–9).

Jones, Richard *Extra Clerk* 21 Dec. 1745–9 Dec. 1748 (Adm. 3/52). Left office 9 Dec. 1748 (SPB, vi f. 7).

Jones, Robert Molesworth *Extra Clerk* 12 Nov. 1842–10 May 1844 (Adm. 12/395). *Third Class Clerk* 10 May 1844–31 March 1855 (Adm. 46/121 no. 1651). *Third Class (First Section) Clerk* 31 March 1855–18 March 1856 (Adm. 12/602; *Navy Lists*). Left office 18 March 1856 on app. as Storekeeper and Agent Victualler, Trincomalee (Adm. 47/25).

Joynes, William *Marshal* 5 July 1660–c. 17 Oct. 1689 (HCA 50/3 ff. 36–7; HCA 50/5 ff. 71–2; HCA 50/6 f. 9). D. by 17 Oct. 1689 (app. of Cheeke).

Keene, Whitshed *Commissioner* 10 April–31 Dec. 1783.

Keltie, Robert *Extra Clerk* 19 June 1795–28 Sept. 1797 (SPB, viii f. 15). Discharged 28 Sept. 1797 (SPB, ix f. 11).

Kempe, Charles Nicholas *Third Class Clerk* 30 Dec. 1853–31 March 1855 (Adm. 12/570). *Third Class (Second Section) Clerk* 31 March 1855–15 March 1856 (Adm. 12/602; *Navy Lists*). *Acting Third Class (First Section) Clerk* 15 March 1856–20 Dec. 1856/20 March 1857 (Adm. 12/618). *Third Class (First Section) Clerk* app. between 20 Dec. 1856 and 20 March 1857 (*Navy Lists*). *Acting Second Class Clerk* 18 July 1861–20 Dec. 1861/20 March 1862 (Adm. 12/698). *Second Class Clerk* app. between 20 Dec. 1861 and 20 March 1862 (*Navy Lists*). *First Class Clerk* 31 March 1870 (Adm. 12/846).

    Private Secretary to First Secretary (Osborne) 13 March 1857–March 1858 (Adm. 12/634); (Paget, Baring, Gordon Lennox) 30 June 1859–Dec. 1868 (Adm. 12/666; Adm. 12/778, 30 April and 17 July 1868).

Kempe, Thomas *Deputy Judge Advocate of the Fleet* 20 June 1740–15 June 1743 (Adm. 6/15 p. 301). *Judge Advocate of the Fleet* 15 June 1743–11 Nov. 1744 (Adm. 6/16 pp. 191–2). D. 11 Nov. 1744 (SPB, iv f. 20).

Kendall, James *Commissioner* 24 Feb. 1696–31 May 1699.

Kennedy, Charles Stewart *Extra Clerk* 29 May 1847–1 Oct. 1850 (Adm. 12/474). *Third Class Clerk* 1 Oct. 1850–31 March 1855 (Adm. 12/522). *Third Class (First Section) Clerk* 31 March 1855–15 June 1859 (Adm. 12/602; *Navy Lists*). *Second Class Clerk* 15 June 1859–31 March 1870 (Adm. 12/666). *First Class Clerk* 31 March 1870 (Adm. 12/846).

Kensington, William (Edwardes) 2nd Lord *Commissioner* 10 Feb. 1806–6 April 1807.

Keppel, Hon. Augustus (cr. Viscount **Keppel** 22 April 1782) *Commissioner* 31 July 1765–11 Dec. 1766. *First Lord* 1 April 1782–30 Jan. 1783; 10 April–31 Dec. 1783.

Kettlewell, John *Watchman* 7 April 1720–28 June 1742 (SPB, i f. 20). Left office 28 June 1742 on app. as Cook Mate, Greenwich Hospital (SPB, v f. 20).

Killigrew, Henry *Commissioner* 15 April 1693–2 May 1694.

Killingworth, William *Counsel* 23 April 1686–14 Sept. 1696 (Sergison MS f. 151). Left office 14 Sept. 1696 (app. of Lechmere; AO 1/1721/138).

King, Thomas *Extra Clerk* 20 March 1782–8 May 1787 (Adm. 3/94). Discharged 8 May 1787 (SPB, viii f. 14); reapp. 9 Oct. 1787 (Adm. 3/103). Res. 5 March 1789 (SPB, viii f. 15).

Kirkpatrick, James *Clerk* 11 Feb. 1717–10 Oct. 1721 (Adm. 2/194 p. 211). Left office 10 Oct. 1721 on app. as Agent Victualler, Dover (Adm. 2/195 p. 384).

Kitchen, William *Gardener* 11 Aug. 1812–1 April 1827 (SPB, xii ff. 69–70). D. 1 April 1827 (SPB, xiv f. 12).

Kite, Thomas *Extra Clerk* 8 April 1777–13 March 1790 (SPB, v f. 7). *Clerk* 13 March 1790–7 Feb. 1800 (Adm. 3/107; SPB, viii f. 13). *Senior Clerk* 7 Feb. 1800–28 Sept. 1807 (SPB, ix f. 81). *Chief Clerk* 28 Sept. 1807–30 June 1813 (SPB, iii f. 8). Ret. 30 June 1813 (SPB, xii f. 12).

Klyne, James *Messenger* 26 Nov. 1799–24 Sept. 1806 (SPB, ix f. 58). *Board Room Messenger* 24 Sept. 1806–5 Jan. 1816 (SPB, iii f. 18). Ret. 5 Jan. 1816 (SPB, xii ff. 63–4).

Knox, Arthur Edward Ellis *Temporary Clerk* 29 Nov. 1861–15 July 1862 (Adm. 12/698). *Third Class (Second Section) Clerk* 15 July 1862–28 Sept. 1866 (Adm. 12/714). *Acting Third Class (First Section) Clerk* 28 Sept.–9 Oct. 1866 (Adm. 12/778). *Third Class (First Section) Clerk* 9 Oct. 1866 (ibid.).

Labouchere, Henry *Civil Lord* 8 June 1832–23 Dec. 1834.

Lambert, A. *Temporary Clerk* app. 17 May 1855 (Adm. 12/602). No further occ.

Lambert, George Thomas *Third Class (Second Section) Clerk* 22 Dec. 1866 (Adm. 12/778).

Laplume *see* **Fetter**

Larkin, George *Deputy Judge Advocate of the Fleet* 18 Aug. 1694–21 Oct. 1697 (SPB, i f. 27). Left office 21 Oct. 1697 (app. of Fawler).

Latimer, Viscount *see* **Osborne**, Viscount

Lauderdale, John (Maitland) 1st Duke of *Commissioner* 9 July 1673–14 May 1679.

Law, Hon. Henry Spencer *Private Secretary to First Lord* (Ellenborough) 16 Jan.–July 1846 (Adm. 12/458).

Lawes, Edward *Third Class Clerk* 1 Nov. 1827–26 Oct. 1829 (SPB, xiv f. 8). Res. 26 Oct. 1829 (ibid.).

Lawes, Thomas *Extra Clerk* 31 Aug. 1744–9 Nov. 1746 (SPB, vi f. 7). D. 9 Nov. 1746 (ibid.).

Lawrence,— *Clerk* occ. as Clerk to Pepys Nov. 1678 (MS Rawlinson A 181 ff. 25–26).

Leader, Robert *Messenger (Marine Pay Department)* 3 July 1809–10 May 1813 (SPB, xii ff. 77–8). Left office 10 May 1813 (ibid.).

Leake, Sir John, kt. *Member of Council* 19 June–28 Oct. 1708. *Commissioner* 8 Nov. 1709–14 Oct. 1714.

Lechmere, Thomas *Counsel* 14 Sept. 1696–18 Feb. 1703 (Adm. 6/4 p. 25). Left office 18 Feb. 1703 (app. of Ettrick; AO 1/1724/145).

Lee, George *Commissioner* 19 March 1742–27 Dec. 1744.

Lee, Sir Thomas, 1st Bart. *Commissioner* 14 May 1679–19 Feb. 1681; 8 March 1689–24 Feb. 1691. D. 24 Feb. 1691.

Leeke, Sir Henry John, kt. *Third Naval Lord* 23 April–28 June 1859.

Lefevre *see* **Shaw Lefevre**

Legatt, John *Watchman* 19 Aug. 1801–25 March 1825 (SPB, iii f. 19). Res. 25 March 1825 (SPB, xiv f. 11).

Legatt, Richard *Watchman* app. 30 March 1825 (SPB, xiv f. 11); still in office 1832 (ibid.). No further occ.

Legge, Hon. Heneage *Counsel* 9 Feb. 1743–4 June 1747 (SPB, vi f. 19). Left office 4 June 1747 on app. as Baron of Exchequer (ibid.; C 66/3622).

Legge, Hon. Henry *Commissioner* 25 April 1745–27 June 1746.

Lemon, John *Commissioner* 17 Jan.–15 May 1804.

Lennox *see* **Gordon Lennox**

Leveson Gower, Hon. John *Commissioner* 30 Jan.–10 April 1783; 31 Dec. 1783–12 Aug. 1789.

Lewis,— *Clerk* occ. as Clerk to Pepys Nov. 1678 (MS Rawlinson A 181 ff. 25–6).

Lilburn, George *Extra Messenger* 26 April–24 Sept. 1806 (SPB, iii f. 17). *Board Room Messenger* 24 Sept. 1806–25 March 1828 (ibid.). Left office 25 March 1828 on app. as Head Messenger, Navy Board (SPB, xiv f. 10). *Head Messenger* 26 July–10 Aug. 1841 (Adm. 12/383). Left office 10 Aug. 1841 (ibid.).

Lindsay, Hon. Hugh *Marshal* 14 March 1815–23 April 1844 (HCA 50/16 f. 68; HCA 50/18 f. 144; HCA 50/20 f. 224). D. 23 April 1844 (Burke, *Peerage*, under Crawford, Earl of).

Lindsay, Sir John, kt. *Commissioner* 10 April–31 Dec. 1783.

Lindsey, Anne *Necessary Woman* pd. from 2 Sept. 1706 by order 3 Sept. 1706 (SPB, i f. 21). D. 12 April 1720 (ibid.).

Lindsey, John *Watchman* pd. from 30 Sept. 1699 by order 28 Dec. 1699 (SPB, i f. 20). D. 5 April 1720 (ibid.).

Lindsey, Mary *Necessary Woman* 27 April 1720–c. 17 Aug. 1722 (SPB, i f. 21). D. by 17 Aug. 1722 (Adm. 2/195 p. 517).

Lisburne, Wilmot (Vaughan) 4th Viscount (cr. Earl of **Lisburne** 18 July 1776) *Commissioner* 28 Feb. 1770–1 April 1782.

Littleton, Fisher *Advocate* 7 Sept. 1693–16 March 1697 (HCA 50/6 ff. 108–9). Left office 16 March 1697 (app. of Newton).

Littleton, Sir Thomas, 2nd Bart. *Commissioner* 19 Feb.–12 April 1681. D. 12 April 1681.

Lloyd, John *Extra Clerk* 21 Dec. 1745–30 April 1749 (Adm. 3/52). Discharged 30 April 1749 (SPB, vi f. 7).

Lloyd, Richard (ktd. 16 Jan. 1677) *Advocate* 19 May 1674–13 Sept. 1685 (HCA 50/4 f. 113; HCA 50/5 f. 56). *Judge* 1 Oct. 1685–28 June 1686 (ibid. ff. 112–16; C 66/3269). D. 28 June 1686 (E. Hatton, *New View of London* (London 1708), i, 156).

Locker, Frederick *Extra Clerk* 8 Oct.–12 Nov. 1842 (Adm. 12/395). *Third Class Clerk* 12 Nov. 1842–31 March 1855 (ibid.). *Third Class (First Section) Clerk* 31 March 1855–14 Oct. 1858 (Adm. 12/602; *Navy Lists*). *Second Class Clerk* 14 Oct. 1858–25 Sept. 1862 (Adm. 12/650). Ret. 25 Sept. 1862 (Adm. 12/714).

Lomas, Thomas *Extra Clerk* 31 Aug. 1841–14 Jan. 1845 (Adm. 12/383). Left office 14 Jan. 1845 on app. as Clerk, Naval Departments, Somerset House (Adm. 12/442).

Losack, Richard *Extra Clerk* 13 March–31 Dec. 1790 (Adm. 3/107). Res. 31 Dec. 1790 (SPB, viii f. 14).

Lovaine, Algernon George (Percy) *styled* Lord *Civil Lord* 8 March 1858–11 March 1859.

Lowry Corry, Hon. Henry Thomas *Civil Lord* 8 Sept. 1841–12 Feb. 1845. *First Secretary* 13 Feb. 1845–13 July 1846 (Adm. 12/442); 9 March 1858–30 June 1859 (Adm. 12/650). *First Lord* 8 March 1867–18 Dec. 1868.

Lowther, Sir John, 2nd Bart. *Commissioner* 8 March 1689–24 Feb. 1696.

Lowther, William (Lowther) *styled* Viscount *Commissioner* 24 Nov. 1809–3 July 1810.

Lushington, Stephen *Judge* 17 Oct. 1838–3 July 1867 (HCA 50/21 ff. 20–1; C 66/4548). Surrendered office 3 July 1867 (HCA 50/24 p. 394).

Lushington, Vernon *Second Secretary* 29 June 1869 (Adm. 12/828).

Lygon, Hon. Frederick *Civil Lord* 11 March–28 June 1859.

Lynn, Francis *Clerk* pd. from 26 Dec. 1702 by order 17 April 1703 (SPB, i f. 42). Left office 2 Feb. 1706 on app. as Secretary, Commissioners of Sick and Wounded (ibid.; *CTB*, xxix, 434).

Lyttelton, Sir Thomas, 4th Bart. *Commissioner* 1 June 1727–5 May 1741.

McCann, Thomas *Temporary Clerk* app. 17 May 1855 (Adm. 12/602). No further occ.

Macgregor, Alpin *Third Class (Second Section) Clerk* 22 Dec. 1866 (Adm. 12/778).

Macgregor, Evan *Temporary Clerk* 13 Aug. 1860–16 Jan. 1862 (Adm. 12/682). *Third Class (Second Section) Clerk* 16 Jan. 1862–20 Sept./20 Dec. 1865 (Adm. 12/714). *Acting Third Class (First Section) Clerk* app. between 20 Sept. and 20 Dec. 1865 (*Navy Lists*). *Third Class (First Section) Clerk* 8 Feb. 1866–31 March 1870 (Adm. 12/778). *Second Class Clerk* 31 March 1870 (Adm. 12/846).

Madden, James *Extra Clerk (Marine Department)* 17 July 1755–5 May 1760 (Adm. 2/1152 pp. 134–5). *Second Clerk (Marine Department)* 5 May 1760–30 June 1782 (Adm. 2/1156 p. 428). *First Clerk (Marine Department)* 30 June 1782–6 Aug. 1789 (Adm. 2/1174 p. 172). Dis. 6 Aug. 1789 (Adm. 2/1179 pp. 499–510).

    First Clerk (Marine Pay Department) 1755–c. 6 Aug. 1789 (*3rd Rept. on Fees*, 117). Probably dis. c. 6 Aug. 1789 (Adm. 2/1179 pp. 499–510).

Malleson, Edward *Extra Clerk* 4 Feb. 1847–4 June 1850 (Adm. 12/474). *Third Class Clerk* 4 June–1 Oct. 1850 (Adm. 46/184 no. 544; Adm. 46/186 no. 1918). Res. 1 Oct. 1850 (Adm. 12/522).

Malpas, George (Cholmondeley) *styled* Viscount *Commissioner* 2 Aug. 1727–19 May 1729.

Man, John *Watchman* 8 April 1777–4 July 1778 (SPB, v f. 27). *Messenger* 4 July 1778–23 June 1788 (ibid.). D. 23 June 1788 (SPB, viii f. 44).

Man, Robert *Commissioner* 23 April 1779–22 Sept. 1780.

Man, Robert *Commissioner* 10 Sept. 1798–19 Feb. 1801.

Markham, John *Commissioner* 19 Feb. 1801–15 May 1804; 10 Feb. 1806–6 April 1807.

Marratt, Richard *Head Messenger* pd. from 24 June 1682 to 24 June 1698 (AO 1/1716/122; SPB, i f. 20). Discharged 24 June 1698 by order 20 Sept. 1698 (SPB, i f. 20).

Marriott, Sir James, kt. *Judge* 12 Oct. 1778–26 Oct. 1798 (HCA 50/12 ff. 212–16; C 66/3772). Left office 26 Oct. 1798 (app. of W. Scott).

Marsden, William *Second Secretary* 3 March 1795–21 Jan. 1804 (SPB, viii f. 12). *First Secretary* 21 Jan. 1804–24 June 1807 (SPB, iii f. 4). Ret. 24 June 1807 (ibid.).

Marsh, Robert *Extra Clerk* 9 Oct. 1787–31 July 1788 (Adm. 3/103). Res. 31 July 1788 (SPB, viii f. 15).

Martin, Richard *Extra Clerk* 25 Jan. 1799–12 Feb. 1801 (SPB, ix f. 11). *Junior Clerk* 12 Feb. 1801–10 April 1806 (ibid. f. 84). D. 10 April 1806 (SPB, iii f. 10).

Martin, William Fanshawe *First Naval Lord* 8 March 1858–28 June 1859.

Mason, Edmund *Deputy Judge Advocate of the Fleet* 12 Nov. 1744–2 March 1745 (Adm. 6/16 pp. 383–4). Left office 2 March 1745 (app. of G. Atkins).

Mason, Gregory *Watchman* pd. from 24 June 1694 by order 26 Sept. 1694 (SPB, ii ff. 50–1). Discharged 24 June 1698 by order 1 Oct. 1698 (SPB, i f. 20).

Maude, Charles John *Third Class (Second Section) Clerk* 10 Dec. 1867 (Adm. 12/794).

Maxwell, Basil *Extra Clerk* 14 Feb. 1782–7 Oct. 1789 (Adm. 3/94). *Second Clerk (Marine Department)* 7 Oct. 1789–c. 3 Aug. 1796 (Adm. 2/1180 pp. 65–6). D. by 3 Aug. 1796 (Adm. 2/1185 p. 493).

Maxwell, Robert *Extra Clerk* 12 June 1780–10 April 1800 (Adm. 3/90). D. 10 April 1800 (SPB, ix f. 10).
  Translator 12 Feb. 1784–8 May 1787 (Adm. 3/99). *Translator of Spanish Papers* 8 May 1787–18 June 1788 (Adm. 3/103; Adm. 17/7). *Translator* 18 June 1788–10 April 1800 (Adm. 3/104).

Mears, Henry *Watchman* 11 March 1720–5 July 1732 (Adm. 2/195 p. 176). *Porter* 5 July 1732–25 May 1756 (SPB, iv f. 20). D. 25 May 1756 (SPB, v f. 22).

Melgund, William Hugh (Elliot Murray Kynynmound) *styled* Viscount *Acting Private Secretary to First Lord* (Minto) occ. from 20 March 1840 to 20 March 1841 (*Navy Lists*).

Melmerby, Thomas *Clerk* pd. from 2 May 1711 by order 16 May 1711 (SPB, i f. 43). Discharged 24 June 1713 by order 27 June 1713 (ibid.).

Melville, Henry (Dundas) 1st Viscount *First Lord* 15 May 1804–2 May 1805.

Melville, Robert (Saunders Dundas) 2nd Viscount *First Lord* 25 March 1812–2 May 1827; 19 Sept. 1828–25 Nov. 1830.

Mends, Matthew Bowen *Extra Clerk* 15 April 1806–15 March 1811 (SPB, iii f. 14). *Junior Clerk* 15 March 1811–5 Feb. 1816 (SPB, xii ff. 25–6). *Second Class Clerk* 5 Feb. 1816–21 June 1821 (SPB, xiii ff. 19–20). Left office 21 June 1821 on app. as Naval Officer, Quebec (ibid.).

Meredith, Sir William, 3rd Bart. *Commissioner* 31 July 1765–11 Dec. 1766.

Meres, Sir Thomas, kt. *Commissioner* 14 May 1679–19 May 1684.

Merryam, John *Watchman* 26 Dec. 1768–15 July 1791 (SPB, v f. 27). D. 15 July 1791 (SPB, viii f. 44).

Metcalf, James *Board Room Messenger* 24 Jan.–25 March 1820 (SPB, xiii ff. 027–8). App. annulled 25 March 1820 (ibid.).

Methuen, Paul *Commissioner* 8 Nov. 1709–20 Dec. 1710.

Middleton, Alexander *Third Class Clerk* 29 June 1830–5 April 1837 (SPB, xiv f. 8). *Second Class Clerk* 5 April 1837–24 July 1846 (Adm. 12/332). D. 24 July 1846 (*Gent. Mag.* (1846), cxix(2), 328).

Middleton, Sir Charles, 1st Bart. (cr. Lord **Barham** 1 May 1805) *Commissioner* 12 May 1794–20 Nov. 1795. *First Lord* 2 May 1805–10 Feb. 1806.

Midlane, Maurice Wemyss *Third Class Clerk* 30 Sept. 1833–7 Nov. 1842 (Adm. 12/

290). *Second Class Clerk* 7 Nov. 1842–22 Feb. 1855 (Adm. 12/395). *First Class Clerk* 22 Feb. 1855–18 Feb. 1858 (Adm. 12/602). Ret. 18 Feb. 1858 (Adm. 12/634, 21 March, 8 and 16 Dec. 1857; Adm. 12/650, 18 Feb. 1858).

Miller, John *Supernumerary Clerk* pd. from 26 Dec. 1813 to 24 June 1814 (SPB, xii ff. 45–6). *Extra Clerk* 30 July 1814–5 Feb. 1816 (ibid. ff. 41–2). *Third Class Clerk* 5 Feb. 1816–2 June 1826 (SPB, xiii ff. 021–2). *Second Class Clerk* 2 June 1826–10 Feb. 1831 (SPB, xiv f. 6). Left office 10 Feb. 1831 on app. as Timber and Store Receiver, Sheerness (ibid.).

Miller, John Vaughan *Third Class (Second Section) Clerk* 23 Nov. 1858–26 April 1865 (Adm. 12/650). *Acting Third Class (First Section) Clerk* 26 April 1865–20 June/ 20 Sept. 1865 (Adm. 12/762). *Third Class (First Section) Clerk* app. between 20 June and 20 Sept. 1865 (*Navy Lists*). *Second Class Clerk* 21 Oct. 1867 (Adm. 12/ 794).
Private Secretary to Second Secretary (Romaine) app. between 20 Sept. and 20 Dec. 1862 (*Navy Lists*). Left office 17 Aug. 1865 (Adm. 12/762).

Miller, William *Third Class Clerk* 15 April 1820–19 Feb. 1824 (SPB, xiii ff. 021–2). D. 19 Feb. 1824 (SPB, xiv f. 7).

Miller, William Charles *Extra Clerk* 28 Oct. 1841–22 July 1846 (Adm. 12/383). *Third Class Clerk* 22 July 1846–31 March 1855 (Adm. 12/458). *Third Class (First Section) Clerk* 31 March 1855–8 Aug. 1868 (Adm. 12/602; *Navy Lists*). D. 8 Aug. 1868 (Adm. 12/810).

Millman, William *Watchman* 4 July 1778–10 Feb. 1781 (SPB, v f. 27). *Head Messenger* 10 Feb. 1781–24 Jan. 1820 (ibid. f. 26). Ret. 24 Jan. 1820 (SPB, xiii ff. 027–8).

Milne, Alexander (ktd. 20 Dec. 1858) *Fourth Naval Lord* 23 Dec. 1847–2 March 1852. *Fifth Naval Lord* 2 March 1852–5 Jan. 1853. *Fourth Naval Lord* 5 Jan. 1853–24 Nov. 1857. *Third Naval Lord* 24 Nov. 1857–23 April 1859. *Fourth Naval Lord* 23 April–28 June 1859. *First Naval Lord* 13 July 1866–18 Dec. 1868.

Milnes, John *Clerk* 29 July 1725–2 May 1751 (Adm. 3/35). *Chief Clerk* 2 May 1751–15 June 1756 (Adm. 3/62). *Deputy Secretary* 15 June 1756–16 Oct. 1759 (Adm. 3/64). Ret. 16 Oct. 1759 (Adm. 3/67).

Minto, Gilbert (Elliot Murray Kynynmound) 2nd Earl of *First Lord* 19 Sept. 1835–8 Sept. 1841.

Mitchell, Sir David, kt. *Commissioner* 31 May 1699–26 Jan. 1702. *Member of Council* 22 May 1702–19 April 1708.

Molyneux, Samuel *Commissioner* 2 Aug. 1727–13 April 1728. D. 13 April 1728 (SPB, iv f. 1).

Monmouth, James (Scott) 1st Duke of *Commissioner* 9 July 1673–14 May 1679.

Montgomery, Alfred *Third Class Clerk* 30 May–4 Sept. 1833 (Adm. 12/290). Res. 4 Sept. 1833 (ibid.).

Montgomery, William Vaughan *Third Class Clerk* 5 June 1824–29 Aug. 1827 (SPB, xiv f. 7). D. 29 Aug. 1827 (ibid.).

Moore, Sir Graham, kt. *Commissioner* 24 May 1816–13 March 1820.

Moore, John *Private Secretary to First Lord* (Somerset) 4 July 1859–24 Nov. 1862 (Adm. 12/666). Res. 24 Nov. 1862 (Adm. 12/714).

Moorsom, Robert *Private Secretary to First Lord* (Mulgrave) 29 June 1807–30 March 1809 (SPB, iii f. 5). *Commissioner* 30 March 1809–3 July 1810.

More O'Ferrall, Richard *First Secretary* 4 Oct. 1839–9 June 1841 (Adm. 12/356). Left office 9 June 1841 on app. as Secretary, Treasury (T 29/438 p. 181).

Moreton, Hon. Wyndham Percy *Third Class Clerk* 16 Aug. 1854–31 March 1855 (Adm. 12/586). *Third Class (Second Section) Clerk* 31 March 1855–22 Oct. 1857 (Adm. 12/602; *Navy Lists*). Res. 22 Oct. 1857 (Adm. 12/634).

Morris, John *Porter* 2 May 1804–1 May 1806 (SPB, iii f. 18). D. 1 May 1806 (ibid.).

Morrison, James *Extra Clerk* 8 Dec. 1764–24 June 1766 (Adm. 3/72). Left office 24 June 1766 on app. as Clerk of Cutting House, Victualling Office (SPB, v f. 7).

Moss, Henry *Extra Clerk* 15 June 1804–14 July 1805 (SPB, iii f. 14). Dis. 14 July 1805 (ibid.).

Moss, Samuel *Extra Clerk* 25 April 1793–3 Aug. 1796 (Adm. 3/110). *Second Clerk (Marine Department)* 3 Aug. 1796–5 Sept. 1809 (Adm. 2/1185 p. 493). Ret. 5 Sept. 1809 (SPB, xii ff. 59–60).

Moss, Samuel *Third Class Clerk (Marine Pay Department)* 20 April–30 June 1831 (SPB, xiv f. 19). Discharged 30 June 1831 (ibid.).

Mostyn, Savage *Commissioner* 6 April–2 July 1757.

Mountain, William John *Extra Clerk* 28 Sept. 1807–5 Feb. 1816 (SPB, iii f. 14). *Third Class Clerk* 5 Feb. 1816–5 June 1824 (SPB, xiii ff. 021–2). *Second Class Clerk* 5 June 1824–25 May 1833 (SPB, xiv f. 6). *First Class Clerk* 25 May 1833–4 Oct. 1847 (Adm. 12/290). Ret. 4 Oct. 1847 (Adm. 12/474).
    Private Secretary to First Secretary (Croker) 22 Jan. 1822–2 June 1826 (SPB, xiii ff. 021–2).

Mulgrave, Constantine John (Phipps) 2nd Lord *Commissioner* 15 Dec. 1777–1 April 1782.

Mulgrave, Henry (Phipps) 3rd Lord *First Lord* 6 April 1807–4 May 1810.

Munday, Joseph *Watchman* 11 Jan. 1800–c. 25 June 1801 (SPB, ix f. 58). D. by 25 June 1801 (SPB, iii f. 19).

Murray, Herbert Harley *Private Secretary to First Lord* (Pakington) 13 March 1858–June 1859 (Adm. 12/650).

Murray, James *Supernumerary Clerk* pd. from 30 Sept. to 25 Dec. 1812 (SPB, xii ff. 45–6).

Neale *see* **Burrard Neale** *and* **Vansittart Neale**

Nepean, Evan (cr. Bart. 16 July 1802) *First Secretary* 3 March 1795–20 Jan. 1804 (SPB, viii f. 12). Res. 20 Jan. 1804 on app. as Chief Secretary, Ireland (SPB, iii f. 4; Adm. 12/109.) *Commissioner* 13 Sept. 1804–10 Feb. 1806.

Nesbitt, William *Extra Clerk* 25 April 1807–30 July 1814 (SPB, iii f. 14). *Junior Clerk* 30 July 1814–1814 (SPB, xii ff. 25–6). D. 1814 (ibid.).

Newbegin, James *Porter* 2 May 1806–4 Nov. 1817 (SPB, iii f. 18). Ret. 4 Nov. 1817 (SPB, xii ff. 65–6).

Newson, John *Clerk* pd. from 30 May 1708 by order 11 June 1708 (SPB, i f. 43). Discharged 24 June 1713 by order 27 June 1713 (ibid.); reapp. 4 Sept. 1713 (ibid.). Discharged 16 Jan. 1715 (ibid.).

Newton, Sir Henry, kt. *Advocate* 16 March 1697–28 Oct. 1714 (HCA 50/6 f. 156; HCA 50/7 ff. 84, 108; HCA 50/8 ff. 23, 81–2, 106–7). *Judge* 1 Dec. 1714–29 July 1715 (ibid. ff. 139–43; C 66/3499). D. 29 July 1715 (SPB, i f. 27).

Nicholas, George *Clerk* pd. from 26 Dec. 1704 by order 20 March 1705 (AO 1/1725/147). Discharged 18 Jan. 1706 by order 21 Jan. 1706 (SPB, i f. 43; AO 1/1726/148).

Nicholas, Henden *Extra Clerk* 26 Aug.–28 Sept. 1807 (SPB, iii f. 14). App. cancelled 28 Sept. 1807 (ibid.).

Nicholl, Sir John, kt. *Judge* 30 May 1833–26 Aug. 1838 (HCA 50/20 ff. 1–7; C 66/4420). D. 26 Aug. 1838 (*Gent. Mag.* (1838), cviii(2), 546).

Nicholls, Thomas *Messenger* 17 Sept. 1714–3 Nov. 1715 (SPB, i f. 43). Discharged 3 Nov. 1715 (ibid.).

Noble, Thomas *Extra Clerk* 23 Feb. 1748–30 April 1749 (SPB, vi f. 7). Discharged 30 April 1749 (ibid.).

Noel, James Gambier *Extra Clerk* 1 May 1852–13 April 1854 (Adm. 12/554). *Third Class Clerk* 13 April 1854–31 March 1855 (Adm. 12/586). *Third Class (Second Section) Clerk* 31 March 1855–4 Sept. 1858 (Adm. 12/602; *Navy Lists*). *Third Class (First Section) Clerk* 4 Sept. 1858–20 Sept./20 Dec. 1862 (Adm. 12/650). *Acting Second Class Clerk* app. between 20 Sept. and 20 Dec. 1862 (*Navy Lists*). *Second Class Clerk* 21 Nov. 1865 (Adm. 12/762).

Norris, Sir John, kt. *Commissioner* 19 March 1718–13 May 1730.

Northumberland, Algernon (Percy) 4th Duke of *First Lord* 2 March 1852–5 Jan. 1853.

Nottingham, Earl of *see* **Finch**, Hon. Daniel

Nutland, John *Porter* 1 April 1820–c. 3 Feb. 1837 (SPB, xiii ff. 029–30). D. by 3 Feb. 1837 (Adm. 12/332).

Nye, James Moses *Extra Messenger* 28 Jan. 1804–24 Sept. 1806 (SPB, iii f. 17). *Board Room Messenger* 24 Sept. 1806–24 Jan. 1820 (ibid. f. 18). *Head Messenger* 24 Jan. 1820–16 July 1841 (SPB, xiii f. 027). Ret. 16 July 1841 (Adm. 12/383).

Oakes, Leonard *Clerk* pd. from 29 Sept. 1704 (AO 1/1725/147; SPB i f. 43). Left, office 21 Feb. 1711 on app. as Muster Master of the Fleet (SPB, i f. 42; Adm. 6/11 f. 110).

Oakes, Thomas *Extra Clerk* app. 13 June 1746 (Adm. 3/54). Pd. to 29 Sept. 1748 (AO 1/1750/197). Left office 12 Feb. (?) 1749 on app. as Agent to French Prisoners at Portsmouth (SPB, vi f. 7).

O'Brien, Lord Edward *Private Secretary to First Lord* (Mulgrave) 19 April 1809–May 1810 (SPB, xii f. 10).

O'Brien, Henry Higgins Donatus *Private Secretary to First Lord* (Graham) 6 Jan. 1853–March 1855 (Adm. 12/570).

O'Brien Stafford, Stafford Augustus *First Secretary* 3 March 1852–6 Jan. 1853 (Adm. 12/554).

O'Ferrall *see* **More O'Ferrall**

Oldner, John *Clerk* pd. from 25 Aug. 1702 by order 25 Dec. 1702 (SPB, i f. 6). Left office 3 Sept. 1713 on app. as Clerk of Cheque, Sheerness (ibid. f. 42; Adm. 6/11 f. 271).

Oldys, William *Advocate* 4 July 1686–7 Sept. 1693 (HCA 50/5 ff. 149–50; HCA 50/6 f. 4). Left office 7 Sept. 1693 (app. of F. Littleton).

Onslow, Sir Richard, 2nd Bart. *Commissioner* 5 June 1690–15 April 1693.

O'Reilly, Charles William *Third Class Clerk* 25 April 1838–30 Dec. 1853 (Adm. 12/344). *Second Class Clerk* 30 Dec. 1853–18 Oct. 1854 (Adm. 12/570). D. 18 Oct. 1854 (death certificate; Adm. 12/586, 19 Oct. 1854).
    Private Secretary to First Secretary (Ward) 13 July 1846–14 June 1848 (Adm. 12/458).

Orford, Earl of *see* **Russell**, Edward

Ormond, James (Butler) 1st Duke of *Commissioner* 9 July 1673–14 May 1679.

Osborn, John (succ. as 5th Bart. 29 June 1818) *Commissioner* 5 Oct. 1812–16 Feb. 1824.

Osborn, Robert *Clerk* 7 June 1716–18 June 1743 (Adm. 2/194 p. 8). *Chief Clerk* 18 June 1743–17 Nov. 1744 (Adm. 3/47; SPB, vi f. 6). *Deputy Secretary* 17 Nov. 1744–1 Aug. 1746 (Adm. 6/16 p. 388). Left office 1 Aug. 1746 on app. as Clerk of Acts, Navy Board (Adm. 3/55).

Osborne, Francis George Godolphin (*styled* Hon. 15 Feb. 1850) *Extra Clerk* 15 March 1848–1 May 1852 (Adm. 12/490). Res. 1 May 1852 (Adm. 12/554).

Osborne, Ralph Bernal *First Secretary* 6 Jan. 1853–9 March 1858 (Adm. 12/570).

Osborne, Thomas (Osborne) 1st Viscount (cr. Viscount **Latimer** 15 Aug. 1673; Earl of **Danby** 27 June 1674) *Commissioner* 9 July 1673–14 May 1679.

Ossory, Thomas (Butler) *styled* Earl of *Commissioner* 26 Sept. 1677–14 May 1679.

Owen, Sir Edward William Campbell Rich, kt. *Member of Council* 12 March–19 Sept. 1828.

Owen, Peter *Messenger* pd. from 25 Dec. 1709 by order 8 April 1710 (SPB, i f. 20). D. 30 May 1716 (ibid.).

Oxenden, Sir George, 5th Bart. *Commissioner* 3 June 1725–2 Aug. 1727.

Pack, Joel *Clerk* pd. from 28 Feb. 1709 by order 24 March 1709 (SPB, i f. 43). Discharged 24 June 1713 by order 27 June 1713 (ibid.).

Paget, Lord Clarence Edward *First Secretary* 30 June 1859–30 April 1866 (Adm. 12/666).

Paget, Hon. Henry *Member of Council* 30 April 1704–28 Oct. 1708.

Pakington, John Slaney *Private Secretary to First Lord* (Sir J. S. Pakington) 16 July 1866–March 1867 (Adm. 12/778).

Pakington, Sir John Somerset, 1st Bart. *First Lord* 8 March 1858–28 June 1859; 13 July 1866–8 March 1867.

Palairet, Elias John *Extra Clerk* 17 Nov. 1757–28 Feb. 1759 (SPB, vii f. 7). Left office 28 Feb. 1759 (ibid.).

Palliser, Sir Hugh, 1st Bart. *Commissioner* 12 April 1775–23 April 1779.

Palmerston, Henry (Temple) 2nd Viscount *Commissioner* 15 Sept. 1766–15 Dec. 1777.

Palmerston, Henry John (Temple) 3rd Viscount *Commissioner* 6 April 1807–26 Oct. 1809. Left office 26 Oct. 1809 on app. as Secretary at War (SPB, xii f. 1).

Paris, John Rose *Extra Clerk* 7 June 1845–8 Oct. 1847 (Adm. 12/442). *Third Class Clerk* 8 Oct. 1847–31 March 1855 (Adm. 12/474). *Third Class (First Section) Clerk* 31 March 1855–21 Feb. 1859 (Adm. 12/602; *Navy Lists*). *Acting Second Class Clerk* 21 Feb.–1 June 1859 (Adm. 12/666). *Second Class Clerk* 1 June 1859–6 Nov. 1866 (ibid.). Ret. 6 Nov. 1866 (Adm. 12/778).

Parker, George *Private Secretary to First Lord* (St. Vincent) 5 Jan. 1802–May 1804 (SPB, iii f. 5).

Parker, Harry (succ. as 6th Bart. c. 1783) *Extra Clerk* 21 Nov. 1752–4 July 1763 (SPB, vii f. 7). *Clerk* 4 July 1763–13 Jan. 1783 (Adm. 3/71). *Chief Clerk* 13 Jan. 1783–25 March 1795 (Adm. 3/96). Res. 25 March 1795 (SPB, viii f. 13).
Extra Clerk (Marine Department) 5 May 1760–30 June 1782 (Adm. 2/1156 p. 428). Res. 30 June 1782 (Adm. 2/1174 p. 172).

Parker, Hyde *First Naval Lord* 2 March 1852–25 March 1854. D. 25 March 1854 (*Gent. Mag.* (1854), cxxxv, 76).

Parker, John *First Secretary* 9 June–10 Sept. 1841 (Adm. 12/383); 21 May 1849–3 March 1852 (Adm. 12/506).

Parker, Sir William, kt. (cr. Bart. 18 Dec. 1844) *Second Naval Lord* 1 Aug.–23 Dec. 1834; 25 April 1835–25 June 1841. *First Naval Lord* 13–24 July 1846.

Parmiter, Thomas Pool *Clerk* pd. from 24 June 1694 by order 26 Sept. 1694 (SPB, ii ff. 50–1). Left office 14 Nov. 1702 on app. as Clerk of Cheque, Sheerness (SPB, i f. 20; Adm. 6/7 f. 60).

Parry, William Edward *Acting Hydrographer* 8 Dec. 1823–16 Jan. 1824 (SPB, xiv f. 9); 22 Nov. 1825–10 Nov. 1826 (ibid.); 1 Nov. 1827–13 May 1829 (ibid.).

Patton, Philip *Commissioner* 15 May 1804–10 Feb. 1806.

Paulet, Lord Henry *Commissioner* 18 May 1813–24 May 1816.

Paulet *see also* **Powlett**

Peake, John *Secretary* (*Naval Works Department*) 25 March 1796–28 Oct. 1807 (SPB, x f. 40). Transferred to Navy Board 28 Oct. 1807 as Extra Assistant to Civil Architect and Engineer of the Navy (SPB, xii ff. 293–4; PC 2/174 pp. 274–6, 284).

Pearce, John *Watchman* 28 June 1742–2 June 1748 (SPB, vi f. 20). Left office 2 June 1748 (ibid.).

Pearce, William *Extra Clerk* 19 Aug. 1778–16 June 1795 (Adm. 3/85). *Clerk* 16 June 1795–7 Feb. 1800 (SPB, viii f. 13). *Senior Clerk* 7 Feb. 1800–1 July 1813 (SPB, ix f. 9). *Chief Clerk* 1 July 1813–22 Aug. 1819 (SPB, xii f. 12). Ret. 22 Aug. 1819 (SPB, xiii ff. 015–16).

Pechell *see* **Brooke Pechell**

Peel, Sir Robert, 3rd Bart. *Civil Lord* 14 March 1855–30 May 1857.

Pelham, Hon. Frederick Thomas *Private Secretary to First Lord* (Northumberland) 3 March 1852–Jan. 1853 (Adm. 12/554). *Fourth Naval Lord* 24 June 1857–8 March 1858. *Second Naval Lord* 28 June 1859–15 June 1861.

Pelham, Kendrick *Clerk* pd. from 26 Dec. 1704 by order 20 March 1705 (SPB, i f. 43; AO 1/1725/147). D. 17 Dec. 1708 (SPB, i f. 43).

Pelham, Thomas *Commissioner* 19 March 1761–1 Jan. 1763.

Pell, William *Messenger* 7 June 1716–26 July 1717 (SPB, i f. 20). Left office 26 July 1717 (ibid.).

Pembroke, Thomas (Herbert) 8th Earl of *First Lord* 20 Jan. 1690–10 March 1692; 4 April 1701–26 Jan. 1702. *Lord High Admiral* 26 Jan.–20 May 1702; 29 Nov. 1708–8 Nov. 1709.

Pembroke, William *Clerk* pd. from 10 June 1707 by order 7 July 1707 (SPB, i f. 43). Left office 4 Feb. 1717 on app. as Clerk of Survey, Portsmouth (ibid. f. 42; Adm. 6/12 f. 87).

Pennell, Charles Henry *Third Class Clerk* 4 July 1825–21 Jan. 1833 (SPB, xiv f. 8). *Second Class Clerk* 21 Jan. 1833–24 May 1847 (Adm. 12/290). *First Class Clerk* 24 May 1847–21 March 1857 (Adm. 12/474). *Chief Clerk* 21 March 1857–13 July 1865 (Adm. 12/634, ret. of J. J. Dyer). Ret. 13 July 1865 (Adm. 12/762).
    Private Secretary to First Secretary (Elliot) 31 May–18 Aug. 1832 (SPB, xiv f. 8).

Pennell, Henry Cholmondeley *Third Class Clerk* 30 Dec. 1853–31 March 1855 (Adm. 12/570). *Third Class* (*Second Section*) *Clerk* 31 March 1855–18 April 1857 (Adm. 12/602; *Navy Lists*). *Third Class* (*First Section*) *Clerk* 18 April 1857–18 July 1861 (Adm. 12/634). *Acting Second Class Clerk* 18 July 1861–20 Dec. 1861/20 March 1862 (Adm. 12/698). *Second Class Clerk* app. between 20 Dec. 1861 and 20 March 1862 (*Navy Lists*). Ret. 22 Jan. 1866 (Adm. 12/778).

Penrice, Henry (ktd. 15 Nov. 1715) *Advocate* 28 Oct. 1714–15 Aug. 1715 (HCA 50/8 f. 138). *Judge* 23 Aug. 1715–19 Dec. 1751 (ibid. ff. 182–7; HCA 50/9 ff. 138–42; C 66/3512, 3573). Left office 19 Dec. 1751 (app. of Salusbury).

Penton, Henry *Commissioner* 30 Dec. 1774–1 April 1782.

Pepys, Samuel *Secretary* occ. from 15 June 1673 to 21 May 1679 (James and Shaw, Admiralty Administration, 182; Pepys Library no. 2849 p. 1; ibid. no. 2856 p. 284) and from 23 May 1684 to 5 March 1689 (Pepys Library no. 2857 p. 3; ibid. no. 2862 p. 598; C 66/3245).

Perceval, Hon. Charles George (succ. as 2nd Lord **Arden** 11 June 1784) *Commissioner* 31 Dec. 1783–19 Feb. 1801.

    Registrar grant in reversion by letters patent under seal of Admiralty court 30 June 1764 (HCA 50/12 ff. 49–51); confirmed by letters patent under great seal 2 July 1764 (C 66/3696); succ. 9 Aug. 1790 (d. of Farrant). D. 5 July 1840.

Perceval, Hon. Spencer *Counsel* 16 Jan. 1795–19 Feb. 1801 (SPB, viii f. 42). Res. 19 Feb. 1801 on app. as Solicitor General (SPB, ix f. 55; C 66/3985).

Perchard, Rachel *Housekeeper* 15 March 1740–12 May 1752 (SPB, vi f. 20). D. 12 May 1752 (SPB, vii f. 22).

Perigal, James *Extra Clerk* 10 Nov. 1780–25 March 1782 (Adm. 3/91). Left office 25 March 1782 on app. as Purser of the *Alfred* Armed Ship (SPB, v f. 7).

Perrier, John *Extra Clerk* 22 May 1841–11 Nov. 1842 (Adm. 12/383). *Third Class Clerk* 11 Nov. 1842–31 March 1855 (Adm. 12/395). *Third Class (First Section) Clerk* 31 March 1855–27 Jan. 1858 (Adm. 12/602; *Navy Lists*). *Second Class Clerk* 27 Jan. 1858–2 March 1870 (Adm. 12/650). Ret. 2 March 1870 (Adm. 12/846).

Pett, Peter *Clerk* pd. from 24 June 1694 by order 15 Feb. 1695 (SPB, ii f. 20). D. c. 12 Feb. 1709 (Adm. 2/188 p. 149).

Pett, Samuel *Clerk* formerly Clerk to Hayter as Clerk of Acts, Navy Board (AO 1/1715/119); transferred to Admiralty as Clerk May 1679 on Hayter's app. as Secretary (MS Rawlinson A 181 f. 250). Probably left office with Hayter Feb. 1680. Probably reapp. as Chief Clerk by Bowles March 1689; occ. from 9 to 26 April 1689 (Adm. 2/377).

    Deputy Judge Advocate of the Fleet 7 Jan. 1692–4 July 1693 (Sergison MS f. 191). Left office 4 July 1693 (app. of J. Burchett).

Phillimore, Joseph *Advocate* 25 Oct. 1834–24 Jan. 1855 (HCA 50/20 ff. 78–9). D. 24 Jan. 1855 (*Gent. Mag.* (1855), cxxxvi, 319).

Phillimore, Robert Joseph (ktd. 17 Sept. 1862) *Advocate* 3 Feb. 1855–3 Sept. 1862 (HCA 50/23 p. 237). Left office 3 Sept. 1862 on app. as Queen's Advocate (app. of T. Twiss; C 66/5014). *Judge* 23 Aug. 1867 (HCA 50/24 pp. 394–402; C 66/5032).

Phillips, Erasmus *Extra Clerk* 25 Sept. 1739–14 Oct. 1742 (Adm. 3/43). *Clerk* 14 Oct. 1742–28 March 1777 (Adm. 3/46). Res. 28 March 1777 (Adm. 12/54; SPB, v f. 6).

Phillipson, John *Commissioner* 13 Dec. 1743–27 Dec. 1744.

Phinn, Thomas *Counsel and Judge Advocate of the Fleet* 17 April 1854–22 May 1855 (Adm. 12/586, under Admiralty Courts). *Second Secretary* 22 May 1855–7 May 1857 (Adm. 12/602). Res. 7 May 1857 (Adm. 12/634). *Counsel and Judge Advocate of the Fleet* 12 Nov. 1863–31 Oct. 1866 (*Navy List*). D. 31 Oct. 1866 (*Gent. Mag.* (1866), clix, 843).

Phipps, Constantine *Counsel* 8 Dec. 1708–19 Nov. 1709 (SPB, i f. 20). Left office 19 Nov. 1709 (app. of G. Townsend).

Phipps, Hon. Edmund *Paymaster of Marines* 16 Jan. 1810–30 Sept. 1812 (Adm. 6/406). Res. 30 Sept. 1812 (ibid.; app. of E. R. Stewart).

Phipps, Pownoll William *Third Class (Second Section) Clerk* 12 Jan.–20 July 1858 (Adm. 12/650). Res. 20 July 1858 (ibid.).

Pickard, J. J. *Index Writer* 9 Jan. 1863 (Adm. 12/730).

Piers, Octavius Barrington *Third Class Clerk* 24 May 1837–18 Nov. 1853 (Adm. 12/332). *Second Class Clerk* 18 Nov. 1853–29 Dec. 1855 (Adm. 12/570). Left office 29 Dec. 1855 on app. as Acting First Class Clerk, Transport Department (Adm. 12/602); reapp. between 20 Dec. 1856 and 20 March 1857 (*Navy Lists*). Res. 15 June 1859 on app. as Storekeeper, Woolwich (Adm. 12/666).

    Private Secretary to First Secretary (Herbert, Lowry Corry) 29 Sept. 1841–July 1846 (Adm. 12/383).

Pigot, Hugh *Commissioner* 1 April 1782–31 Dec. 1783.

Pinfold, Charles *Advocate* 14 Nov. 1751–17 Feb. 1756 (HCA 50/11 ff. 78–9). Left office 17 Feb. 1756 on app. as Governor, Barbados (ibid. f. 107; C 66/3651).

Pinfold, Thomas *Advocate* 13 Sept. 1685–4 July 1686 (HCA 50/5 f. 112). Left office 4 July 1686 on app. as King's Advocate (ibid. f. 149).

Pitt, John *Commissioner* 17 Nov.–13 Dec. 1756.

Pitt, Thomas *Commissioner* 20 April 1763–21 Dec. 1765.

Pitts, Robert *Messenger (Marine Pay Department)* 19 May 1813–12 Oct. 1826 (SPB, xii ff. 77–8). D. 12 Oct. 1826 (SPB, xiv f. 21).

Pole, Sir Charles Morice, 1st Bart. *Commissioner* 10 Feb.–23 Oct. 1806.

Pole *see also* **Wellesley Pole**

Pollock, William *Extra Clerk* 1 Jan. 1759–24 June 1763 (Adm. 3/66). Salary ceased 24 June 1763 (SPB, v f. 7). App. Clerk to Earl of Egremont as Secretary of State May 1763 (*Calendar of Home Office Papers 1760–5*, 285; *1st Rept. on Fees*, 19).

Porter, Charles (ktd. 25 Jan. 1686) *Counsel* 4 July 1685–23 April 1686 (Sergison MS f. 147). Left office 23 April 1686 on app. as Lord Chancellor, Ireland (ibid. f. 151).

Potter, Hugh *Registrar* app. May 1639 (Corbett MS, v pp. 81–9). Removed from office 1644 (ibid.); reapp. 6 Sept. 1660 (HCA 50/3 ff. 34–5). D. c. 12 Feb. 1662 (M. F. Keeler, *The Long Parliament, 1640–41 : a Biographical Study of its Members* (Philadelphia 1954), 312).

Potts, Robert *Watchman* 29 Sept. 1786–24 June 1788 (SPB, viii f. 44). *Messenger* 24 June 1788–11 Feb. 1798 (ibid.). D. 11 Feb. 1798 (SPB, ix f. 58).

Powdick, John *Extra Clerk* 14 Dec. 1756–31 Dec. 1759 (SPB, vii f. 7). Left office 31 Dec. 1759 (ibid.).

Powell, Charles *Board Room Messenger* 25 March 1828–c. 15 Jan. 1833 (SPB, xiv f. 14). D. by 15 Jan. 1833 (Adm. 12/290, app. of Sivewright).

Powell, James *Messenger* 6 Aug. 1792–26 Nov. 1799 (SPB, viii f. 44). Left office 26 Nov. 1799 on app. as Head Messenger, Navy Board (SPB, ix f. 58).

Powlett, Lord Harry *Commissioner* 21 June 1733–19 March 1742.

Powlett *see also* **Paulet**

Pratt, Benoni *Watchman* pd. from 26 Dec. 1704 by order 27 March 1705 (SPB, i f. 20). D. by 11 March 1720 (Adm. 2/195 p. 176).

Pratt, Hon. John Jeffreys (*styled* Viscount **Bayham** 13 May 1786) *Commissioner* 18 July 1782–10 April 1783; 31 Dec. 1783–12 Aug. 1789.

Prescott, Henry *Second Naval Lord* 20 July–23 Dec. 1847.

Price, Thomas *Third Class Clerk* 1–24 May 1837 (Adm. 12/332). Res. 24 May 1837 (ibid.).

Priest, C. *Board Room Messenger* 19 June 1850–23 Sept. 1860 (Adm. 12/522). Ret. 23 Sept. 1860 (ibid.).

Priestman, Henry *Commissioner* 5 June 1690–31 May 1699.

Primrose, Edward Montagu *Temporary Clerk* 11 Nov. 1862–1 Feb. 1866 (Adm. 12/714). *Third Class (Second Section) Clerk* 1 Feb. 1866–27 Oct. 1868 (Adm. 12/778). *Third Class (First Section) Clerk* 27 Oct. 1868 (Adm. 12/810).

Proby, Charles John *Third Class Clerk* 13 March 1841–19 Oct. 1854 (Adm. 12/383). *Second Class Clerk* 19 Oct. 1854–29 Jan. 1862 (Adm. 12/586). Ret. 29 Jan. 1862 (Adm. 12/714).

Pulteney, Daniel *Commissioner* 30 Sept. 1721–3 June 1725.

Pybus, Charles Small *Commissioner* 27 June 1791–25 July 1797.

Raines, Sir Richard, kt. *Judge* 17 Dec. 1686–1 June 1689 (HCA 50/5 f. 154; C 66/3290). Left office 1 June 1689 (app. of Hedges).

Rainsford, Francis *Receiver of Droits* 31 July 1691–13 Sept. 1695 (HCA 50/6 ff. 53–6). Dis. 13 Sept. 1695 (ibid. f. 129).

Ram, Andrew *Clerk* 29 Aug. 1716–6 April 1751 (Adm. 2/194 p. 89). Ret. 6 April 1751 (Adm. 3/62).

Randall, Robert *Extra Clerk* 15 June 1804–4 Sept. 1809 (SPB, iii f. 14). *Junior Clerk* 4 Sept. 1809–5 Feb. 1816 (SPB, xii ff. 23–4). Ret. 5 Feb. 1816 (ibid.).

Raymond, Arthur Mills *Extra Clerk* 25 March 1782–8 May 1787 (SPB, viii f. 14). Discharged 8 May 1787 (ibid.); reapp. 9 Oct. 1787 (Adm. 3/103). *Junior Clerk* 11 April 1800–3 May 1804 (SPB, ix f. 82). *Senior Clerk* 3 May 1804–27 April 1807 (SPB, iii f. 8). Ret. 27 April 1807 (ibid.).

Regins, William *Clerk* pd. from 26 Dec. 1704 by order 20 March 1705 (SPB, i f. 43). Discharged 29 Sept. 1705 by order 13 Dec. 1705 (ibid.).

Reke, Samuel *Mechanist of Naval Works* 25 March 1796–16 Oct. 1799 (Adm. 6/25). D. 16 Oct. 1799 (SPB, x f. 40).

Reynolds, Elizabeth *Necessary Woman* 26 May 1767–19 July 1775 (SPB, v f. 27). D. 19 July 1775 (ibid.).

Reynolds, John *Clerk* pd. from 28 Feb. 1709 by order 24 March 1709 (SPB, i f. 43). Discharged 24 June 1713 by order 27 June 1713 (ibid.).

Reynolds, John Eliot *Extra Clerk* 25 Sept. 1761–8 Aug. 1765 (SPB, vii f. 7). D. 8 Aug. 1765 (SPB, v f. 7).

Reynolds, William *Extra Clerk* 18 Jan. 1790–11 April 1800 (Adm. 3/107). *Junior Clerk* 11 April 1800–30 April 1807 (SPB, ix f. 83). *Senior Clerk* 30 April 1807–16 Dec. 1815 (SPB, iii f. 9). Ret. 16 Dec. 1815 (SPB, xii ff. 13–14).

Rich, Nathaniel *Clerk* pd. from 25 June 1698 by order 3 Aug. 1698 (SPB, i f. 6). D. c. 25 March 1700 (ibid.; Adm. 20/74 no. 578).

Rich, Sir Robert, 2nd Bart. *Commissioner* 16 Nov. 1691–1 Oct. 1699. D. 1 Oct. 1699.

Richards, George Henry *Hydrographer* 19 Sept. 1863 (Adm. 12/730).

Richards, Peter *Third Naval Lord* 3 June 1854–2 April 1857.

Riley, Richard *Extra Clerk* 19 June 1795–19 Dec. 1800 (SPB, viii f. 15). *Junior Clerk* 19 Dec. 1800–28 Sept. 1807 (SPB, ix f. 83). *Senior Clerk* 28 Sept. 1807–5 Feb. 1816 (SPB, iii f. 9). *First Class Clerk* 5 Feb. 1816–14 May 1832 (SPB, xiii ff. 017–18). Ret. 14 May 1832 (SPB, xiv f. 5).

Roberts,— *Clerk* occ. as Clerk to Pepys Nov. 1678 (MS Rawlinson A 181 ff. 25–6).

Roberts, James *Board Room Messenger* 5 Aug. 1868 (Adm. 12/810).

Roberts, Mary *Necessary Woman* 17 Aug. 1722–c. 19 Dec. 1729 (SPB, iv f. 20). D. by 25 Dec. 1729 (ibid.; app. of C. Clack).

Robinson, Anne *Necessary Woman* 15 May 1816–c. 26 March 1823 (SPB, xii ff. 67–8). D. by 26 March 1823 (SPB, xiv f. 12).

Robinson, Sir Christopher, kt. *Judge* 22 Feb. 1828–21 April 1833 (HCA 50/17 ff. 266–71; C 66/4334). D. 21 April 1833 (*Gent. Mag.* (1833), ciii(1), 465).

Robinson, Hon. Frederick John *Commissioner* 3 July 1810–5 Oct. 1812.

Robinson, Robert *Extra Clerk* 11 Sept. 1770–12 June 1782 (Adm. 3/77). *Clerk* 12 June 1782–7 Feb. 1800 (Adm. 3/95). *Senior Clerk* 7 Feb. 1800–2 May 1804 (SPB, iii f. 7). Ret. 2 May 1804 (ibid.).

Robinson, Sir Robert Spencer, kt. *Second Naval Lord* 18 Dec. 1868.

Robinson, William *Extra Clerk (Marine Pay Department)* 1 Oct. 1800–11 Dec. 1819 (SPB, xii ff. 75–6). *Second Class Clerk (Marine Pay Department)* 11 Dec. 1819–10 April 1831 (SPB, xiii ff. 037–8). Left office 10 April 1831 (SPB, xiv f. 64).

Robson, William Frogatt *Solicitor* 8 Dec. 1843–15 Jan. 1862 (HCA 50/22 ff. 44–5). Superseded 15 Jan. 1862 (Adm. 3/714, app. of Skirrow).

Rock, William *Deputy Judge Advocate of the Fleet* 6 May 1703–9 Dec. 1706 (Adm. 6/7 f. 122). D. 9 Dec. 1706 (SPB, i f. 27).

Roebuck, George *Inspector of Telegraphs* 23 April 1796–23 Aug. 1816 (SPB, ix f. 11). Office discontinued 23 Aug. 1816 (SPB, xii ff. 55–6).

Rogers, Burchett *Extra Clerk (Marine Department)* 17 July 1755–c. 26 April 1770 (Adm. 2/1152 pp. 134–5). D. by 26 April 1770 (Adm. 2/1165 p. 1).

Rogers, Heigham *First Clerk (Naval Works Department)* 5 July 1804–28 Oct. 1807 (SPB, iii f. 25). Transferred to Navy Board 28 Oct. 1807 as Clerk, Secretary's Department (PC 2/174 pp. 274–6, 284; SPB, xii ff. 191–2).

Rogers, John *Messenger* 26 July 1717–c. 25 March 1734 (SPB, i f. 20). D. by 25 March 1734 (SPB, vi f. 20).

Romaine, William Govett *Second Secretary* 7 May 1857–19 June 1869 (Adm. 12/634). Ret. 19 June 1869 (Adm. 12/828).

Roney, Cusack Patrick *Third Class Clerk* 17 Feb. 1841–16 Dec. 1844 (Adm. 12/383). Res. 16 Dec. 1844 (Adm. 12/426).
  Private Secretary to First Secretary (More O'Ferrall, Parker) 13 March–Sept. 1841 (Adm. 12/383, 13 March and 9 June 1841).

Rooke, Sir George, kt. *Commissioner* 2 May 1694–26 Jan. 1702. *Member of Council* 22 May 1702–11 June 1705.

Ross, Charles *Commissioner* 31 July–25 Nov. 1830.

Rothery, Henry Cadogan *Registrar* 10 Nov. 1853 (HCA 50/23 pp. 102–7).

Rous, Hon. Henry John *Fourth Naval Lord* 17 Feb.–13 July 1846.

Rouse, John *Extra Clerk* 6 Sept. 1809–5 Feb. 1816 (SPB, iv ff. 39–40). *Third Class Clerk* 5 Feb. 1816–17 July 1821 (SPB, xiii ff. 021–2). *Second Class Clerk* 17 July 1821–14 May 1832 (ibid. ff. 019–20). *First Class Clerk* 14 May 1832–15 Dec. 1834 (SPB, xiv f. 5). Ret. 15 Dec. 1834 (Adm. 12/298).

Rowley, Sir Charles, kt. *Third Naval Lord* 23 Dec. 1834–25 April 1835.

Rowley, William (ktd. 12 Dec. 1753) *Commissioner* 22 June 1751–17 Nov. 1756; 6 April–2 July 1757.

Rupert, Prince *Commissioner* 9 July 1673–14 May 1679.

Russell, Edward (cr. Earl of **Orford** 7 May 1697) *Commissioner* 5 June 1690–23

Jan. 1691. *First Lord* 2 May 1694–31 May 1699; 8 Nov. 1709–4 Oct. 1710; 14 Oct. 1714–16 April 1717.

Russell, Philip   *Clerk* pd. from 26 March 1697 by order 9 June 1697 (SPB, i f. 6). Discharged 24 June 1698 by order 15 July 1698 (ibid.).

Russell, Lord William   *Commissioner* 10 Feb. 1806–6 April 1807.

Rutherford, Thomas L.   *Third Class Clerk* 13 Oct. 1837–31 Oct. 1840 (Adm. 46/ 54 no. 3711). Res. 31 Oct. 1840 (Adm. 12/368).

Ryan, Anthony   *Solicitor* 16 June 1747–2 Jan. 1749 (SPB, vi f. 19). D. 2 Jan. 1749 (ibid.).

Ryder, Alfred Phillips   *Private Secretary to First Lord* (Somerset) 24 Nov. 1862–27 April 1863 (Adm. 12/714).

Ryland, Frederick   *Extra Clerk* 17 July 1813–5 Feb. 1816 (SPB, xii ff. 41–2). *Third Class Clerk* 5 Feb. 1816–10 Feb. 1831 (SPB, xiii ff. 021–2). *Second Class Clerk* 10 Feb. 1831–29 April 1833 (SPB, xiv f. 6). Dis. 29 April 1833 (Adm. 12/290).
   Private Secretary to First Secretary (Croker) 2 June 1826–Nov. 1830 (SPB, xiv f. 7).

Sacheverell, William   *Commissioner* 8 March 1689–20 Jan. 1690.

Sadler, James   *Chemist of Naval Works* 25 March 1796–28 Oct. 1807 (Adm. 6/25). Office abolished 28 Oct. 1807 on transfer of Naval Works Department to Navy Board (PC 2/174 pp. 274–6, 284; SPB, iii f. 24).

St. Vincent, John (Jervis) 1st Earl of   *First Lord* 19 Feb. 1801–15 May 1804.

Salusbury, Thomas (ktd. 18 Nov. 1751)   *Advocate* 9 Aug. 1748–14 Nov. 1751 (HCA 50/11 f. 65). *Judge* 19 Dec. 1751–28 Oct. 1773 (ibid. ff. 79–84; C 66/3634). D. 28 Oct. 1773 (SPB, v f. 26).

Sandford, Thomas   *Watchman* 16 July 1791–28 July 1801 (SPB, viii f. 44). D. 28 July 1801 (SPB, iii ff. 18–19).

Sandwich, John (Montagu) 4th Earl of   *Commissioner* 27 Dec. 1744–26 Feb. 1748. *First Lord* 26 Feb. 1748–22 June 1751; 20 April–16 Sept. 1763; 12 Jan. 1771–1 April 1782.

Sandys, Hon. Edwin   *Commissioner* 6 April–2 July 1757.

Saul, Joseph   *Third Class Clerk* 19 June–3 July 1832 (SPB, xiv f. 8). Left office 3 July 1832 on app. as Third Class Clerk, Accountant General of Navy (Adm. 12/ 284).

Saunders, Sir Charles, kt.   *Commissioner* 31 July 1765–15 Sept. 1766. *First Lord* 15 Sept.–11 Dec. 1766.

Saunders, Samuel   *Clerk* pd. from 24 June 1694 by order 26 Sept. 1694 (SPB, ii ff. 50–1). Pd. to 25 Dec. 1695 (Adm. 20/63 no. 104).

Saunders Dundas, Hon. Richard (ktd. 4 Feb. 1856)   *Private Secretary to First Lord* (Melville) 4 Oct. 1828–Nov. 1830 (SPB, xiv f. 4); (Haddington) 29 Jan. 1845– Jan. 1846 (Adm. 12/442). *Third Naval Lord* 5 Jan. 1853–3 June 1854. *Second Naval Lord* 3 June 1854–8 March 1855; 2 April–24 Nov. 1857. *First Naval Lord* 24 Nov. 1857–8 March 1858. *Second Naval Lord* 8 March 1858–28 June 1859. *First Naval Lord* 28 June 1859–3 June 1861. D. 3 June 1861 (Adm. 12/698, 4 June 1861).

Savile, Henry   *Commissioner* 20 Jan. 1682–19 May 1684.

Sayer, Charles   *Extra Clerk* 19 June 1795–19 Dec. 1800 (SPB, viii f. 15). *Junior Clerk* 19 Dec. 1800–4 Sept. 1809 (SPB, ix f. 84). *Senior Clerk* 4 Sept. 1809–5 Feb. 1816 (SPB, xii ff. 13–14). *First Class Clerk* 5 Feb. 1816–8 Dec. 1821 (SPB, xiii ff. 017–18). Ret. 8 Dec. 1821 (ibid.).

Sayer, Everard   *Proctor* 5 Aug. 1727–3 Feb. 1745 (HCA 50/9 f. 129). D. 3 Feb. 1745 (*Gent. Mag.* (1745), xv, 108).

Sayer, Exton   *Advocate* 30 March 1727–21 Sept. 1731 (HCA 50/9 ff. 101, 133). D. 21 Sept. 1731 (*Gent. Mag.* (1731), i, 405).

Sayer, George   *Proctor* 14 May 1718–5 Aug. 1727 (HCA 50/8 f. 215). Left office 5 Aug. 1727 (app. of Everard Sayer).

Sayer, Valentine   *Extra Clerk* 2 Dec. 1767–24 Jan. 1769 (Adm. 3/75). D. 24 Jan. 1769 (SPB, v f. 7).

Scott, George   *Extra Clerk* 26 Aug. 1807–5 Feb. 1816 (SPB, iii f. 14). Ret. 5 Feb. 1816 (SPB, xii ff. 37–8).

Scott, James   *Third Class Clerk* 13 April 1854–31 March 1855 (Adm. 12/586). *Third Class (Second Section) Clerk* 31 March 1855–14 Oct. 1858 (Adm. 12/602; *Navy Lists*). *Third Class (First Section) Clerk* 14 Oct. 1858–13 July 1865 (Adm. 12/650). *Acting Second Class Clerk* 13 July 1865–20 Sept./20 Dec. 1865 (Adm. 12/762). *Second Class Clerk* app. between 20 Sept. and 20 Dec. 1865 (*Navy Lists*).

Scott, Thomas   *Watchman* 10 Feb. 1781–29 Sept. 1786 (SPB, v f. 27). Res. 29 Sept. 1786 (SPB, viii f. 44).

Scott, William (ktd. 3 Sept. 1788; cr. Lord **Stowell** 17 July 1821)   *Advocate* 21 May 1782–4 Sept. 1788 (HCA 50/13 ff. 734). Left office 4 Sept. 1788 on app. as King's Advocate (C 66/3846). *Judge* 26 Oct. 1798–22 Feb. 1828 (HCA 50/14 ff. 99–104; C 66/3952). Left office 22 Feb. 1828 (app. of C. Robinson).

Scudamore Stanhope, Chandos Scudamore   *Private Secretary to First Lord* (Childers) 16 July 1870 (Adm. 12/846).

Seddon, Samuel   *Solicitor* 24 Jan. 1749–29 May 1778 (SPB, vi f. 19). Res. 29 May 1778 (SPB, v f. 28).

Sedgwick, Charles   *Extra Clerk* 25 July 1797–29 Sept. 1800 (SPB, ix f. 11). Res. 29 Sept. 1800 (ibid.).

Senior, Joseph   *Third Class Clerk* 16 Nov. 1854–31 March 1855 (Adm. 12/586). *Third Class (Second Section) Clerk* 31 March 1855–27 Aug. 1859 (Adm. 12/602; *Navy Lists*). *Third Class (First Section) Clerk* 27 Aug. 1859–20 Sept./20 Dec. 1865 (Adm. 12/666). *Acting Second Class Clerk* app. between 20 Sept. and 20 Dec. 1865 (*Navy Lists*). *Second Class Clerk* 8 Feb. 1866 (Adm. 12/778).

Seppings, Nicholas Lockyer   *Third Class Clerk* 11–19 June 1832 (SPB, xiv f. 8). Left office 19 June 1832 on app. as Third Class Clerk, Accountant General of Navy (Adm. 12/284).

Sewell, Thomas   *Extra Clerk* 29 April–25 Nov. 1741 (SPB, vi f. 7). Discharged 25 Nov. 1741 (ibid.).

Seymour, Edward   *Commissioner* 9 July 1673–14 May 1679.

Seymour, Frederick Beauchamp Paget   *Private Secretary to First Lord* (Childers) 22 Dec. 1868–16 July 1870 (Adm. 12/810).

Seymour, Sir George Francis, kt.   *Third Naval Lord* 8 Sept. 1841–22 May 1844.

Seymour, George Henry   *Third Naval Lord* 13 July 1866–18 Dec. 1868.

Seymour, Lord Hugh   *Commissioner* 7 March 1795–10 Sept. 1798.

Seymour, Walter Richard   *Third Class (Second Section) Clerk* 29 June 1859–5 Aug. 1861 (Adm. 12/666). Res. 5 Aug. 1861 (Adm. 12/698).

Shaftesbury, Anthony Ashley (Cooper) 1st Earl of   *Commissioner* 9 July 1673–31 Oct. 1674.

Shaw Lefevre, George John   *Civil Lord* 9 May–13 July 1866.

Sheffield, W. E. *Metal Master of Naval Works* 26 April 1803–28 Oct. 1807 (Adm. 6/28 ff. 135–6). Office abolished 28 Oct. 1807 on transfer of Naval Works Department to Navy Board (PC 2/174 pp. 274–6, 284; SPB, iii f. 25).

Shepherd, George *Extra Clerk* 3 May 1804–15 April 1806 (SPB, iii f. 13). *Junior Clerk* 15 April 1806–5 Feb. 1816 (ibid. f. 11). *Second Class Clerk* 5 Feb. 1816–15 June 1824 (SPB, xiii ff. 019–20). Ret. 15 June 1824 (SPB, xiv f. 6).

Shepherd, Henry John *Counsel and Judge Advocate of the Fleet* 2 June 1828–7 Feb. 1845 (SPB, xiv ff. 15–16). Left office 7 Feb. 1845 on app. as Commissioner of Bankruptcy (app. of Godson; *London Gazette* no. 20436).

Sherer, Richard *Clerk* pd. from 21 Aug. 1710 by order 22 Oct. 1710 (SPB, i f. 43). Discharged 24 June 1712 by order 9 July 1712 (ibid.).

Sheridan, Charles Kinnaird *Third Class Clerk* 19 Jan. 1833–1 May 1847 (Adm. 12/290). Res. 1 May 1847 (Adm. 12/332).

Sheridan, Francis Cynric *Third Class Clerk* 10 Feb. 1831–31 May 1832 (SPB, xiv f. 8). Res. 31 May 1832 on app. as Secretary to Earl of Mulgrave as Governor of Jamaica (ibid.; Adm. 12/284).

Sheridan, John *Third Class Clerk* 22 Aug. 1840–30 Dec. 1853 (Adm. 12/368). *Second Class Clerk* 30 Dec. 1853–18 Oct. 1865 (Adm. 12/570). Ret. 18 Oct. 1865 (Adm. 12/762).

Shovell, Sir Cloudesley, kt. *Member of Council* 26 Dec. 1704–22 Oct. 1707. D. 22 Oct. 1707 (SPB, i f. 1).

Sivewright, George *Board Room Messenger* 15 Jan. 1833–1854 (Adm. 12/290). *Head Messenger* probably app. 1854; first occ. 1855 (*Royal Kal.* (1855), 199). Ret. 15 Feb. 1864 (Adm. 12/746).

Skinner, Peter *Clerk* occ. as Clerk to Pepys 1 Jan. 1687 (Pepys Library no. 2867 p. 13).

Skirrow, Charles Fletcher *Solicitor* 15 Jan.–12 May 1862 (Adm. 12/714). Left office 12 May 1862 (app. of Bristow).

Smith,— *Temporary Clerk* app. 24 Oct. 1857 (Adm. 12/634). No further occ.

Smith, Charles *Extra Clerk* 3 May 1804–20 May 1805 (SPB, iii f. 13). Left office 20 May 1805 (ibid.).

Smith, James *Watchman* 19 Aug. 1801–5 May 1822 (SPB, iii f. 19). D. 5 May 1822 (SPB, xiv f. 11).

Smith, Joseph *Deputy Judge Advocate of the Fleet* 16 Oct. 1668–c. 25 Dec. 1671 (Adm. 2/1734 f. 46). Pd. to 25 Dec. 1671 (AO 1/1712/108; AO 1/1713/111, 112).

Smith, Needham *Extra Clerk* 25 Aug. 1773–1 April 1777 (Adm. 3/80). D. 1 April 1777 (SPB, v f. 7).

Smith, Sarah *Housekeeper* 14 March 1832–28 May 1851 (SPB, xiv f. 12). D. 28 May 1851 (Adm. 12/538).

Smith, William *Index Writer* 9 Jan. 1863 (Adm. 12/730).

Smyth, John *Commissioner* 27 June 1791–12 May 1794.

Somerset, Edward Adolphus (Seymour) 12th Duke of *First Lord* 28 June 1859–13 July 1866.

Southerne, James *Clerk* app. Clerk to W. Coventry c. 25 June 1660 (*The Diary of Samuel Pepys*, ed. R. Latham and W. Matthews, i (London 1970), 183); probably served Coventry as Chief Clerk throughout his period as Secretary; in service of Pepys, probably as Chief Clerk; signed Secretary's letters 30 and 31 Oct. and 6 Nov. 1673 (Pepys Library no. 2849 pp. 276, 277, 285). *Secretary* occ. from 16 Jan. 1690 to 4 Aug. 1694 (Adm. 2/378, 385).

Deputy Judge Advocate of the Fleet 23 Jan. 1675–12 March 1677 (Adm. 2/1737 p. 214). Left office 12 March 1677 on app. as Clerk of Acts, Navy Board (Adm. 2/1738 f. 92).

Spalding, Augustus Frederick Montagu *Third Class Clerk* 24 Feb.–31 March 1855 (Adm. 12/602). *Third Class (Second Section) Clerk* 31 March 1855–27 Aug. 1859 (ibid.; *Navy Lists*). *Acting Third Class (First Section) Clerk* 27 Aug. 1859–18 July 1861 (Adm. 12/666). *Third Class (First Section) Clerk* 18 July 1861–22 Jan. 1866 (Adm. 12/698). *Acting Second Class Clerk* 22 Jan.–28 Sept. 1866 (Adm. 12/778). *Second Class Clerk* 28 Sept. 1866 (ibid.).

Spence, John *Extra Clerk* 3 May–5 June 1804 (SPB, iii f. 14). Res. 5 June 1804 (ibid.); reapp. 9 Sept. 1805 (ibid.). Res. 25 Aug. 1807 (ibid.).

Spencer, A. L. *Temporary Clerk* app. 17 Sept. 1859 (Adm. 12/666). No further occ.

Spencer, Lord Charles *Commissioner* 8 March 1768–16 July 1779.

Spencer, George John (Spencer) 2nd Earl *First Lord* 19 Dec. 1794–19 Feb. 1801.

Spencer, Hon. Robert Cavendish *Private Secretary to Lord High Admiral* (Clarence) 13 Sept. 1827–Sept. 1828 (SPB, xiv f. 4).

Spike, Abraham *Watchman* 4 Nov. 1742–4 Feb. 1761 (SPB, vi f. 20). D. 4 Feb. 1761 (SPB, vii f. 23).

Spike, Samuel *Watchman* 16 Feb. 1761–20 Dec. 1772 (SPB, vii f. 23). D. 20 Dec. 1772 (SPB, v f. 27).

Spriggs, Charles *Extra Clerk* 26 Jan. 1776–22 April 1780 (SPB, v f. 7). Dis. 22 April 1780 (ibid.).

Stables, John *Extra Clerk* 3 May–10 June 1804 (SPB, iii f. 13). Res. 10 June 1804 (ibid.).

Stafford *see* O'Brien Stafford

Stanhope, Hon. John *Commissioner* 26 Feb.–3 Dec. 1748. D. 3 Dec. 1748 (SPB, vi f. 2).

Stanhope *see also* Scudamore Stanhope

Stanley, Hon. Frederick Arthur *Civil Lord* 3 Sept.–18 Dec. 1868.

Stanley, Hans *Commissioner* 26 Sept. 1757–31 July 1765.

Stansfeld, James *Civil Lord* 5 May 1863–22 April 1864.

Stanyan, Abraham *Commissioner* 14 Oct. 1714–16 April 1717.

Stapylton *see* Chetwynd Stapylton

Stephens, Philip (cr. Bart. 13 March 1795) *Clerk* 6 April 1751–16 Oct. 1759 (Adm. 3/62). *Second Secretary* 16 Oct. 1759–18 June 1763 (Adm. 3/67). *Secretary* 18 June 1763–13 Jan. 1783 (d. of Cleveland; Adm. 3/71, 4 July 1763). *First Secretary* 13 Jan. 1783–3 March 1795 (Adm. 3/96). *Commissioner* 7 March 1795–23 Oct. 1806.

Steward, Gabriel *Paymaster of Marines* 4 June 1778–9 Jan. 1792 (Adm. 6/406). D. 9 Jan. 1792 (*Gent. Mag.* (1792), lxii(1), 91).

Stewart, Edward *Private Secretary to First Lord* (Graham) 11 Dec. 1830–26 May 1831 (SPB, xiv f. 4).

Stewart, Hon. Edward Richard *Paymaster of Marines* 30 Sept. 1812–20 July 1813 (Adm. 6/406). Res. 20 July 1813 (ibid.; app. of Doyle).

Stewart, Houston *Third Naval Lord* 9 Feb. 1850–13 Feb. 1852. *Second Naval Lord* 13 Feb.–2 March 1852.

Stirling, Sir James, kt. *Third Naval Lord* 13 Feb.–2 March 1852.

Stokes, Henry Graham *Proctor* 11 Oct. 1866 (HCA 50/24 ff. 380–1).

Stowell, Lord *see* **Scott**, William

Strafford, Thomas (Wentworth) 1st Earl of *First Lord* 30 Sept. 1712–14 Oct. 1714.

Strahan, William *Judge Advocate of the Fleet* 13 Sept. 1711–22 Dec. 1714 (Adm. 6/11 f. 60). Left office 22 Dec. 1714 (Adm. 6/12 f. 10). *Advocate* 20 March 1742–25 May 1748 (HCA 50/10 f. 192). D. 25 May 1748 (SPB, vi f. 19).

Stuart, Horace Noel *Third Class (Second Section) Clerk* 11 Dec. 1868 (Adm. 12/810).

Styan, William *Board Room Messenger* 17 Feb. 1864 (Adm. 12/746).

Swabey, Henry Birchfield *Registrar* 7 Aug. 1840–9 Nov. 1853 (3 & 4 Vict. c 66, s 3; HCA 50/23 pp. 82–3). Res. 9 Nov. 1853 (HCA 50/23 pp. 82–3).

Swainson, Edwin Newcome *Third Class Clerk* 30 Dec. 1853–31 March 1855 (Adm. 12/670). *Third Class (Second Section) Clerk* 31 March 1855–14 Dec. 1857 (Adm. 12/602; *Navy Lists*). *Third Class (First Section) Clerk* 14 Dec. 1857–20 Dec. 1861/20 March 1862 (Adm. 12/634). *Acting Second Class Clerk* app. between 20 Dec. 1861 and 20 March 1862 (*Navy Lists*). *Second Class Clerk* app. between 20 Sept. and 20 Dec. 1862 (ibid.).
    Private Secretary to Second Secretary (Phinn, Romaine) 16 March 1857–20 Sept./20 Dec. 1862 (Adm. 12/634, 16 March and 9 May 1857; *Navy Lists*).

Taylor, James *Watchman* app. 6 May 1822 (SPB, xiv f. 11); still in office 1832 (ibid.). No further occ.

Temple, Richard (Grenville Temple) 2nd Earl *First Lord* 17 Nov. 1756–6 April 1757.

Templeman, George *Extra Clerk* 15 March 1811–5 Feb. 1816 (SPB, xii ff. 41–2). *Third Class Clerk* 5 Feb. 1816–30 Dec. 1826 (SPB, xiii ff. 021–2). Ret. 30 Dec. 1826 (SPB, xiv f. 7).

Thomas, Charles Inigo *Temporary Clerk* 14 June 1865–18 May 1866 (Adm. 12/762). *Third Class (Second Section) Clerk* 18 May 1866–2 Dec. 1869 (Adm. 12/778). *Third Class (First Section) Clerk* 2 Dec. 1869 (Adm. 12/828).

Thompson, Edward *Commissioner* 5 May 1741–19 March 1742.

Thompson, William *Messenger* pd. from 25 June 1697 by order 11 Oct. 1697 (SPB, i f. 20). *Porter* pd. from 25 June 1698 by order 20 Sept. 1698 (ibid.). Discharged 16 Sept. 1714 by order 17 Sept. 1714 (ibid.).

Thomson, John Deas *Private Secretary to First Lord* (Barham) 8 May 1805–Feb. 1806 (SPB, iii f. 5).

Thorburn, Richard *Librarian* 26 April 1862 (Adm. 12/714, 11 Jan. 1862; PC 2/255 p. 362).

Thornton, Robert *Marshal* 30 Oct. 1811–14 March 1815 (HCA 50/15 f. 219). Left office 14 March 1815 (app. of H. Lindsay).

Thurtle, Samuel *Extra Clerk* 14 Nov. 1796–19 Dec. 1800 (SPB, ix f. 11). *Junior Clerk* 19 Dec. 1800–15 March 1811 (ibid. f. 84). *Senior Clerk* 15 March 1811–5 Feb. 1816 (SPB, xii ff. 15–16). *First Class Clerk* 5 Feb. 1816–26 Aug. 1841 (SPB, xiii ff. 017–18). Ret. 26 Aug. 1841 (Adm. 12/383).

Tindall, Matthew *Deputy Judge Advocate of the Fleet* 30 May–8 Nov. 1689 (Sergison MS f. 162). Left office 8 Nov. 1689 (app. of C. Jenkins).

Torrington, Earl of *see* **Herbert**, Arthur

Torrington, Viscount *see* **Byng**, Sir George

Townsend, George *Counsel* 19 Nov. 1709–11 June 1711 (SPB, i f. 20). Left office 11 June 1711 (app. of Ettrick); reapp. 18 Jan. 1715 (SPB, i f. 20). D. 22 Sept. 1726 (SPB, iv f. 19; *Hist. Reg. Chron.* (1726), xi, 37, 38).

Townsend, William *Proctor* 29 May 1820–11 Oct. 1866 (HCA 50/16 f. 240). Res. 11 Oct. 1866 (HCA 50/24 p. 380).

Townshend, Hon. Charles *Commissioner* 9 April 1754–29 Dec. 1755.

Townshend, Charles *Commissioner* 31 July 1765–28 Feb. 1770.

Townshend, Hon. John *Commissioner* 1 April–18 July 1782; 10 April–31 Dec. 1783.

Townshend, Hon. John Thomas *Commissioner* 12 Aug. 1789–26 April 1793.

Tranter, Thomas *Messenger* 31 July 1751–3 July 1760 (SPB, vii f. 22). D. 3 July 1760 (ibid.).

Trentham, Granville (Leveson Gower) *styled* Viscount *Commissioner* 18 Nov. 1749–22 June 1751.

Trevelyan, George Otto *Civil Lord* 18 Dec. 1868–12 July 1870.

Trevor, John *Commissioner* 19 March 1742–9 Sept. 1743. D. 9 Sept. 1743 (SPB, vi f. 2).

Troubridge, Sir Edward Thomas, 2nd Bart. *Fourth Naval Lord* 25 April 1835–22 July 1837. *Third Naval Lord* 22 July 1837–25 June 1841. *Second Naval Lord* 25 June–8 Sept. 1841.

Troubridge, Sir Thomas, 1st Bart. *Commissioner* 19 Feb. 1801–15 May 1804.

Troughton, John *Extra Clerk* in office by 19 Dec. 1728 (Adm. 3/37). *Clerk* 19 Dec. 1728–7 Nov. 1738 (ibid.). Res. 7 Nov. 1738 (Adm. 3/43).

Tucker, Benjamin *Private Secretary to First Lord* (St. Vincent) 17 April 1801–5 Jan. 1802 (SPB, ix f. 80). *Second Secretary* 21 Jan.–21 May 1804 (SPB, iii f. 5). Left office 21 May 1804 (ibid.); reapp. 10 Feb. 1806 (ibid.). Left office 5 April 1807 (ibid.).

Tucker, John *Gardener* 12 March 1741–26 Feb. 1786 (SPB, vi f. 20). D. 26 Feb. 1786 (SPB, viii f. 44).

Tucker, John *Paymaster of Marines* 19 April 1757–4 June 1778 (Adm. 6/406 pp. 45–6). Left office 4 June 1778 (app. of Steward).

Tufnell, Henry *Private Secretary to First Lord* (Minto) 23 Sept. 1835–6 Nov. 1839 (Adm. 12/308). Left office 6 Nov. 1839 on app. as Commissioner, Treasury (C 66/4580).

Tupper, Carré Cook *Extra Clerk* 12 Feb. 1807–15 March 1811 (SPB, iii f. 14). *Junior Clerk* 15 March 1811–5 Feb. 1816 (SPB, xii ff. 25–6). Ret. 5 Feb. 1816 (ibid.).

Turner, Sir Charles, kt. *Commissioner* 14 Oct. 1714–16 April 1717.

Turner, William (ktd. 26 Feb. 1664) *Advocate* 29 Oct. 1661–c. 18 Oct. 1670 (HCA 50/3 f. 216). D. by 18 Oct. 1670 (Prob. 11/334 f. 142).

Twiss, Horace *Counsel and Judge Advocate of the Fleet* 9 Feb. 1824–1 June 1828 (SPB, xiv f. 15). Left office 1 June 1828 on app. as Under Secretary of State, Colonial Office (ibid. f. 16; D. M. Young, *The Colonial Office in the Early 19th Century* (London 1961), 263).

Twiss, Travers *Advocate* 3 Sept. 1862–27 Aug. 1867 (HCA 50/24 pp. 210–12). Left office 27 Aug. 1867 on app. as Queen's Advocate (ibid. pp. 403–4).

Upsal, Richard *Second Clerk* (*Naval Works Department*) 22 May 1797–5 Jan. 1801 (SPB, x f. 40). *First Clerk* (*Naval Works Department*) 5 Jan. 1801–24 June 1804 (ibid.). Res. 24 June 1804 (SPB, iii f. 25).

Vanbrugh, Edward *Extra Clerk* in office by 15 Nov. 1740 (SPB, vi f. 7; Adm. 3/44, 13 Nov. 1740). Res. 11 Feb. 1742 (SPB, vi f. 7).

Vansittart Neale, Henry James *Temporary Clerk* 4 Aug. 1862–13 Dec. 1865 (Adm.

12/714). *Third Class (Second Section) Clerk* 13 Dec. 1865–14 Aug. 1868 (Adm. 12/762). *Third Class (First Section) Clerk* 14 Aug. 1868 (Adm. 12/810).
    Private Secretary to Second Secretary (Romaine, Lushington) 15 Oct. 1866 (Adm. 12/778; Adm. 12/828, 2 July 1869).

Varney, John *Extra Clerk* in office by 10 Oct. 1721 (Adm. 3/32). *Clerk* 10 Oct. 1721–29 Sept. 1725 (ibid.). D. 29 Sept. 1725 (SPB, iv f. 7).

Vaughan, Edward *Commissioner* 14 May 1679–19 Feb. 1681.

Vaughan, John (Vaughan) *styled* Lord (succ. as 3rd Earl of **Carbery** 3 Dec. 1686) *Supernumerary Commissioner* 17 April–19 May 1684. *Commissioner* 8 March 1689–23 Jan. 1691.

Villiers, Hon. George *Paymaster of Marines* 19 March 1792–16 Jan. 1810 (Adm. 6/406). Res. 16 Jan. 1810 (ibid., app. of E. Phipps).

Villiers, George Bussy (Villiers) *styled* Viscount *Commissioner* 19 March 1761–1 Jan. 1763.

Villiers, Hon. Thomas (cr. Lord **Hyde** 3 June 1756) *Commissioner* 24 Dec. 1748–17 Nov. 1756.

Vismes *see* de Vismes

Wager, Sir Charles, kt. *Commissioner* 19 March 1718–21 June 1733. *First Lord* 21 June 1733–19 March 1742.

Walbanke, John *Clerk* probably served throughout Pepys' first period as Secretary June 1673–May 1679; occ. 11 and 25 Nov. 1678 (MS Rawlinson A 181 ff. 184, 16); probably served as Chief Clerk to Brisbane throughout his period as Secretary Feb. 1680–May 1684; signed Secretary's letters 17 July 1681 and 17 May 1684 (Adm. 2/1753, 1754); probably continued in office as Chief Clerk by Pepys May 1684. D. in office between 3 and 16 Dec. 1686 (A. Bryant, *Samuel Pepys: the Saviour of the Navy* 2nd ed. (London 1949), 207–8; Prob. 11/385 f. 174).
    Deputy Judge Advocate of the Fleet 26 Feb. 1684–14 Oct. 1686 (Sergison MS f. 145). Pd. to 14 Oct. 1686 (AO 1/1717/126).

Walbanke, Richard *Clerk* brother of J. Walbanke who had employed him 'for many years under him before his death' in 1686 (A. Bryant, *Samuel Pepys: the Saviour of the Navy* 2nd ed. (London 1949), 208; Prob. 11/385 f. 174); occ. as Clerk to Pepys 1 Jan. and 19 Nov. 1687 (Pepys Library no. 2867 p. 13; Rawlinson A 177 f. 129).

Waldron, Richard *Watchman* pd. from 25 Dec. 1704 by order 20 March 1705 (SPB, i f. 20). D. 4 Oct. 1719 (ibid.).

Walker, Edward Allen *Third Class Clerk* 7 Aug. 1826–14 April 1827 (SPB, xiv f. 8). Res. 14 April 1827 (ibid.).

Walker, George *Clerk* pd. from 30 May 1708 by order 11 June 1708 (SPB, i f. 43). D. 21 Oct. 1709 (ibid.).

Walker, Michael *Supernumerary Clerk* pd. from 26 Dec. 1811 to 25 Dec. 1816 (SPB, xii ff. 45–6).

Walker, Sir Walter, kt. *Advocate* probably app. 1670 on d. of W. Turner; d. in office by 19 May 1674 (HCA 50/4 f. 113).

Wall, William *Supernumerary Clerk* pd. from 26 Dec. 1811 to 25 Dec. 1813 (SPB, xii ff. 45–6).

Wallace, Thomas *Commissioner* 25 July 1797–10 July 1800.

Waller, Thomas *Second Clerk (Marine Pay Department)* probably app. 1797; first occ. 1798 (*Royal Kal.* (1798), 131). Left office by 31 Dec. 1807 (app. of G. Gardner).

Walpole, Horatio (Walpole) *styled* Lord *Commissioner* 17 June 1811–5 Oct. 1812.

Walpole, Robert *Member of Council* 11 June 1705–25 Feb. 1708. Left office 25 Feb. 1708 on app. as Secretary at War (Adm. 2/187 p. 21).

Ward, Edward *Extra Clerk* 24 Feb. 1757–8 Nov. 1760 (SPB, vii f. 7). Left office 8 Nov. 1760 (ibid.).

Ward, Henry George *First Secretary* 13 July 1846–21 May 1849 (Adm. 12/458). Left office 21 May 1849 on app. as Lord High Commissioner, Ionian Islands (*London Gazette* no. 20973).

Ward, Robert *Commissioner* 6 April 1807–17 June 1811.

Ward, Swinburne *Extra Clerk* 8 Oct. 1847–18 Nov. 1853 (Adm. 12/474). *Third Class Clerk* 18 Nov. 1853–22 March 1855 (Adm. 12/570). Res. 22 March 1855 (Adm. 12/602).

    Private Secretary to First Secretary (Parker) 21 May 1849–March 1852 (Adm. 12/506).

Warren, Edward C. *Third Class Clerk* 11–14 June 1832 (Adm. 12/284). Left office 14 June 1832 on app. as Third Class Clerk, Accountant General of Navy (ibid.).

Warren, Thomas *Clerk* pd. from 24 June 1694 by order 26 Sept. 1694 (SPB, ii ff. 50–1). Left office 31 July 1695 on app. as Secretary to Sir George Rooke as Admiral of the Fleet (Adm. 20/65 no. 264).

Warrender, Sir George, 4th Bart. *Commissioner* 5 Oct. 1812–8 Feb. 1822.

Warter, John *Solicitor* 26 June 1703–2 Dec. 1718 (SPB, i f. 20). Discharged 2 Dec. 1718 (ibid.).

Warton, Sir Michael, kt. *Commissioner* 8 March 1689–20 Jan. 1690.

Washington, John *Hydrographer* 25 Jan. 1855–3 Sept. 1863 (Adm. 12/602). Res. 3 Sept. 1863 (Adm. 12/730).

Waters, Edmund *First Clerk* (*Marine Pay Department*) occ. from 1795 to 1797 (*Royal Kal.* (1795), 131; ibid. (1797), 131). *Deputy Paymaster of Marines* occ. from 1798 to 1807 (ibid. (1798), 131; ibid. (1807), 158). *First Clerk* (*Marine Pay Department*) probably app. 1807 (SPB, xii ff. 73–4). Res. 29 Sept. 1808 (ibid.).

Weaver, James Frederick *Board Room Messenger* 29 July 1868 (Adm. 12/810).

Weaver, William Henry *Office Keeper* (*Marine Pay Department*) 11 Dec. 1827–1 July 1831 (SPB, xiv f. 21). Left office 1 July 1831 (ibid.).

Webb, Daniel C. *Second Clerk* (*Marine Pay Department*) occ. from 1795 to 1797 (*Royal Kal.* (1795), 131; ibid. (1797), 131). *First Clerk* (*Marine Pay Department*) occ. from 1798 to 1807 (ibid. (1798), 131; ibid. (1807), 158).

Webster, William Charles *Extra Clerk* 17 Aug. 1756–7 Aug. 1758 (Adm. 3/64). Res. 7 Feb. 1758 (ibid.).

Wellesley Pole, Hon. William *First Secretary* 24 June 1807–12 Oct. 1809 (SPB, iii f. 4).

Wemyss, David (Wemyss) 4th Earl of *Member of Council* 19 April–28 Oct. 1708.

Werden, John (cr. Bart. 28 Nov. 1672) *Secretary* occ. from 2 July 1672 to 15 June 1673 (James and Shaw, Admiralty Administration, 182).

West, Algernon Edward *Third Class Clerk* 30 Dec. 1853–31 March 1855 (Adm. 12/570). *Third Class* (*Second Section*) *Clerk* 31 March 1855–18 April 1857 (Adm. 12/602; *Navy Lists*). *Third Class* (*First Section*) *Clerk* 18 April 1857–20 June/20 Sept. 1862 (Adm. 12/634). *Second Class Clerk* app. between 20 June and 20 Sept. 1862 (*Navy Lists*). Res. 10 May 1866 on app. as Deputy Director of Military Funds, India Office (Adm. 12/778; *The Indian Army and Civil Service List* (Jan. 1867), viii).

West, Temple *Commissioner* 17 Nov. 1756–6 April 1757; 2 July–9 Aug. 1757. D. 9 Aug. 1757 (SPB, vi f. 2).

Westcomb, Gregory *Clerk* 17 Jan. 1715–19 Dec. 1728 (Adm. 2/193 pp. 127–8). D. 19 Dec. 1728 (*Hist. Reg. Chron.* (1728), xiii, 63).

Wharton, Hon. Goodwin *Commissioner* 5 June 1697–31 May 1699.

Whiffen, John *Third Class Clerk* 11–19 June 1832 (SPB, xiv f. 8). Left office 19 June 1832 on app. as Third Class Clerk, Accountant General of Navy (Adm. 12/284).

Whish, George Clinton *Third Class (Second Section) Clerk* 11 Aug. 1858–20 June/ 20 Sept. 1862 (Adm. 12/650). *Acting Third Class (First Section) Clerk* app. between 20 June and 20 Sept. 1862 (*Navy Lists*). *Third Class (First Section) Clerk* 2 Jan. 1864–6 Nov. 1866 (Adm. 12/746). *Acting Second Class Clerk* 6 Nov. 1866–7 May 1867 (Adm. 12/778). *Third Class (First Section) Clerk* 7 May 1867–2 Feb. 1869 (Adm. 12/794). Ret. 2 Feb. 1869 (Adm. 12/828).

Whitbread, Samuel *Civil Lord* 28 June 1859–27 March 1863.

White, William *Watchman* 3 June 1748–25 Dec. 1768 (SPB, vi f. 20). D. 25 Dec. 1768 (SPB, v f. 27).

Whittaker, Edward *Solicitor* 2 March 1692–7 July 1699 (SPB, i f. 20). Discharged 7 July 1699 (Adm. 2/180 pp. 45–6).

Whittaker, Thomas *Clerk* pd. from 18 Nov. 1695 by order 18 March 1696 (SPB, i f. 6). Discharged 24 June 1698 by order 15 July 1698 (ibid.).

Wild, Alfred *Board Room Messenger* 23 April 1864 (Adm. 12/746).

Wilder, Francis *Extra Clerk* 3 May 1804–24 April 1807 (SPB, iii f. 13). Res. 24 April 1807 (ibid.).

Willes, John William Shippen *Temporary Clerk* 21 Sept. 1859–2 Sept. 1861 (Adm. 12/666). *Third Class (Second Section) Clerk* 2 Sept. 1861–26 May 1863 (Adm. 12/698). Res. 26 May 1863 (Adm. 12/730).

Willett, Augustus Saltern *Extra Clerk* 26 Nov. 1766–9 March 1771 (SPB, v f. 7). Res. 9 March 1771 on app. as Agent Victualler to West India Squadron (ibid.).

Williams, Griffith *Agent of Marines* 16 April 1767–c. 3 July 1791 (Adm. 6/406). D. by 3 July 1791 (Adm. 2/1181 p. 311).

Williams, John *Clerk* pd. from 25 June 1697 to 25 March 1700 (SPB, i f. 6).

Williamson, Sir Joseph, kt. *Commissioner* 31 Oct. 1674–14 May 1679.

Wilson, Henry James Carrington *Temporary Clerk* 20 Jan.–11 Nov. 1862 (Adm. 12/714). *Third Class (Second Section) Clerk* 11 Nov. 1862–9 Oct. 1866 (ibid.). *Acting Third Class (First Section) Clerk* 9 Oct.–6 Nov. 1866 (Adm. 12/778). *Third Class (First Section) Clerk* 6 Nov. 1866 (ibid.).

Winch, Sir Humphrey, 1st Bart. *Commissioner* 14 May 1679–19 May 1684.

Winchester, Charles *Watchman* 11 Feb. 1784–10 Jan. 1800 (SPB, v f. 27). D. 10 Jan. 1800 (SPB, ix f. 58).

Winchester, John *Extra Messenger* 13 Aug. 1795–29 Sept. 1803 (SPB, viii f. 43). Left office 29 Sept. 1803 (SPB, iii f. 17).

Winchilsea, Daniel (Finch) 8th Earl of *First Lord* 19 March 1742–27 Dec. 1744; 6 April–2 July 1757.

Winnington, Francis *Solicitor* 4 April 1733–16 June 1747 (SPB, vi f. 19). Left office 16 June 1747 (app. of Ryan).

Winnington, Thomas *Commissioner* 13 May 1730–22 May 1736.

Winter, John *Agent of Marines (Portsmouth)* 9 Nov. 1756–9 April 1763 (Adm. 6/406 p. 33). Discharged 9 April 1763 (ibid.; app. of Clevland).

Winter, Nicholson *Board Room Messenger* probably app. 1854; first occ. 1855 (*Royal Kal.* (1855), 199). *Head Messenger* 17 Feb. 1864 (Adm. 12/746).

Wishart, Sir James, kt. *Member of Council* 20 June–28 Oct. 1708. *Commissioner* 20 Dec. 1710–14 Oct. 1714.

Wolley, Henry *Third Class Clerk* 11 June 1832–20 April 1838 (Adm. 12/284). *Second Class Clerk* 20 April 1838–30 Dec. 1853 (Adm. 12/344). *First Class Clerk* 30 Dec. 1853–1 April 1869 (Adm. 12/570). Ret. 1 April 1869 (Adm. 12/828).

Wolley, Thomas *Third Class Clerk* 3 May 1833–13 March 1841 (Adm. 12/290). *Second Class Clerk* 13 March 1841–12 April 1854 (Adm. 12/383). *First Class Clerk* 12 April 1854–31 March 1870 (Adm. 47/23). *Chief Clerk* 31 March 1870 (Adm. 12/846).

Private Secretary to First Secretary (More O'Ferrall) 17 Feb.–13 March 1841 (Adm. 12/383).

Wood, Charles (succ. as 3rd Bart. 31 Dec. 1846) *First Secretary* 27 April 1835–4 Oct. 1839 (Adm. 12/308). *First Lord* 8 March 1855–8 March 1858.

Woolley, John *Messenger* 3 Oct. 1729–31 July 1751 (SPB, iv f. 20). Left office 31 July 1751 on app. as Porter, Greenwich Hospital (SPB, vii f. 22).

Woolley, Joseph *Extra Messenger* 11 April 1800–26 April 1806 (SPB, iii f. 17). *Messenger* 26 April–24 Sept. 1806 (ibid.). *Board Room Messenger* 24 Sept. 1806–19 May 1813 (ibid.). Left office 19 May 1813 on app. as Head Messenger, Navy Board (SPB, xii ff. 63–4, 295–6).

Worcester, Henry (Somerset) *styled* Marquess of *Commissioner* 24 May 1816–15 March 1819.

Worth, George *Third Class Clerk* 6 Nov. 1824–14 May 1832 (SPB, xiv f. 7). *Second Class Clerk* 14 May 1832–26 Aug. 1841 (ibid. f. 6). *First Class Clerk* 26 Aug. 1841–16 Aug. 1854 (Adm. 12/383). Ret. 16 Aug. 1854 (Adm. 12/586).

Wren, Matthew *Secretary* occ. from 4 Sept. 1667 to 14 June 1672 (James and Shaw, Admiralty Administration, 182). D. 14 June 1672 (*The Bulstrode Papers 1667–75* (London 1897), i, 237).

Wright, Charles *Extra Clerk* 21 Jan. 1757–25 Aug. 1773 (SPB, vii f. 7). *Clerk* 25 Aug. 1773–16 June 1795 (Adm. 3/80). *Chief Clerk* 16 June 1795–27 Sept. 1807 (SPB, viii f. 13). D. 27 Sept. 1807 (SPB, iii f. 7).

Wright, George *Messenger* pd. from 21 April 1708 by order 21 June 1708 (SPB, i f. 20). D. 21 Feb. 1711 (ibid.).

Wright, Henry *Extra Clerk* 27 Oct. 1787–11 April 1800 (Adm. 3/103). *Junior Clerk* 11 April 1800–3 May 1804 (SPB, ix f. 83). *Senior Clerk* 3 May 1804–30 July 1814 (SPB, iii f. 9). Ret. 30 July 1814 (SPB, xii ff. 13–14).

Wright, Robert *Counsel* pd. from March 1673 to 24 June 1678 (AO 1/1713/113; AO 1/1715/119). Discharged 29 Dec. 1679 (Adm. 2/740 pp. 270–3).

Yonge, Sir George, 5th Bart. *Commissioner* 15 Sept. 1766–28 Feb. 1770.

Yonge, Sir William, kt. *Commissioner* 1 June 1728–13 May 1730.

York, James (Stuart) 1st Duke of *Lord High Admiral* originally app. c. 1649 (James and Shaw, Admiralty Administration, 19 n. 4); office granted by letters patent 29 Jan. 1661 (C 66/2932). Surrendered office 15 June 1673 (*CSPD 1673*, 374).

Yorke, Charles Philip *First Lord* 4 May 1810–25 March 1812.

Yorke, Henry Francis Redhead *Temporary Clerk* 4 Sept. 1865–27 Sept. 1866 (Adm. 12/762). *Third Class (Second Section) Clerk* 27 Sept. 1866–31 March 1870 (Adm. 12/778). *Third Class (First Section) Clerk* 31 March 1870 (Adm. 12/846).

Yorke, Hon. John   *Commissioner* 21 Dec. 1765–15 Sept. 1766.

Yorke, Sir Joseph Sydney, kt.   *Commissioner* 3 July 1810–2 April 1818.

Young, William   *Clerk* 21 June 1717–11 Aug. 1727 (Adm. 2/194 p. 292). Left office 11 Aug. 1727 on being attached exclusively to Sixpenny Office as Commissioner (Adm. 3/36; Adm. 6/13 ff. 7, 151; SPB, iv f. 7).

Young, William   *Commissioner* 20 Nov. 1795–19 Feb. 1801.

Zouche, Richard   *Judge* 4 Feb.–1 March 1661 (HCA 50/3 f. 119). D. 1 March 1661 (T. Faulkner, *A Historical and Topographical Account of Fulham* (London 1813), 86).

Index of Offices and Departments